Hell On A Hill Top

Hell On A Hill Top

America's Last Major Battle In Vietnam

On The East Flank Of The A Shau Valley
March–July 1970
The 324B Division Surrounds The 101st
Airborne's Currahee Battalion

Major General
Benjamin L. Harrison
US Army, Retired

iUniverse, Inc.
New York Lincoln Shanghai

Hell On A Hill Top
America's Last Major Battle In Vietnam

iUniverse, Inc.

For information address:
iUniverse, Inc.
2021 Pine Lake Road, Suite 100
Lincoln, NE 68512
www.iuniverse.com

ISBN: 0-595-32730-3 (pbk)
ISBN: 0-595-66675-2 (cloth)

Printed in the United States of America

For the soldiers who fought at Ripcord. For my beautiful, loving and incredibly supportive wife, Carolyn. For our children, Ben and Laura, our grandchildren Sean, Mark, Michelle, Katie, Madelaine and Christian, and our great grandchildren Hayden, Dylan and Madison.

Contents

Preface

Ripcord: THE LAST OFFENSIVE

"I still had one battalion left. I had used only two battalions from my 3rd Regiment. One battalion had been operating east of the Bo River," responded Major General Chu Phuong Doi, whose entire 324B Division had been committed since 19 May 1970 to "concentrate its main forces to attack and destroy Operating Base 935." After three hours of questioning, General Doi had been asked by the author while visiting Doi in Cao Bang, Vietnam 26 May 2004, "What would you have done if we had not evacuated Firebase Ripcord on 23 July?" His response seemed like a most uncharacteristic admission that his division, which had once consisted of nine infantry battalions, had been ground down to only one fully combat capable battalion.

In the Vietnamese spring of 1970 the U.S. Army's 101st Airborne Division—the "Screaming Eagles"—prepared for America's last offensive of the Vietnam War. While the dwindling number of the remaining American forces deployed in Vietnam withdrew from the battlefield and stood down awaiting formal movement orders to return to their home shores, the 101st Airborne Division made war plans to mount a major offensive in the enemy's bastion of strength, the infamous A Shau Valley and the rugged mountains of the Annamite Chain in Northern I Corps of Vietnam which formed the wedge between the countries of South Vietnam, Laos and North Vietnam.

Only the US Army's 1st Brigade, 5th Infantry Division (Mechanized) in Quang Tri and the 1st Infantry Division, Army of the Republic of Vietnam (ARVN) stood with the 101st in this large, hotly contested battle area. Just within the past 12-months American forces in northern I Corps plummeted in numbers: two Marine Corps divisions, the 3rd Marine Division which had long held the bloody Demilitarized Zone on the 17th Parallel and the 1st

Marine Division in southern I Corps withdrew, leaving a vacuum of vast proportions.

Simultaneously, as the American forces withdrew, the North Vietnamese reinforced their two crack infantry divisions and regional Communist\Viet Cong forces in this strategically critical area with two additional regular People's Army of Vietnam (PAVN) divisions. Charged with destroying all enemy forces that sought to enter their sanctuaries of the Annamite Mountains and disrupt their build-up, the NVA were ready to fight anyone and pay any price in the lives of its soldiers in the fulfillment of this vital mission.

General Creighton Abrams, Commander U.S. Military Assistance Command (COMUSMACV), charged the 101st Airborne Division with undertaking offensive operations in this hornet's nest of the enemy as a means to buy time to allow the military forces of South Vietnam to develop into more effective fighting units, as well as to shield the overall process of Vietnamization. Richard M. Nixon campaigning in 1968, and as President in 1969, promised to strengthen the South Vietnamese military and weaken the forces of North Vietnam. The 101st Airborne Division's mission called for the Screaming Eagles to enter NVA sanctuaries, conduct spoiling attacks, and to disrupt enemy lines of communication and supply.

The 101st Airborne Division, already spread perilously thin by tripling the size of their Area of Operations (AO), made plans to send the Division's 3rd Brigade into the northern highlands. The 3rd Brigade planned to combat air assault into a series of locations, establish fire support bases, and seek out and destroy an enemy whose strength intelligence estimates at the time, had grossly underestimated.

In sharp contrast to Korea, "The Forgotten War," the war in Vietnam seems destined never to be forgotten. Thousands of books have been written about the ten-year Vietnam War; actually, more books written than the number of major battles fought during the entire war. Only one book, Keith Nolan's superb *RIPCORD Screaming Eagles Under Siege Vietnam, 1970,* has been written about the last major battle fought by US ground forces in Vietnam; and it published thirty years after the battle. Until now, no English language book addressed North Vietnamese Army accounts of its last major battle with American ground forces. Drawn from books and documents published in the Socialist Republic of Vietnam, in the Vietnamese language, and interviews conducted by the author with officers of the North Vietnamese Army/People's Army of Vietnam (NVA/PAVN), the "other side of the story" can now be included.

This is the story of the brave and courageous American infantrymen, airmen, and artillerymen who invaded the enemy's rear areas along the Ho Chi Minh Trail in March-July 1970 against a vastly larger, determined, dedicated and disciplined enemy force, engaged in some of the bloodiest combat of the entire war. The battle for Ripcord involved twenty-six different US Army units in either direct combat or supporting roles, but always the principal combatant unit remained the 2nd Battalion, 506th Infantry—the "Currahees." Currahee is a Cherokee Indian word for "Stand Alone." The 506th Infantry Currahees of World War II became well known in books and film as the "Band of Brothers." This story tells of the Vietnam generation Currahee Band of Brothers and the enemy opposing them during America's last major ground offensive of the Vietnam War.

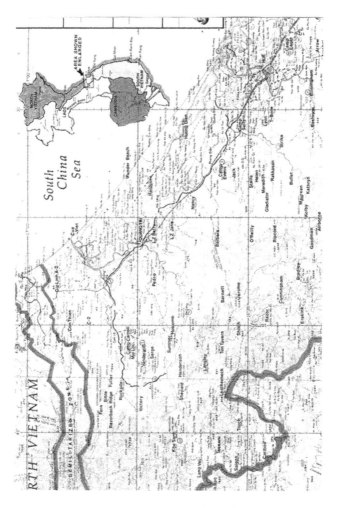

Northern Part of South Vietnam Including 3rd Brigade Area of
Operations

Glossary

AA antiaircraft fire

ADC assistant division commander

AIT advanced individual training

AKA aka also known as

AK-47 standard communist 7.62mm auto-matic rifle; a version with a folding metal stock was known as an AK-50

AO area of operations

ARA aerial rocket artillery

Arc Light bombing mission by B-52 Stratofortresses

arty artillery

ARVN Army of the Republic of Vietnam

ASP ammunition supply point

blivet rubberized bag used for transporting and storing fuel and water

CA combat assault

C&C command-and-control helicopter

CAR15 shortened, all-metal version of the M16 5.56mm automatic rifle

C4 plastic explosives

CG commanding general

Chalk designation by number of a lift helicopter in flight sequence

Chinook nickname for the CH47 transport helicopter

CO commanding officer

Cobra nickname for the AH-1G helicopter gunship

COSVN Central Office for South Vietnam for Communist operations in the RVN

CP command post

CS tear gas

DEROS date eligible for return from overseas

DISCOM Division Support Command

div arty division artillery

DMZ demilitarized zone

DOW died of wounds

EOD explosive ordnance disposal

El pay grade for recruit private

E2 pay grade for private

E3 pay grade for private first class

E4 pay grade for corporal or specialist fourth class

E5 pay grade for sergeant or specialist fifth class

E6 pay grade for staff sergeant or specialist sixth class

E7 pay grade for sergeant first class

E8 pay grade for first sergeant or master sergeant

E9 pay grade for sergeant major or command sergeant major

FA field artillery

FAC forward air controller

FDC fire direction center

FO forward observer

Front North Vietnamese name for area of military operations

FSB fire-support base

G1 personnel officer at division or higher level

G2 intelligence officer at division or higher level

G3 operations officer at division or higher level

G4 logistics officer at division or higher level

HE high explosive

H&I harassing and interdicting artillery and mortar fires

HHC Headquarters & Headquarters Company

Huey nickname for the UH-1 helicopter

Intruder nickname for the A6 all-weather Navy/Marine fighter-bomber

JP4 aviation fuel

KIA killed in action

Kit Carson Scout former NVA or Viet Cong soldier who came to the ARVN side and worked with US forces

klick kilometer

LAW light antitank weapon

LNO liaison officer

LOH light observation helicopter

LP listening post

LRRP long-range reconnaissance patrol

LZ landing zone

MA mechanical ambush

MACV Military Assistance Command Vietnam

Mic radio microphone

MG machine gun

MIA missing in action

MR Military Region, usually one or more Provinces

M16 standard U.S. 5.56mm automatic rifle

M60 standard U.S. 7.62mm light machine gun

M79 standard U.S. 40mm grenade launcher

M203 M16 rifle modified with 40mm grenade launcher under barrel

NCO noncommissioned officer (pay grades E4 to E9)

NDP night defensive position

NLF National Liberation Front

NVA North Vietnamese Army

OBE overtaken by events

OCS Officer Candidate School

OP observation post

Op or ops operations

OPCON Operational Control, usually a temporary tasking

PAVN People's Army of Vietnam, same as NVA

Phantom nickname for the F-4 jet fighter-bomber

Pink Team one scout helicopter (from the white platoon) and one

Cobra gunship (from the red platoon).

POL petroleum-oil-lubricant

PRC 25 standard infantry radio

PSDF Province Security Defense Force

PSP pierced steel planking

R&R rest-and-recreation leave

REMF rear-echelon motherfucker

RF/PF Regional Force/Popular Force local forces of RVN

RIF **reconnaissance in force**

ROTC Reserve Officer Training Corps.

RPG rocket-propelled grenade

RPD standard communist 7.62mm machine gun

RTO radiotelephone operator

RVN Republic of Vietnam

SAM Surface to air missile

Shake and Bake nickname for graduates of the Noncommissioned Officer Candidate School

S1 personnel officer at battalion or brigade level

S2 intelligence officer at battalion or brigade level

S3 operations officer at battalion or brigade level

S4 logistics officer at battalion or brigade level

SITREP situation report

Six the commander of the unit

SOI signal operating instructions

SSI special signal intercept

SVN South Vietnam, same as RVN

Tri-Thien-Hue Theater The PAVN designation for military operations in Quang Tri Province, Thua Thein Province and Hue City

TOC tactical operations center

USAF United States Air Force

USARV United States Army Vietnam

USMA United States Military Academy at West Point, New York

VC Viet Cong

WIA wounded in action

WP white phosphorus

X0 **executive officer**

Unit Map Symbols

D Co, 2nd Bn, 501st Inf

Enemy, in this instance, Peoples Army of Viet Nam (PAVN) are shown as double lines or broken lines. In color, enemy is red and friendly blue.

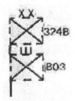

Location of the Command Posts of the 324B Division and 803rd Infantry Regiment, PAVN. Each of the three regts of the 324B had about 1800 men and a division total of about 7800.

2nd Battalion, 506th Infantry Regiment. US infantry bns had four rifle companies, each with a field strength of 90 to 120 men. Each bn had a 81mm mortar platoon with 6 tubes and a bn reconnaissance platoon of about 25 men.

6th Regional Force Regiment, originally Viet Cong, but after Tet 1968, mostly North Vietnamese Peoples Army regulars. The 6th Regt had three to eight infantry bns.

B Co, 2nd Bn, 506th Inf

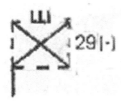

29th Inf Regt (minus), PAVN. For the Ripcord battle, the 29th had one bn operating a few kms east along the Bo River.

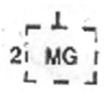

Each PAVN bn had a machine gun co.

The 7th Sapper Bn was a large, specially trained, strongly supported, PAVN Military District (Corps) force attached to the 324 Division for the Ripcord battle.

Each co has six tubes of mortars equivalent to US 4.2 in mortars. Gen Doi said he had four companies of 120mm mortars at Ripcord.

Each PAVN inf bn had a platoon of six 82mm mortars.

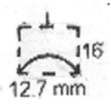

16th Anti-Aircraft Bn had three companies with .51 caliber anti-aircraft machine guns.

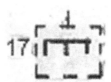

17th Engineer Co of the 324B Div.

Prologue

The primary sources for the North Vietnamese Army's story, the view from Hanoi, of *Hell On A Hill Top* consist of unit histories, books, official documents and interviews with officers of the People's Army of Vietnam (PAVN). The People's Army Publishing House and Institute of Military History printed most of the available books and documents. Both agencies operate under the Ministry of Defense in Hanoi, as government owned and controlled enterprises. The books and documents were normally printed in small numbers with limited distribution. The ability to identify what had been published and then to obtain copies proved both challenging and formidable, which developed into a frustrating two-year research effort.

To more fully comprehend the strategy (national policy and military doctrine) and tactics (the method of employing forces in combat) of the People's Army of Vietnam, one must review, not only the history of the Vietnamese Communist Party (the *La Dong* Party), but also the cultural and military history of the Vietnamese people, as well as, the organization and command structure of the military forces of North Vietnam.

How the PAVN developed their national strategy, or more accurately, how the Communist Party Politburo dictated that national strategy to the military commanders, how foreign countries influenced the development of that strategy, and how the strategy evolved over time, all must be appreciated to understand the execution of PAVN strategy and tactics on the battlefield. The 1970 battle for Fire Support Base Ripcord witnessed a dramatic shift in both PAVN strategy and tactics. Normally, PAVN forces avoided decisive engagement with US forces. Their strategy attempted to wear down the enemy over time, hit and withdraw, favoring the tactical shock and surprise of the ambush. However, the battle for Ripcord saw a significant shift in these timeworn tactics. Why did the PAVN choose to attack the 101st Airborne Division, the only remaining full strength US division in South Vietnam in 1970? Why did the PAVN risk costly defeat when it was obvious the US forces were in the process of withdrawing from the conflict? How much were they willing to risk in terms of both men and material resources? More critically, how do we find the answers to these questions?

Requests for Information from the Vietnamese Embassy in Washington—

Having read the splendid book, *We Were Soldiers Once...and Young*, by Lieutenant General Harold G. Moore, Retired, and Joseph L. Galloway (later made into a hit movie), I recalled that the authors sought the views of the North Vietnamese Army commanders who fought against them. They achieved this during two trips made to Vietnam. When I got the great news that Keith Nolan would be writing of the story of the battle for Fire Support Base Ripcord, I immediately thought of Moore and Galloway who included the enemy side of their battle. Early in my discussions with Keith Nolan, I suggested that the North Vietnamese side of the battle for Ripcord should be included in his upcoming book. Keith informed me that his publisher would not finance the research and that he simply could not do it.

Chuck Hawkins, a Ripcord Association stalwart, lived in the Washington, DC area, so I asked him if he could help Nolan find the enemy story of Ripcord. Chuck had already discussed this issue with Keith Nolan. In May 1998, Chuck wrote the Vietnamese Embassy in Washington requesting information related to the Ripcord battle. The Embassy promptly replied that they had forwarded his request to the Veterans Association of Vietnam (VAV) for help. Chuck never heard from the VAV. In February 1999, I wrote Vietnamese Ambassador Le Van Bang in Washington with specific requests to which I received no response at all. I asked a senior officer living in the Washington, DC area for help. He responded that he would be happy to help, but he did not want to go to the Vietnamese Embassy. Next, I went to a Ripcord veteran serving on the staff of an important United States Senator who said that his current position made asking the Vietnamese Embassy for help was both sensitive and unattractive. Strike-three on the home field of Washington.

A newsletter produced by the Texas Tech University Vietnam Center contained an article which noted that Senior Colonel Vo Dinh Quang, Defense Attaché, Embassy of Vietnam visited the Texas Tech University Vietnam Center in June 1999. I wrote in August 1999 to the Defense Attaché requesting help in conducting research for Nolan's book, which failed to illicit a response from Senior Colonel Quang. With great reluctance, I concluded that maybe that hill is just too steep to climb and maybe Nolan doesn't really need the enemy side of Ripcord for his book. Besides, the book was due to be published in less than a year.

The Great Ripcord Association Reunion in October 2000—

Enthusiasm for the Ripcord Association reunion, scheduled for Shreveport, Louisiana in October 2000, greatly surged with the July 2000 publication of *RIPCORD Screaming Eagles Under Siege Vietnam 1970*. Over twice the number of regular attendees registered for this celebration. Coordinated locally by Jim Campbell and his wife Mary, and with the assistance of many members and friends of the Association, the reunion was a spectacular success. Jim was a platoon leader in C Co, 2/506th during the Ripcord battle. Now a successful practicing attorney in Shreveport, he started in the fall of 1999 to make the 30-year anniversary reunion of the Ripcord battle a celebration of all American veterans who have served their country. Jim especially wanted to have a proper welcome home for the Vietnam veterans; something that most of them had never experienced. With the help and sometimes guidance of Fred Spaulding, who had planned, coordinated, and managed the previous four reunions, Jim marched out with full speed and purpose. Early on he involved the civic leaders of Shreveport and Bossier City. Jim gained financial backing from friends and several civic organizations. Many members of Jim's law firm along with their families and friends eagerly helped him. The print and local television news media provided excellent coverage prior to and each day of the reunion.

Jim Campbell was a friend and admirer of First Lieutenant J. Robert Kalsu who was killed in action during the Ripcord battle. Bob was the only NFL player killed in Vietnam. (Bob was actually the only professional athlete to give his life for his country in Vietnam.) As the Buffalo Bills' Rookie of the Year in 1969, Kalsu knew he could have avoided Vietnam, but he chose to honor his commissioning oath and serve his country. Campbell knew that National Football League great Rocky Bleier who played for the Pittsburg Steelers organization, was also a wounded Vietnam veteran and holder of four Super Bowl champion rings. At Jim's invitation, Rocky changed his travel schedule and spoke in moving tribute to First Lieutenant J. Robert Kalsu. Bob had been on Ripcord for several weeks and took command of A Battery, 2nd

Battalion, 11th Field Artillery on 21 July, just two days prior to his death and four days before the birth of his only son. Even after thirty years, Bob's widow, Jan, still shied away from the public eye and did not attend the reunion, but Bob's son and daughter attended with appropriate honors.

Mrs. Wilma Knight provided another moving highlight during the reunion when, on behalf of all Gold Star Mothers, she placed a wreath at the memorial plaque to honor her son, Private First Class Wieland Norris. Norris was killed in the Ripcord fight right after he volunteered to walk point for an A Co, 2/506th patrol. Wieland's brother, the famous Chuck Norris, also attended and became quite emotional after briefly talking with the media.

For many, this reunion both inspired us and evoked many emotions. The questions and concerns of our soldiers who fought the Ripcord battle about what really happened on the enemy side of the fight, multiplied by Nolan's book, strongly reinforced the need for the view from Hanoi. We fought for a just and honorable cause and we wanted to know more. Vietnam veteran Ken Mullholland wrote in the Wall Street Journal May 23, 1997, that the thousands of Americans who died in the 40 years of the Cold War did not die in vain. He said, "Our involvement in places like Korea and Vietnam should be recorded as the most honorable and unselfish sacrifice any great power has undertaken." Mullholland believed that our willingness to fight convinced the Soviets that a move to seize Central Europe would have been met with resolve by Americans. He said, "Those who died in the named and unnamed battles of the Cold War, made the supreme sacrifice for a cause every bit as just as the ones fought for at Valley Forge, Gettysburg and Omaha Beach." (Appendix A)

A New Ray of Hope for Getting the North Vietnamese Side of the Battle—

A chance meeting in April 2000 in Fort Worth at the annual national convention of the Army Aviation Association of America with Lieutenant General Teddy Allen, Retired, brought a sparkling new ray of hope for our quest for the North Vietnamese view. Teddy said he was doing business in Vietnam and had been there several times. I told him of our research predicament and he said he would try and help.

Two weeks later I received an email from Major General Greg Gile, Retired, an associate of Teddy Allen's currently working in Vietnam. Greg advised that Colonel Nguyen Ba Van, Retired, and living in Cu Chi fought in the Ripcord area in 1970 as a soldier in the North Vietnamese Army and is now working with General Allen's company in Vietnam and is eager to try and help with my research.

Gen Gile stated for Colonel Van to approach the Vietnamese government, he needs a letter from me requesting Colonel Van do the following:

1. Obtain permission from the Ministry of Defense to open the files and documents of the battles in and around Doc Mieu and US Fire Support Base Ripcord from March 1970 through December 1970.

2. Collect all information and details reasonably available on the battles to include maps, documents, strategies and battle results.

3. Find and identify participants during the requested period and set up meetings and interviews with former commanders and participants to obtain a clear and accurate description of how the battle was fought and the results.

4. Support a visit to the site by Keith Nolan and or myself should that be deemed appropriate.

This was indeed good news. Even better, General Allen returned from Vietnam saying he had met with Col Van who told him that there was a lot of information about Ripcord at the War Information Center in Quang Tri. Van could escort me to Quang Tri and then he would arrange a meeting in Hanoi with Senior General Van Tien Dung who was in command of all North Vietnamese forces in the Ripcord battle and who, later, succeeded Senior General Vo Nguyen Giap as commander of all the North Vietnamese Army. It sounded too good to be true—and it was.

Col Van advised through Teddy's interpreter, Nguyen Ba Bang, that assistance would not be forthcoming from the Ministry of Defense unless the US Ambassador requested it from the Ministry of Foreign Affairs. I made the appropriate request to the American Embassy in Hanoi.

General Allen checked with the American Embassy in Hanoi and they had not received my 15 September 2000 letter. Teddy faxed a copy to the Embassy. He also stated that he was planning to return to Vietnam on 1 December 2000 and invited me to join him. General Allen wisely cautioned, "I don't think you can accomplish all you want to do, with just one trip." He told Col Van that I would pay his expenses—Van did not expect any pay from me. (General Allen had learned from his interpreter that Col Van had already accumulated expenses of $700. I gave a check to Teddy and he had it delivered to Van. While interviewing Van on 4 June 2001, I verified that all his expenses had been fully reimbursed by the $700, which made him very happy.)

With these fresh and encouraging contacts, now seemed to be a most propitious time to try and make the trip while Teddy and his interpreter would be available to help me. I told Teddy that I would meet him in Ho Chi Minh City on 1 December 2000. This meant leaving Texas on 29 November 2000. Teddy made hotel and transportation arrangements for my arrival into Ho Chi Minh City at 9:20 pm on 1 December 2000. Additionally, I sent another letter by fax and air mail to Ambassador Douglas B. (Pete) Peterson on 19 November 2000 once again asking for his endorsement of my visit and to request assistance from the Ministry of Foreign Affairs.

About this time, at the behest of my friend Lieutenant General John H. Cushman, Retired, I was contacted by Courtney Frobenius. Courtney had worked for Jack as an advisor in Vietnam's IV Corps area. He had also commanded a rifle platoon and company on an earlier tour in the 9th Infantry Division. Courtney lived in Vietnam three years, 1995–1998. He is semi-fluent in the language and is a highly respected expert on Vietnam, the people, culture, government, and military.

Leaving in ten days for a Communist country half way around the world presented me with a challenge. Thanks to the Vietnamese Embassy web site and FedEx, I obtained a visa for my 29 November 2000 departure.

As our car arrived at the curb at the Killeen Airport on 29 November 2000, my wife, Carolyn, had a transient ischemic attack (TIA). A horrible shock and scare for us both. I later learned that the minor stroke was over prior to her arrival at the Scott and White Hospital Emergency Room. The CT Scan showed no apparent damage. Doctors considered this a fortunate warning sign and prescribed a blood thinner in hope of preventing a stroke in the future. After some adjustment to her medications, she fully recovered and continues to do quite well. A happy ending, but nonetheless a painful blow to both of us.

Unfortunately, my call to General Allen in Ho Chi Minh City did not get to him in his hotel until about the time my transportation arrived at the Ton Son Nhut Airport. I rescheduled my Vietnam visit for March 2001, or so I thought.

Rescheduling of the Visit—

On 5 December I received the following email from US Ambassador to Vietnam Peterson:

> I hope we have not let your request slip through the cracks. Upon your initial request, I asked my staff to work with the Ministry of Foreign Affairs to facilitate your trip. As far as I know we have had no word from them. My Military Attaché is out of pocket at the moment so I can't give you a good update. I'll check with the Ministry again myself to see if they have any response for us. It may be OBE for you now as I see you are to be in HCMC on or about the 30th of November. I regret we have not followed up with this closely. Let me know if everything is alright or if we need to pursue this further.
> I responded to Ambassador Peterson:
> Thank you for your interest, vital support and personal follow-up. No, my request did not drop through the cracks. Your staff has been right on top of it and very helpful. Ms Lavay Miller advised me that you had asked Deputy Chief of Mission, Dennis G. Harter, to personally pass my letters sent to you on to Ambassador Bang in Hanoi. She also advised that Ambassador Bang said he'd talk with Nugyen Manh Hung of the Ministry of Foreign Affairs Americas Department.

I responded to Ambassador Peterson by email, explaining Carolyn's TIA and my rescheduling for March 2001.

Rescheduling of the Visit Number Two—

Now that I knew the name and position of the Vietnamese official who might help us, I thought it appropriate to try and make direct contact. I sent a detailed letter and an autographed copy of Keith Nolan's *RIPCORD, Screaming Eagles Under Siege Vietnam 1970* to Mr. Nguyen Manh Hung, Director, Americas Department, Ministry of Foreign Affairs. Happily, I received a letter from Director Hung dated 18 January 2001 that acknowledged receipt of the book and welcomed my visit. Unhappily, he suggested that I reschedule the visit for the latter part of April and contact Mr. Luong Thanh Nghi, Deputy Director, Vietnam Foreign Press Center, for assistance.

I called Mr. Luong Thanh Nghi by telephone on 5 February 2001. Following this introductory conversation, I faxed Nghi a proposed detailed itinerary using their dates of 15–25 April 2001. (Appendix B) Encouraged by Col Van's earlier proposal that interviews and discussions could be arranged with

Senior General Van Tien Dung and his division, regimental and battalion commanders, I sent a list of 23 questions dealing with the battle for Ripcord. These questions were translated into Vietnamese by General Allen's interpreter and provided to Col Van. The questions were never answered.

On 23 February, Tran Le Tien of the Foreign Press Center, Ministry of Foreign Affairs sent an email saying that my 5 February letter and proposed itinerary had been received and that he, Tien, would be "the instrument of Mr. Luong Thanh Nghi" and "We are starting to coordinate with other sides for the visit."

Rescheduling of the Visit For the Third Time—

I thought the trip was finally set for 15 April until 28 March, two weeks before departure. On that date, Tien informed me by email, that the dates they had suggested were no longer acceptable. Tien said: "Your message has arrived and unfortunately I would like to inform that the timing of your trip from 15-to-25 April seems to be inconvenient for us as you know we all will be getting stuck with some other big events from mid April till early of May. So please plan your visit a little bit later." Tien did not mention it, but I learned later that the National Party Congress coincided with the dates of my scheduled visit.

A third visa request to the Vietnamese Embassy in Washington proposed a 1–10 June 2001 visit. Very fortunately for me, this timing allowed Lieutenant Colonel Fred Spaulding, Retired, to accompany me. Fred was the 3rd Brigade S-3 Air as a captain in 1970. An experienced combat soldier and officer, Fred had been a sergeant first class in the Rangers prior to attending Officer Candidate School at Fort Benning. He was on his third tour in Vietnam and had commanded five infantry rifle companies before joining the 3rd Brigade staff at Camp Evans. He spent a great deal of time in the brigade scout helicopters flying in the Ripcord area. Fred knew the AO and he knew the brigade. A key officer to the Brigade, Fred proved critical in the planning and execution of the evacuation of FSB Ripcord on 23 July 1970—a talented professional and very courageous soldier.

Mr. Tien informed me by email that Senior General Tien Van Dung probably would not have time for me and that they were having difficulty locating commanders who had fought in the battle for Ripcord. I again suggested that they get in touch with Col Nguyen Ba Van. I also noted the fact that the People's Army of Vietnam was well known for its accurate record keeping and the participants of the Ripcord battle should be relatively easy to identify. Also, at this time, I again appealed to Mr. Nguyen Manh Hung, Director, Americas Department of the Ministry of Foreign Affairs, for help, stating that the time for my rescheduled visit was fast approaching.

Mr. Luong Thanh Nghi responded that they had located Major General Chu Phuong Doi, former commander of the 324B Division, living in Cao Bang several hundred miles north of Hanoi near the border with China. Nghi said that was about a ten-hour automobile drive from Hanoi. I responded that I would pay General Doi's expenses and a consulting fee if he would meet me in Hanoi. Nghi said that Doi was 80 years old and did not want to travel. As no airline serviced Cao Bang and considering that a road trip would take at least two days of our limited time to visit General Doi not knowing if it would be at all productive in any event, we abandoned that lead.

Frustrations Continue—

By now serious doubts crossed my mind about whether or not the effort and expense of a trip back to Vietnam was really worth it. On 29 May from out of the electronic blue came an email from John Lally, St. Paul, Minnesota, that brought me back to focus on the purpose of my quest. Lally's email follows:

> I just came across the Currahees website after three decades of being out of contact with old comrades from my 1970 tour of duty. I was delighted to find your e-mail address listed, because I've been waiting 30 years to apologize to you. You won't remember the incident, but I certainly do.
>
> In 1970–71, I was a buck sergeant squad leader in Alpha, 1/506th, a former college history teacher sorely out of place and very resentful that my education was going to waste. You were, I believe, fairly new as commander of 3rd Brigade and flew your Huey out to hump the boonies with our platoon. When our company commander, Captain Bauer, sent me out from our night defensive position to fetch you, I made the decision that our journey back from the LZ would test your commitment to the men in the field. I directed my point man to take us through the toughest part of the jungle back to the NDP [night defensive position], and he certainly did.
>
> That night and the next day, you showed us what real leadership was by how you behaved and the things you taught us. When my squad escorted you back to the LZ for pickup, you again impressed me with your intelligence and humanity. We sat on the LZ for 30 minutes or so and talked education, politics and many other topics. Sergeant and Colonel...man to man. I felt ashamed for having made the journey so difficult, but didn't have the nerve to apologize then.

Our paths crossed again a few months later at Camp Evans. I'd been hurt during an air assault and was just getting out of the hospital and walking back to the company area, dressed in my still-muddy fatigues, no helmet, boots un-bloused because of my bandages. A Military Police second lieutenant—the only one I saw in RVN with a gold metal bar [insignia of a second lieutenant]—stopped me to chew me out for being so grubby. As I stood at attention in the hot sun waiting to tell him why I was in that condition, you came along, called me by name after so much time, and inquired about my health. After a brief conversation, you sent me on my way and, according to friends who were nearby, helped the lieutenant understand the responsibilities of being a leader. Of course, this only made me feel worse about my indiscretion earlier.

I know you won't remember these incidents, but both are among my most vivid memories of Vietnam. I'm happy to hear you earned your stars, because you demonstrated for me dimensions of leadership I'd never seen demonstrated, and which I've tried to emulate in my management roles since then.

Sir, I hope you are well and enjoying a well-deserved retirement. It was an honor to serve under you.

In a follow-on email, John Lally said:

Thanks for asking about what's happened since 1970. My career goals changed after Vietnam. I returned to school to work on a PhD and taught college for three years, but found the classroom—and frankly, academic attitudes towards Vietnam vets—very confining. For the last 20 years or so I've been an executive in state government, currently as Chief Information Officer (computer geek!) for the Minnesota Department of Human Services and formerly as Deputy Commissioner for the Department of Revenue—cultures as dissimilar as the Army and higher education! I live in a suburb of St. Paul, have been married to a teacher for nearly 28 years, and will have two kids in college next year.

About your trip: I've read some of Nolan's writings, and applaud your attempts to get a 360-degree perspective on the war—I used to teach the British viewpoint on the American Revolution, which was eye-opening to some students who grew up on the cherry tree and Boston Tea Party diet of patriotic conventions.

Back On Target—

By chance, another bit of encouraging news came from the US Army Command and General Staff College's January/February 2001 Military Review. It contained an article by Merle L. Pribbenow, a former CIA officer who had been stationed in Saigon. The article, "The Fog of War: The Vietnamese View of the Ia Drang Battle," included several references to the People's Army

Publishing House in Hanoi which provided welcome hope that some published North Vietnamese account of the battle for Ripcord might exist.

Courtney Frobenius, who sensed my growing frustration, suggested another possible approach. While living in Vietnam, Courtney became acquainted with Colonel Pham Van Dinh. Dinh, as a Lieutenant Colonel in the South Vietnamese Army, commanded the 56th Infantry Regiment and Camp Carroll in 1972, keys to defense against an enemy attack across the northern border, the Demilitarized Zone (DMZ). The North Vietnamese attacked in what became known as the Easter Offensive of 1972. Supported by tanks and self-propelled artillery, the NVA attack focused on Camp Carroll. After fighting off several enemy assaults and receiving massive incoming fire, Lieutenant Colonel Dinh and his officers chose to surrender the 56th Regiment and Camp Carroll with its 21 artillery pieces. His soldiers were taken prisoner and the North Vietnamese flew Dinh to Hanoi. The North Vietnamese, recognizing the political impact of Lt Col Dinh's surrender, made him a colonel in the People's Army of Vietnam and proclaimed him a national hero of North Vietnam. Following his surrender, Colonel Dinh encouraged other South Vietnamese officers "to get in touch with the NLF forces and return to the people,"

Courtney suggested that Dinh might be of significant help to me on my visit. Dinh, currently residing in Hue, enjoyed a unique position with the current communist government and he was now living in Hue. Colonel Dinh spoke English and proved thoroughly familiar with military terms and the conduct of the war. Now, counting heavily on finding pertinent documents at the People's Army Publishing House and the War Information Center in Quang Tri just north of Hue, I immediately agreed to hire Dinh. The fact that I had known Dinh in 1971 when I was the Senior Advisor to the 1st Infantry Division, ARVN, during Operation Lam Son 719 and Dinh was the executive officer of the 54th Infantry Regiment also helped.

At the time, Trang Frobenius, Courtney's wife, was in Hanoi escorting a group of students from the University of Southern Mississippi. Courtney contacted her and asked her to make arrangements with Colonel Dinh when she visited Hue. Mrs. Frobenius gave advanced pay and travel money to Colonel Dinh on my behalf. Dinh met Fred and myself at the airport in Ho Chi Minh City on 3 June 2001 and traveled with us to Hanoi and back to Hue.

Still trying to work the system, the American Ambassador personally endorsed my trip and the Ministry of Foreign Affairs officially sanctioned me as a welcome visitor. In April, I again suggested to Mr. Luong Thanh Nghi that he contact Col Nguyen Ba Van as Van had already been working on my visit. To my surprise, Nghi said, "We already talked with Colonel Nguyen Ba Van, but he could not give any feasible information for the search."

Unhappily disturbed by this, I asked Courtney if he could use the telephone numbers supplied by General Allen to try and get in touch with Col Van. Courtney's wife, Trang, called and spoke with Van. She sent me the following email:

"1. Col Van sent you a letter via surface mail 1/2 month ago to advise you of the general status of the trip. [I never received the letter.]

"2. Col Van has already visited Quang Tri for sightseeing and research.

"3. Col Van went to Hanoi 2-times.

"4. Col Van has called Mr. Nghi but was informed that Mr. Nghi has already moved. (This made no sense as I was still in touch with Nghi.) Col Van concluded saying, "Truthfully, the request from Mr. Harrison too big and too difficult to be done because some of the things relate to national secrets."

Apparently the Ministry of Foreign Affairs told Col Van to butt out!

More bad news. On 31 May, the day before our departure, Nghi emailed me that Senior General Dung's recent hospitalization precluded my visiting him. Nghi also said they had not been able locate anyone for me to interview other than Col Van in Cu Chi. Of course, General Teddy Allen's business contact in Vietnam and not the Ministry of Foreign Affairs had been the one who located and put me in contact with Col Van.

Discouraged, but not yet defeated, we pressed on for our visit to Vietnam in June 2001 in search of the North Vietnamese Army (NVA) or People's Army of Vietnam (PAVN) side of the battle for Ripcord.

Telling the Whole Story—

Our trip to Vietnam turned out quite productive to our pleasant surprise. Since the trip, a significant number of PAVN and other North Vietnamese documents have been gathered and translated. As revealing as the documents are, serious inconsistencies with the dates and sequence of events in the battle for Ripcord remain when compared with US documents and my personal experiences during the battle. And there are certain significant differences that exist in the reports of battle outcomes with respect to losses in men and materiel. Commenting on his reporting of the battle for Ripcord, Keith Nolan said,

"I have never encountered a Vietnam battle as dramatic, tragic, convoluted and bewildering as Ripcord."[1]

To facilitate the readers chronologically understanding the Ripcord battle from both sides, the author cites translated official North Vietnamese documents and interview interpretations and provides parenthetical comments. In addition to Hanoi's view, the author includes US reports of actions, personal observations made both during and after the battle, and add some aviation after-action reports, which were not available to Keith Nolan in the writing of his book.

After preparing the manuscript and readying it for publication, a press-stopping opportunity presented itself.

Another Chance to Interview Major General Chu Phuong Doi—

In November 2003, Professors Andrew Wiest and Brian O'Neil asked me to accompany their University of Southern Mississippi Vietnam War Studies Program as a war veteran-guest lecturer for three weeks in the late spring of 2004. Flattered, but still having fresh memories of a grueling eleven-day visit to Vietnam in 2001, I agreed with the caveat that General Doi is still alive and that there is a fair chance that I can interview him. This launched a search by Courtney Frobenius's Vietnam-IndoChina Tours Company. Fortuitously, Bui Cao Son (Sonny) of the HaiVan Travel Company of Hanoi sought a business relationship with Courtney and eagerly to accepted the challenge.

Sonny established that Doi, alive at age 83 resided in his home in a very remote area ten kilometers west of Cao Bang, three hundred kilometers north of Hanoi near the border with China. Doi is a retired brigadier general in the People's Army of Vietnam. His rank is equivalent to major general in the US Army. Respectfully, I have chosen to call him major general.

I provided Sonny with an introductory letter and a set of questions to be translated but not to be given to Gen Doi until I could present them. Sonny responded that going to A35 (their secret police contact) of the Ministry of the Interior, as they normally did, did not work in this case. Gen Doi told Sonny that he required permission from the Ministry of Defense for the interview with me. Sonny then advised me that he could not accompany me, but would provide Vu Binh Hau as my guide/interpreter. Courtney Frobenius cautioned me that "Binh is police or a puppet for them."

On 9 May, Sonny sent the following email (verbatim as he sent it):

Dear Sir, After going around, we came back to our normal way: directly contact related offices and get their permission (we had a Ministry of Defense official to let Gen Doi know that it's no need for him requiring MoD's permission since he's retired now).

We have permission for you to Cao Bang now after sending official dispatch to:

1. Tourism and Commerce Department of Cao Bang: Dispatch No: 21/ TMHV and got agreement by Dispatch No 188/TMDL (Mr. Do Trong Banh—Vice Director)

2. Immigration Department of Cao Bang: Dispatch No: 20/TMHV

3. Veteran Association of Cao Bang. Dispatch No: 22/TMHV.

I have talked to Gen Doi and following is his ideas:
If you arrive early evening of 25th May (between 7.00 PM—7.30 PM), you could go directly to Gen Doi's home (6 miles away from hotel) for short meeting (Gen Doi politely refused dinner invitation on 25th May). And next morning he (not with family or friend) could meet in Bang Giang hotel and may have lunch with you if the talk lasts to lunchtime.
If you arrive late, then the meeting should be arrange next morning. (I will contact Gen Doi and our guide to see if they can arrive in town in time early enough for the meeting).
Gen Doi also reminded us to bring our own water bottles for self use at his home.
    After Sonny's message, Courtney observed 13 May:
Everyone is in the loop now. The Ministry of the Interior (MI) chief-eye has a meeting today with the University of Southern Mississippi tour operator about this "Mr. Harrison" and what he is doing by going to Cao Bang to meet General Doi. We are advised that this will insure that USM will be put on the watch list with them keeping a good eyeball on you.

At last ready to join the USM study program we departed the States on schedule, 17 May. Notwithstanding my eagerness to get on up to Hanoi and Cao Bang, we had a most interesting and productive visit to the Ho Chi Minh City and Mekong Delta areas. Appendix D contains the names of the participants and a brief report of the university study group trip.

On Tuesday, 25 May, I had a 4 AM get-up for a 6:20 flight for Hanoi, while the students left on a 10:30 flight. I arrived in Hanoi at 8:30, and was met by Vu Binh Hau, translator/guide and driver, Teo, in a stick shift Toyota.

We left from the airport on the north side of Hanoi for Cao Bang—one of the most remote provinces in VN. No airport, only a 300 kilometer, frequently washed out, very narrow rough road through beautiful mountains with narrow valleys filled with lush crops of rice, corn and sugar cane. Our party arrived at Cao Bang at 5 PM, having made good time, or so they said. Hau called Gen Doi and he invited us to his home, located ten kilometers west of Cao Bang near the Bang River.

I remained apprehensive since he turned down my invitation to host his family for dinner in Cao Bang. I was certain that he was going to check me out and then decide if he would meet with me Wed morning. To my most pleasant surprise, our critical meeting proved quite warm and cordial from the very start. His wife, 77, and brother, 75, daughter and granddaughter all gathered there. It is customary in Vietnam to ask one's age when first introduced.

(Author)

Mrs. Doi, Guide Vu Binh Hau, Major General Chu Phuong Doi, Author

Following a customary sharing of tea, I presented him with Hennessey Cognac, Johnny Walker Black Label Scotch, Nolan's book, RIPCORD, my Ripcord coin, my picture autographed to him, a nicely wrapped gift for his wife and one for his daughter. After drinking the customary tea, he said he could no longer drink Cognac and offered beer instead. (He might just sell that bottle of Cognac—$60 in the duty-free store.)

He said he was most appreciative of my coming to Cao Bang. A very, very modest home, it was and is, the home of his family. His son, still in the People's Army, has a nicer, newer house next door.

For some time, we generally discussed both the French War and the American War. I gave him a translation of my questions and the two maps Courtney had prepared for me relative to the French War in his area in 1950 and '52. He put on different glasses stating he had lost the sight in his left eye and that he had gone to Moscow for surgery on his right eye. He smiled saying it was a very nice gift from the Russians. (This is the only time I have ever heard any Vietnamese give credit to the Russians for anything. Notwithstanding the 55,000 Soviets actually in North Vietnam facilitating the war, and billons of dollars provided in supplies and equipment, no papers or books published in the Socialist Republic of Vietnam have ever given any credit to the Russians for their absolutely vital support.)

Doi's wife was smiling and happy to join in the conversation. Several times Gen Doi told me how pleased he was to have me come visit him in his home. He emphasized this with a story of an American veterans group that a few years ago, wanted him to come to Hanoi for talks. He said with a bit of arrogance, "I told them if they wanted to talk to me, they must come to Cao Bang!" I told him that it was I who made that request in 2001. He sat back and smiled broadly and proclaiming he was most happy that I had come to his home this time. He announced he would come to my hotel in the morning. I asked what time and he requested the driver to come at 6 AM. We left in good cheer.

After freshening up at the hotel, Hau, Teo, and I walked around town to find a place for Internet connections, but could not locate one. We had an okay dinner and then went to bed early. The Bang Giang Hotel, considered as the best in town, had air-conditioned rooms only after you closed the windows and turned on the air. However, the lobby and dining areas lacked air-conditioning. I noted several mosquitoes in my room, but did not elect to deploy the mosquito net stored in a cabinet over the head of the bed. The best hotel in town did not take credit cards, did not convert dollars to Dong (Vietnamese currency), or take payment in dollars. Fortunately, the HaiVan travel company paid for all room charges on my behalf.

Waking up early presented no problem as my second-story room over-looked the street market right under my window where vendors sold live ducks and geese beginning at about 5 AM.

Gen Doi promptly arrived at the hotel at 7 AM and immediately announced he could work for only two hours. He enthusiastically talked about his joining Ho Chi Minh 19 Dec 1946 at the age of 24. Ho Chi Minh had returned to Vietnam in 1940 and lived in the Pac Bo caves near Cao Bang. By the time of the battle of Dong Khe, led personally by Ho Chi Minh, Doi rose to the rank of battalion commander in the *Viet Minh*. (In all of our discussions, Gen Doi always referred to his army as the *Viet Minh*, not PAVN or People's Army. He was, and is, hard core, dedicated to the *Viet Minh* purpose of freeing his country from foreign powers. (The *Viet Minh* owed its birth and growth to support given Ho Chi Minh by the Chinese Communist Party.)

Gen Doi provided details of the very significant defeat of LePaige in 1950. Doi was next a battalion commander with the *Pathet Lao* between 1952 and 1954. He said that Ho Chi Minh personally placed him in command of the 209th Regiment at the battle of Dien Bien Phu in 1954. He presented me with a picture made of himself in uniform at the just observed 50th Anniversary of their great victory of Dien Bien Phu. (The cropped picture is on the back of the dust cover.)

Doi remained in the Dien Bien Phu area as a regimental commander until given command of the 324B Division in 1965. He said his mission in 1967 and 1968 was to draw the American Marines into battle along Route 9, in the highlands, to relieve the pressure on the *Viet Cong* forces operating in the highly populated coastal areas. This Hanoi directed strategy evolved into the famous hill fights of 1967 and eventually into the prolonged siege of Khe Sanh in 1968.

He then went on to my questions that he had studied the night before. He cleared up some of the confusion of the official PAVN history of the 324B Division. When I asked a question about what the 1992 published history book said in obvious error, he would reply, "I was not there when they wrote this." I will provide Gen Doi's recollections as the battle for Ripcord unfolds.

I

The Vietnam War in 1970

US Army and Marine ground forces accelerate withdrawal from the battlefield as Hanoi pushes major People's Army reinforcements into South Vietnam.

1

Strategic Setting of Fire Support Base Ripcord

The overarching strategy for US forces in the Vietnam War in 1970 was "Vietnamization" of the war. This meant turning over the war to the South Vietnamese government and its military forces. For this strategy to succeed, the Army of the Republic of Vietnam (ARVN) had to become stronger and the US forces could best buy time for this strategy by weakening the North Vietnamese forces. US forces could do this by restricting the flow of men and materials from North Vietnam into South Vietnam, destroying enemy base areas and defeating North Vietnamese forces on the field of battle. US and ARVN forces struck a long overdue blow across the border into North Vietnamese base areas in Cambodia on 29 April 1970. American public outrage and Congressional pressure caused President Richard M. Nixon to shut down the operation and order the withdrawal of US forces from Cambodia by 30 June 1970. Concurrently, the Nixon administration accelerated the withdrawal schedule of US forces from Vietnam. Nonetheless, the imperative for US forces to help the Republic of Vietnam in Vietnamization did not change.

The only offensive campaign for all of Vietnam planned by the US Military Assistance Command Vietnam (USMACV) for the summer of 1970 called for the 101st Airborne Division with the support of the Army of the Republic of Vietnam (ARVN) 1st Infantry Division, to conduct operations in the A Shau Valley, the North Vietnamese "warehouse area" and against the branches of the Ho Chi Minh Trail coming into South Vietnam in both Quang Tri and Thua Thien Provinces.

Available intelligence about North Vietnamese forces in this area lacked sufficient detail. With the Paris Peace Talks under way for a year, the North Vietnamese sought to strengthen their negotiating position by "liberating" more areas in South Vietnam. Their strategy would not include withdrawal or slackening of operations.

An integral part of the US plan required allied forces operating in the mountains northeast of the A Shau Valley to locate and destroy the logistic facilities and interdict lines of communication of the 803d and 29th NVA Regiments.

Fire Support Base Ripcord scheduled to be re-opened in March 1970, became the key forward operational base in the division's summer offensive plan. Mutually supporting firebases were to be opened at Bradley, Airborne, and Kathryn to support operations in the enemy's rear service areas. Neither Bradley, a mountaintop southwest of Ripcord, very near the A Shau Valley, nor Airborne, well to the south of Ripcord, were opened. Kathryn, although opened, remained too far to the rear to support operations in or around Ripcord. So much for the grand plan. The Division Commander, noting the enemy's fierce resistance to the opening of Ripcord, simply did not want to pick any more fights by reopening more fire support bases near the A Shau with a Division whose assets were already too thinly spread out.

Major General John M. Wright, the Commanding General of the 101st Airborne Division, ordered the 3rd Brigade to initiate the USMACV offensive named TEXAS STAR, on 1 April 1970 in coordination with the 1st Infantry Division, ARVN. Reconnaissance and patrol action began in early March.

To the eyes of the American commanders, the tactical AO defined the first line of defense between the North Vietnamese Army (NVA) base areas spreading across the Laotian border into Vietnam and the famous Ho Chi Minh Trail through northwest South Vietnam and just across the border into Laos. (None of the old fire support bases west and north of Carroll, Barnett, O'Reilly, Gladiator, Ripcord and Rakkasan were occupied in 1970.) The Government of the Republic of Vietnam (RVN) controlled areas along the thin ribbon of coastal littoral lying astride Highway 1 along the South China Sea. The Brigade's mission was to engage the enemy and destroy his offensive capabilities against the ARVN controlled populated areas.

To the troopers in the boonies, the AO looked thick, hot, steaming in the day, cold and wet at night, triple canopy, insect filled jungle with an occasional view of back-breaking hills to climb in wet boots with a 70 to 80 pound rucksack on their back, grenades and ammo magazines on their chest and a rifle welded to their hand. To the grunt on the ground the land mass appeared as a vast and barely permeable array of single, double and triple canopy jungle interlaced with sheer mountains and steep basaltic cliffs.

To those fortunate enough to view it from a helicopter, the AO looked like a lush green carpet of jungle vegetation, broken only by the occasional cleared hilltop of currently occupied or more likely, abandoned fire support bases, and pockmarked by giant holes created by bombs dropped from Goliath B-52's in the course of the war over a span of years. On the western horizon, stood the picturesque but imposing set of high ridgelines outlining the A Shau Valley. The surreal beauty of the green mountains fades as the grunt all too quickly recalls how brief his helicopter ride will be.

Over flying the AO as the brigade commander, the beauty of the passing countryside only briefly held my attention as I considered the awesome brigade mission as part of the division's Operation TEXAS STAR. The mission "to counter the threat presented by the enemy's eastward thrust out of the A Shau Valley and toward the populated lowlands" required troops on the ground to follow up on intelligence leads and deny the enemy free reign in this rugged and remote area where he sought to create and re-supply forward base facilities. To order young soldiers into this coliseum of death, where they would meet young soldiers of our enemy, each seeking to kill the other, weighed heavily as an awesome burden of command.

Because of the withdrawal of both US Marine Divisions and the redeployment of the 1st Cavalry Division out of the northern provinces of South Vietnam, the 3rd Brigade of the 101st Airborne Division in 1970 had a very large piece of the Vietnam War. The math is easy. Where once three US divisions were fully engaged, now there is one division, and more enemy. The 3rd Brigade's Area of Operations (AO) spanned from the former US Marine combat bases at Khe Sanh and Fire Support Base (FSB) Shepard, both facing north towards the Demilitarized Zone (DMZ) at the 17th parallel in the far northwest corner of South Vietnam in Quang Tri Province. The AO extended in a southerly direction past FSB Barnett and FSB O'Reilly where American troops were stationed in supporting roles to the Army of the Republic of Vietnam (ARVN) 1st Infantry Division, past FSB Gladiator, down to FSB Ripcord in Thua Thien Province at the northeastern mouth of the A Shau Valley. From here, the AO went east to FSB Rakkasan and Camp Evans, the base camp of the 3rd Brigade, just northwest of the ancient Imperial Citadel Hue. From Camp Evans the AO followed a northerly course to the 3rd Brigade's alternate Command Post at Camp Carroll immediately south of the Cam Lo River in the southern DMZ area. The 3rd Brigade Area of Operations was about 1300 square kilometers or 800 square miles. Interestingly, this approximated the size of the AO for the entire 1st Cavalry Division when America launched its first ground force offensive in the Ia Drang Valley in October-November 1965.

Conventionally organized, the primary fighting force of the 101st Airborne Division consisted of three infantry brigades, each with three infantry battalions. Not so conventionally, these infantry forces were airmobile and moved about the battlefield on the rotary wings of the three helicopter battalions of the 101st Aviation Group. In 1968, the 3rd Battalion, 506th Infantry was detached from the division and assigned to II Field Force and employed in the Central Highlands of South Vietnam. In 1970, three infantry battalions were assigned to the 1st Brigade and employed in the southern portion of Thua Thien Province with one of these battalions normally committed to be the Division Reserve as a Rapid Reaction Force. Two infantry battalions were assigned to the 2nd Brigade and conducted pacification operations in the populated coastal area of Thua Thien Province. The remaining three infantry battalions were assigned to the 3rd Brigade and fought in the northern and western portions of the Division AO.

During part of the June-August 1970 period, the 3rd Brigade had operational control of six of the eight airmobile infantry battalions in the division (frequently, as many as four infantry battalions at the same time) as well as a brief period of control of the division air cavalry squadron—all of whom were engaged in bitter contact with the regular army forces of North Vietnam. The 3rd Brigade AO fought a conventional war against regular army units of North Vietnam who were equipped with long-range mortars and rockets, recoilless rifles, heavy machine guns and antiaircraft weapons. The overall mission of US Forces in Vietnam focused on counterinsurgency, but in the Third Brigade AO, we were trying to repel or destroy a formidable, conventional, invading army.

The 2nd Battalion, 502nd Infantry and the 2nd Squadron, 17th Cavalry conducted operations in the Khe Sanh-FSB Shepard area. The 1st Battalion, 506th Infantry occupied and conducted operations in the FSB Kathryn area and later, in the FSB Rakkasan area. The 1st Battalion, 501st Infantry opened and conducted operations in the FSB Gladiator area. The 2nd Battalion, 501st Infantry, from time to time, operated north, west and south of FSB Ripcord and conducted a coordinated battalion attack on Hill 1000. The 2nd Battalion, 506th Infantry Currahees on and around FSB Ripcord, conducted the most intense and sustained combat operations. After the 2nd Battalion, 506th Infantry evacuated FSB Ripcord and was placed in Reserve on 23 July, the 3rd Battalion, 187th Infantry opened and conducted operations in the FSB Jack area. The 1st and 2nd Regiments of the 1st Infantry Division, Army of the Republic of Vietnam (ARVN) and the 1st Brigade, 5th Infantry Division (Mechanized) also conducted operations in parts of this AO, mostly in the lowlands to the north and to the east. An armor/mechanized infantry battalion task force from the 1st Brigade, 5th Infantry Division (Mechanized) was briefly under the operational control of the 3rd Brigade.

The 3rd Brigade AO was quite large and quite busy throughout the summer of 1970. My notes show that between 23 June and 31 August, during my first 69 days in command, the 3rd Brigade conducted the following operations:

- 16 Battalion sized combat air assaults to multiple Landing Zones.

- 15 Battalion sized extractions from multiple Pick-Up Zones.

- 4 Fire Support Bases were opened.

- 6 Fire Support Bases were closed.

The units and fire support bases of the 3rd Brigade during this very intense period of operations, June—August 1970, can be seen in the sketch below:

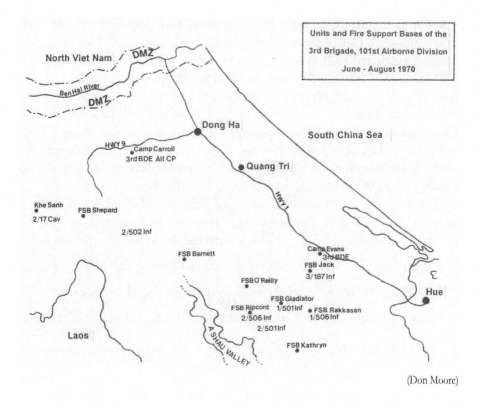

(Don Moore)

The former Republic of South Vietnam was made up of 44 provinces. The province that claimed the most Americans killed was Quang Tri, which bordered on both North Vietnam and Laos. Fifty-four percent of all Americans killed in Vietnam died in the four northernmost provinces, which in addition to Quang Tri were Thua Thien, Quang Nam and Quang Tin. All of them shared borders with Laos. An additional six provinces accounted for another twenty-five percent of the Americans killed in action (KIA). Those six also shared borders with either Laos or Cambodia or had contiguous borders with provinces that did. The remaining 34 provinces accounted for just twenty-one percent of US KIA. These numbers should dispel the notion that South Vietnam was some kind of flaming inferno of violent revolutionary dissent. The overwhelming majority of Americans killed, died in border battles against regular NVA units. The policies established by President Lyndon B. Johnson and Secretary of Defense Robert S. McNamara did not allow the American soldiers to cross those borders and destroy America's enemy forces. Expressed in WW II terms; this is the functional equivalent of having sent the American soldiers to fight in Europe during WW II, but restricting them to Italy, France, Belgium, and Holland, and not letting them cross the borders into Germany, the source of the problem. General Curtis LeMay aptly defined Johnson's war policy in South Vietnam by saying that "We are swatting flies in the South when we should be going after the manure pile in Hanoi."[2]

After the fiasco of the 1961 Bay of Pigs invasion of Cuba, President John F. Kennedy confided to James Reston of The New York Times, "Now we have a problem in making our power credible, and Vietnam is the place,"[3] President Kennedy increased the advisory and support effort from a few hundred to twelve thousand in 1962. Attention was focused on Vietnam and a high priority of effort was established. President Lyndon B. Johnson continued the policy of increasing the advisory and support efforts and then, in 1965, ordered Marine and Army infantry combat troops deployed to Vietnam and authorized a buildup in South Vietnam of a half a million Americans.

Five years later, in 1970, the US military in Vietnam was into the second year of President Richard Nixon's ordered unilateral withdrawals. The 1968 *Tet* offensive, by the *Viet Cong* and NVA that turned the entire South Vietnamese countryside into a combat zone, seemed to us in 1970 like another war from another era. The whole world knew that the United States was getting out of Vietnam. Yet, here we were, in daily contact with a fierce and determined enemy, but no one except those in the 101st Airborne Division seemed to know about it. There were reasons. The Brigade AO was 500 miles north of Saigon, Headquarters for the US Military Assistance Command Vietnam (USMACV) and the concentration point for US and world news media representatives. Even more cogent, on 29 April1970, USMACV launched Operation *Toan Thang* (Vietnamese meaning Total Victory) 43 into the supposedly neutral, off-limits territory of Cambodia. World news media immediately focused on this operation. Also, the fact that the same 3rd Bde, 101st Airborne was taking significant casualties in an area near the previous and costly battle for Hamburger Hill (10–20 May 1969) was not something that USMACV wanted to call to the attention of the news media.

Operation *Toan Thang* 43 into Cambodia was led by then Brigadier General Robert M. Shoemaker with major elements of the 1st Cavalry Division. The 25th Infantry Division provided both an armored and a mechanized infantry battalion. The US 11th Armored Cavalry Regiment and the ARVN 1st Armored Cavalry Regiment provided the reconnaissance and first assault force. The ARVN 3rd Airborne Brigade provided the initial reserve for the attack. The total force of assault troops was about ten thousand US and five

thousand ARVN. At the peak of operations in Cambodia, the South Vietnamese had about twenty-nine thousand and the US had about nineteen
thousand troops in the operation. War protestors focused on Cambodia. On
10 May 1970, over 80,000 people attended an anti-war demonstration in
Washington, DC. The demonstrators also protested the tragic deaths of four
students at Kent State University in Ohio and two students at the predomi-
nantly black Jackson State College in Jackson, Mississippi. Unrest in the
United States was widespread and provoked powerful emotions.

While the Cambodian incursion grabbed the attention of the entire world,
another battle of significant impact took place at Fire Support Base Ripcord
and was virtually ignored. Neither USMACV nor the 101st Airborne Division
called attention to it. It was a very long way from Saigon. Travel to 101st Airborne Division Headquarters was difficult. Travel to Ripcord was dangerous
and impossible without military assistance, to include helicopters.

All military commanders in 1970 were well aware of growing disenchant-
ment with the Vietnam War. American public support of their military fell in
a steep decline. It was exacerbated by the Viet Cong/North Vietnamese Army
Tet 1968 general offensive throughout the countryside and in the principal cities that many in the media wrongly interpreted as a major US military setback.
The May-June 1970 Cambodia 'incursion' failed in its political purpose. The
November 1969 revelations of the March 1968 My Lai massacre and the
deaths of students at Kent State and Jackson State in May 1970 were repug-
nant to the American public. Nothing, however, was more prominent in the
minds of US commanders in the field in 1970, than the Battle of Hamburger
Hill in May 1969.

In May 1969, just one year before Ripcord, Major General Melvin Zais,
Commanding General, 101st Airborne Division directed the 3rd Brigade to
conduct Operation APACHE SNOW on the high ground on the far-western
side of the A Shau Valley to deny the enemy a sanctuary/warehouse area in
this highly important part of the Ho Chi Minh Trail. Colonel Joseph Conmy,
then 3rd Brigade Commander, ordered Lieutenant Colonel Weldon "Tiger"
Honeycutt's 3rd Battalion, 187th Infantry to assault Dong Ap Bia, Hill 937.
The 29th Regiment of the PAVN defended the steep slopes of the hill from
well dug-in and fortified bunkers. A time-tested battlefield rule of thumb
requires a minimum of a three-to-one favorable force ratio to go on the offensive. Here, the ratio was reversed; one battalion attacked three enemy battalions that held the well-fortified high ground. Dedicated and disciplined
American soldiers followed their brave leaders in seven separate assaults up the

rain soaked, slippery hill. Three more US/ARVN battalions joined the fight before the 3/187th finally reached the peak of Dong Ap Bia. The cost in lives for the US soldiers was 56 dead and over 400 wounded. The high cost in US casualties proved especially grievous by the repeated "friendly fire" incidents involving helicopter gunships firing on US troops in conditions of rain-induced poor visibility. To the astonishment and some bitterness of the exhausted soldiers on the hill, Dong Ap Bia was abandoned as the 101st Airborne Division withdrew from the A Shau Valley.

General Westmoreland declared the Dong Ap Bia battle a tactical victory with a body count of over 10 enemy KIA for each American soldier lost. The US high command had maintained that if we kill ten of the enemy for every single friendly loss, we are bound to win. Seeds of doubt were cast on the battlefield. Even though a tactical victory, as was Tet one year earlier, the attrition theory of war as applied to Hanoi, no longer seemed appropriate.

For the first time in US history, an American Army battle victory was denounced on the floor of the United States Senate. This was the real world of 1970 in which our brave and dedicated soldiers fought the battle of Ripcord.

The Infamous "Body Count"—

Much has been said about "body count" in the Vietnam War. Many have criticized commanders for "demanding" body count as a way of showing higher headquarters that their unit was doing well in the fighting. The accuracy of body count varied significantly throughout this long war depending on which unit, in what part of Vietnam, and who the senior commander was at the time. There was, undoubtedly, some distortion, exaggeration, and out-and-out fabrication.

In the better units, and the 101st Airborne Division was certainly one of the best, body count generally was fairly accurate. This was because the senior commanders, at the least the ones I observed first hand, did not put a premium on body count. The troops understood that reporting estimated number of enemy killed would not be accepted without tangible evidence of bodies, weapons, and other equipment recovered from the battlefield.

It is also understandable that the body count might be distorted a bit for morale purposes of the fighting grunts. In 1966, I observed my 10th Combat Aviation Battalion gunships killing enemy soldiers that I verified myself by low and slow flight over the engagement area. At the next briefing at the 101st Command Post, I heard that such and such rifle company killed "X" number of NVA in that exact same fight without any credit given to the gunships. I raised no objections. Sometimes infantry battalion commanders, like Frank "Gunslinger" Dietrich, admitted after the briefing that they knew it was our gunships that were responsible for the enemy KIAs, but the troops needed credit for the kills to boost morale.

The news media from the very start, focused on body count. Body count was used by some, to measure "success" in the war and, fairly frequently, the media used it to deride commanders for the way they were conducting the war. The media alleged that commanders pushed their troops unnecessarily or improperly to generate high body count. In rare and exceptional cases, this may have indeed been true.

It is interesting to note how "body count" got started. It was not by self-serving commanders in the field nor the statistics mesmerized "whiz kids" of Secretary Robert McNamara, but the practice was directed from the highest National Military Command Authority. The demand came directly from the White House from President Lyndon Johnson.

On April 8, 1965 President Johnson asked Gen Earle Wheeler, Chairman of the Joint Chiefs of Staff, "How many *Viet Cong* have we killed since you were here last time?" Later the President wanted to know "how many *Viet Cong* have been killed since the 1st of Jan and how many Vietnamese have been killed by the *Viet Cong* and how many Americans?"[4] From that date forward, the Chairman of the Joint Chiefs was provided daily with friendly and enemy losses, which came to be known as "body count."

Body Count continues—

In 2003 and 2004, the news media announced body count in Iraq several times a day.

The Isolation of the Ripcord Battle—

In addition to the significant distance from Saigon to Ripcord, the difficulty of travel, the personal danger, and competing newsworthy stories, news media personnel were not welcomed in the 101st Airborne Division AO. A lesson was learned at Dong Ap Bia—Hamburger Hill that taking heavy casualties and providing that unpleasant news, especially at this time of the war-wind-down, to the American public, brought down sharp criticism and scrutiny on the already unfortunate unit. Captain Fred Spaulding, the Brigade S-3 Air during the battle for Ripcord, recalls that a team of reporters and photographers from NBC reached Camp Evans in early July 1970, but 101st Airborne Division Headquarters would not allow them to visit FSB Ripcord. Even Army combat photographers and reporter soldiers were not permitted to visit Ripcord. One Army team made it out to Ripcord sneaking aboard a helicopter, but were quickly ordered out of the area when detected. This was indeed extraordinary censorship in a here-to-fore uncensored war.

Lam Son 719—The South Vietnamese Thrust Into Laos—

The North Vietnamese counterattacked in the wake of Cambodia with pressure from Laos towards the coastal littoral cities in Military Region 1. The natural route from the Ho Chi Minh Trail diverted into South Vietnam through the A Shau Valley of Thua Thien Province.[5] The attack axis was from the vicinity of Hamburger Hill right into the heart of the 3rd Brigade AO.

The decision by the President of the Republic of Vietnam to launch a major South Vietnamese Army and Marine offensive from Khe Sanh along Route 9 into Laos to seal off the Ho Chi Minh Trail was a bold initiative of the Saigon government. If successful, it not only would disrupt the Ho Chi Minh Trail, but also prove with high visibility that the process of Vietnamization of the war was working. The decision was of immediate tactical and strategic significance to the 3rd Brigade. We generally did not know this in the brigade, even as classified information, until January 1971 just before Lam Son 719 began on 8 Feb 1971. The operation called for the establishment of a series of fire support bases along Route 9 to Tchepone, Laos.

Apparently the North Vietnamese intelligence was much better than our brigade intelligence. Senior South Vietnamese officials began to discuss the plan for operations into Laos well before any participation of top-level US personnel. Security leaks in the RVN government were large and legend. General Creighton Abrams, (COMUSMACV) conducted the first reported meeting to discuss countermeasures against the NVA buildup in Laos on 8 December 1970. Classified Top Secret, only six invited senior US general officers attended.

The NVA in Hanoi knew or anticipated this major offensive and planned "The Southern Laos—Route 9 Counter-Offensive Campaign" and started taking action six-months earlier in June 1970. This was a "Secret Document for PAVN Internal Distribution." The PAVN high command began to reinforce the 968th Division for its mission of security for the Ho Chi Minh Trail in Central and Southern Laos near Khe Sanh and the A Shau Valley, bordering and into the 3rd Brigade AO.[6] These reinforcements for the 968th Division strengthened the re-supply lines and base areas of the PAVN units operating against the 3rd Brigade. The increase in late June and early July 1970 of PAVN air defense weapons and 120mm mortars around the Ripcord area were a manifestation of this strategic move by Hanoi, and completely unknown to the 3rd Brigade until we found ourselves on the receiving end of the increased firepower.

There is still speculation on who knew what and when and what were the real intentions of the NVA in this strategic area, now more important than ever, because of the closure of the port at Sihanoukville, Cambodia as the primary entry point for supplies to the Viet Cong and NVA in southern South Vietnam. Whether the NVA were planning offensive or defensive operations, this portion of the Ho Chi Minh Trail was absolutely vital to North Vietnam. Major combat continued in the Ripcord area in 1970 as we gave little thought to the fact that parties to the Paris Peace Talks would meet on 21 January 1971 for the one-hundredth time.

(Ripcord Association)

Fire Support Base Ripcord June 1970.

The fire support base may look small in the above picture, but it was a fairly large base, about the size of four football fields and "home" to a battalion headquarters (for a short time also an ARVN battalion headquarters), a battalion medical aid station, one battery of six-105mm howitzers, one battery of six-155mm howitzers, the 2/506th Recon Plat, a quad 50mm machine gun section, three platoons (twelve tubes total) of 81mm mortars, two 90mm recoilless rifles, a platoon of engineers, and three helicopter landing pads controlled by a team of Pathfinders.

The two pictures below were taken in July 1996 by the JTF-FA team in Vietnam working on the case of the missing bodies of Staff Sgt Lewis Howard, Jr. and PFC Charles E. Beals, D Co, 2/506th Inf. Sgt Gary Radford, the soldiers' platoon sergeant when they were wounded and presumed dead on 7 July 1970 on Hill 1000, accompanied the JTF-FA team on the July 1996 search effort. Unfortunately, no bodies were found.

(JTF-FA)

FSB Ripcord taken from Hill 1000 July 1996.

The above picture of FSB Ripcord was taken from Hill 1000 in July 1996. The hill is still bare of vegetation 26 years after the battle. The picture below from the vicinity of Ripcord shows the two critical peaks of Hill 1000.

(JTF-FA)

Hill 1000 taken from the vicinity of FSB Ripcord July 1996.

Units Assigned to 3rd Brigade, 101st Airborne Division, with their rear base at Camp Evans, and normally under the Operational Control of the 3rd Brigade:

3rd Battalion, 187th Infantry "Rakkasans"
1st Battalion, 506th Infantry "Currahees"
2nd Battalion, 506th Infantry "Currahees"
3rd Brigade Reconnaissance and Security Platoon
3rd Brigade Aviation Section

Units sometimes placed temporarily under the Operational Control of the 3rd Brigade On Order of the Division Commander:

1st Battalion, 501st Infantry "Geronimo"
2nd Battalion, 501st infantry "Drive On"
2nd Battalion, 502nd Infantry "Strike Force"
2nd Squadron, 17th Air Cavalry

A Troop, 2nd Squadron, 17th Air Cavalry "Assault"
B Troop, 2nd Squadron, 17th Air Cavalry "Banshee"
C Troop, 2nd Squadron, 17th Air Cavalry "Condor"

Units in support of the 3rd Brigade:

158th Assault Helicopter Battalion (all companies based at Camp Evans.)
C Company, 158th Assault Helicopter Battalion "Phoenix" in Direct
    Support
A Company, 158th Assault Helicopter Battalion "Ghostriders"
B Company, 158th Assault Helicopter Battalion "Lancers"
D Company, 158th Assault Helicopter Battalion "Redskins"
101st Assault Helicopter Battalion
A Company, 101st Assault Helicopter Battalion "Comancheros"
B Company, 101st Assault Helicopter Battalion "Kingsmen"
C Company, 101st Assault Helicopter Battalion "Black Widows"
D Company, 101st Assault Helicopter Battalion "Hawks"
159th Assault Support Helicopter Battalion "Liftmasters"
A Company, 159th Assault Support Helicopter Battalion "Pachyderms"
B Company, 159th Assault Support Helicopter Battalion "Varsity"
C Company, 159th Assault Support Helicopter Battalion "Playtex"
2nd Battalion, 319th Field Artillery 105mm in Direct Support
C Company, 4th Battalion, 77th Aerial Rocket Artillery "Griffins" in Gen-
eral Support Reinforcing 2/319th Arty (Based at Camp Evans.)
A Battery, 2nd Battalion, 11th Artillery in General Support Reinforcing
    2/319th Arty
A Battery, 1st Battalion, 39th Artillery in General Support Reinforcing
    Division Arty
A Battery, 2nd battalion 94th Artillery in General Support XXIVth Corps
3rd Forward Supply and Support Element, 101st Division Support
    Command in Direct Support
Support Team, 501st Signal Battalion in Direct Support
Support Team, 101st Military Intelligence Detachment
3rd Detachment, 265th Radio Research Unit
58th Infantry Platoon (Scout Dog)
Unite States Air Force Tactical Air Control Party, 20th Tactical Air
    Support Squadron

2

Strategic Setting of PAVN Forces in the Ripcord Area in 1970

The Central Party Committee of the *Lao Dong* has always dictated the military strategy of North Vietnam. The strategy has been influenced by the history and culture of the Vietnamese people and by foreign Communist countries. The strategy has changed over time, as has the influence of certain foreign countries. How this complex process has evolved is covered later in the book, but first, we will cut to Hanoi's military strategic setting in the 3rd Brigade's AO in 1970.

The Quang Tri Province and Thua Thien Province Theater—

Hanoi's People's Army of Vietnam referred to the Quang Tri Province and Thua Thien Province Theater of operations as the Tri-Thien-Hue Theater or sometimes, the Tri-Thien Theater. It was known as the B4 Front. B5 Front was also in Quang Tri Province in the north running between the DMZ and Highway 9. The two provinces in the Tri-Thien Theater included all of the 3rd Brigade's Area of Operations. In 1985 the Thuan Hoa Publishers in Hue City, under the editorial supervision of The Committee for the Final Report on the War in the Tri-Thien-Hue Theater, Chief Editor: Kieu Tam Nguyen, produced a report covering three periods. We will look at a portion of the Second Period, from the beginning of 1970 until the end of 1971. Robert J. Destatte translated this document.

Second Period of The Tri-Thien-Hue Theater-From the beginning of 1970 to the end of 1970.

Editorial Note: The words are those of the 1985 Communist Committee for the Final Report on the War in the Tri-Thien-Hue Theater. (*I will provide editorial clarification with parenthetical comments in italics. Take note of the integration of military/political/civil imperatives as discussed in Enemy Situation.*)

General:
    Defeated in the mountainous regions, the enemy (*US and ARVN forces*) withdrew to strengthen his lines in the piedmont region while employing all manner of ruthless pacification methods. The enemy foolhardily initiated an operation (in 1971-Lam Son 719) in the Highway 9-Southern Laos region, which was an important test of his strategy to "Vietnamize the war"

    We continued to attack the enemy, defeated his operations in the mountain forests (at high point 935 (*FSB Ripcord*), Coc Bai (*FSB O'Reilly*), Da Ban (*FSB Barnett*), etc.), step-by-step restored our position and strength in the three strategic regions, and helped defeat the enemy's operation in the Highway 9-Southern Laos region. Thereafter we were able to control the mountain forests, make inroads into the piedmont region, push our movement in the lowlands forward a new step, and prepare for the 1972 strategic (*Easter*) offensive which achieved a decisive victory. (*The 1972 Offensive was a costly defeat for the PAVN and proved that the South Vietnamese could effectively defend their country with appropriate US fire support and re-supply with Advisor presence in ARVN and SVN Marine units.*)

Enemy (*US/ARVN*) situation:
    During the two year period 1970–1971, the American imperialists frantically implemented the Nixon clique's strategy to 'Vietnamize the war:'

1.   They made efforts to pacify and control the populace and to transform the lowlands and cities into a large secure rear base area.

2.   They engaged in military adventures by expanding the war into Cambodia and striving to disrupt our strategic commo-liaison corridor [i.e., the HCM Trail] in an effort to cut off our supplies from the North, to prevent our regular forces from assembling for large attacks, and to return the South to a state of guerrilla warfare of decreasing intensity.

3.   They strove to build the puppet military into a force strong enough to replace American forces.

4.   They made efforts to build a puppet government that was strong from
     top to bottom.

To carry out these strategic intentions, the Americans engineered a
coup against Sihanouk, swept aside Cambodian neutralism, and then
opened a large operation (50,000 Americans and 50,000 puppets) (*The
actual numbers were 19,000 US and 29,000 ARVN.*) into Cambodia, hoping
to destroy our rear bases and push (*North*) Vietnamese regular forces back
(March 1970). Next, they initiated an operation into the Indochina tri-border area in the vicinity of Attopeu, Laos (*west of Dak To*). Then in January
1971 (*actually initiated 8 February 1971*) they opened a large-scale operation in the Highway 9-Southern Laos region.

In parallel with the various large operations and new military adventures, the Americans and puppets carried out successive "accelerated pacification," "special pacification," "community self-defense pacification," and
"local development" plans with an unprecedented level of violence.

After going through two years of continuous enemy counterattacks and
ruthless pacification efforts we entered 1970 in the *Tri-Thien-Hue* Theater
with the enemy still trying to pacify the lowland plains, block us in the
piedmont areas, and destroy us in the mountain forests. He concentrated
his regular forces along Highway 9, strengthened his defensive lines on
Highways 9 and 12, and dug in on high points in the intermediate defense
line (the mountain forests) (*these high points are FSBs Ripcord, O'Reilly and
Barnett*) in an effort to block our regular forces from attacking and to
destroy our strength in the three strategic regions.

Friendly (*PAVN*) situation:

In January 1970, the 18th Plenum of the Central Party Committee
reviewed the situation since *Tet Mau Than* 1968, and outlined a new direction requiring that we "step up attacks throughout the three strategic
regions, making the rural areas the primary focal point for attack, and correctly employ a strategy based on the principles of protracted struggle to
strive for a decisive victory in a relatively short period of time." With regard
to fighting, the Central Party Committee clearly set out guidelines that "we
must continue to step up conventional fighting by regular forces until there
are positive improvements in the local guerrilla warfare movement, and to
emphasize the strategic importance of rear service operations…" With
regard to political guidance, "While focusing on the three strategic regions
we must strengthen the Party's leadership in the urban and rural areas,
mobilize popular uprising movements, strive to gain and retain control of
the populace, and defeat the enemy's rural pacification plans."

The Central Party Committee also laid out concrete guidelines for
action in the event the American imperialists took the risk of expanding the
war into Laos and Cambodia. Central Party Resolution No. 18 was an
extremely sound change of direction in military strategy that dated back to

Tet 1968, and established the basis for huge new successes and changes that would increasingly favor us in our Theater during 1970 and 1971.

On 18 March 1970, the Region Party Committee studied and implemented Central Party Resolution No. 18 by laying out a general mission that we must 'defeat Vietnamization in the Tri-Thien region, develop new power and strength, carry out combined arms attacks, and bring about big changes.' The Region Party Committee stressed: 'Pacification is the most important scheme in the enemy's strategic doctrine, it is the backbone of his policy of Vietnamization; therefore, 'the defeat of pacification is the crucial central mission of the entire Party, the entire armed forces, and the entire population at the present time.' To carry out this central mission the Region and Military Region Party Committees pronounced that: 'parallel with building up the strength of the revolution, we must step-by-step intensify the movement to disrupt pacification in the lowland rural areas; however, the deciding factor will be for us to concentrate on control of the mountain forests (*This "deciding factor" clearly made destruction of Ripcord the PAVN's top priority. While the US was planning a major offensive, the PAVN was also planning a new strategy of going on the offensive.*), and from there restore our position in the three strategic regions and develop the combined military and political strength with which to defeat the enemy's pacification program.

(Major General Chu Phuong Doi told me during our 26 May 04 discussions, that Lieutenant General Tran Van Quang was given command of Military District 4 and placed in direct control of the offensive against Firebase Ripcord.)

To carry out this resolution, the Military *(Tri-Thien)* Region Party Committee issued the following major guidelines for 1970:

• Get a firm grasp of the enemy's operational procedures, take the initiative to defeat his operations in the mountainous regions and our commo-liaison corridors (*HCM Trail*); and defeat his tactics of occupying high points, leap-frogging with helicopters, and ambushing us in the piedmont region.

• Strengthen the regular forces so they will have sufficient strength to initiate campaigns, giving priority to upgrading district armed forces and village guerrillas.

• Promote movements to shoot down helicopters and produce foodstuffs (five million manioc tubers). (*This is the root of the cassava plant with a thick skin and is boiled like a potato.*)

Military Region also declared that progress in 1970 must be a high priority and must be solid. Military Region split 1970 into two periods. Phase

1 (from January to June) primarily would be a period in which we would establish our military posture. Phase 2 (from June forward) would be a period in which we would expand our new posture (*The siege and attack to destroy Ripcord began the first day of Phase 2, on 1 July.*).

The theater operational plan for 1970 was divided into three phases, focused primarily on the mountain forests.

Spring phase, from January to March 1970:

(*The Tri-Thien Theater plan had succeeding phases of April to June and then June to August. Theater forces included in the plan were the 324B Division, 304B Division and the 5th, 6th and 8th Regiments of Regional Forces.*)

Military Region Headquarters decided to continue the attack and apply strong pressure to the enemy's entire defense line in order to force him to respond in many different locations at the same time. Meanwhile we would gradually move our local force units down to operate in the lowland foot-hills to provide direct support to our grass-roots movement aimed at disrupting the enemy's pacification campaign. At the same time the Military Region would use its own main force units to attack and shatter a number of the important links in the enemy defensive network in order to cause it to disintegrate and collapse. Building on this foundation we would open a gateway down to the lowlands.

Higher authority assigned responsibility for carrying out this mission to two units:

• 324Bth Division was responsible for attacking and destroying the enemy's operational base on Hill 935 (*FSB Ripcord*) in *Thua Thien*.

• 304B Division would attack and destroy the enemy base at Da Ban (*FSB Barnett*) in Quang Tri. (Footnote: During this period the High Command assigned 304B Division to Military Region Tri-Thien in order to be able to draw on its forces to work the 324B strategic supply line.) (*This was a very important factor in how the 324B Division could concentrate its combat forces for operations against Ripcord. The 304B Division would protect the 324B supply and services operations and provide porters for food, ammunition and other supplies and medical support.*)

(*Stepping down from theater one echelon to the division level, we find a significantly more sober appraisal by the 324B Division of the PAVN.*)

Strategic Setting of the 324B Division in the Ripcord Area—

The 324B Division Leadership and Party Current Affairs Committee, Senior Colonel Nguyen Van Tao and Senior Colonel Pham Van Long and authors:

Lt Col Dao Quang Doi and Captains Nguyen Thong and Vo Viet Hoa provided this history to People's Army Publishing House, *Hanoi,* for publication in1992. Former CIA Officer Merle Pribbenow has translated it. Comments by Pribbenow are enclosed in [ ], my comments are italics in ().

The translated history reads:

In addition to directing the defeat of the enemy's (*reference here is to the 3rd Brigade, 101st Airborne Division*) large operation in the area of Ap Bia Mountain [Hamburger Hill], the 324B Division was also forced to make an arduous effort to overcome unprecedented difficulties, especially in preparing the battlefield, ensuring logistics support, and feeding and caring for its troops.

From the end of 1969 onward, the enemy (*US/ARVN*) was able to control the lowlands and the foothills. (*A rare admission of the failure of the 1968 and 1969 Tet Offensives.*) He launched a series of operations up into the mountain jungles to destroy our supply caches, savagely attacked Group 559's strategic supply route [the *Ho Chi Minh* Trail], sent aircraft to spray defoliants to kill the forest, ruin our crops, and kill or contaminate our livestock in order to completely destroy our logistics supply sources and supply stockpiles. In the *Tri-Thien* area, because of both enemy actions and natural disasters, our people suffered a long period of protracted starvation. The people had to share with one another individual manioc roots, ears of corn, bowls of rice gruel, and jungle vegetables. They burned clumps of grass and ate the ashes in place of salt. Many people died of starvation, and some villages lost one third of their population.

If the people were hungry, then the soldiers were even hungrier. The little bit of rice and salt available had to be reserved for our front-line troops and to feed the starving civilian population. Some units ate rice gruel and jungle vegetables instead of rice for months at a time.

The enemy tightly sealed off the entrance points from the jungles into the lowlands. Every ton of rice the division obtained from the lowlands cost us the lives of six or seven men.

(*Another unusual admission. Troops at Division level certainly see the war differently from the staff at Theater level. US and ARVN operations had successfully denied the PAVN access to food stores in the piedmont and coastal populated areas. This is a most rare statement that the PAVN ever had lives lost. Our US Army salt tablets don't seem too bad compared to ashes from clumps of burned grass.*)

Nature was no kinder to us than the enemy. Torrential rains ruined our manioc and corn crops, which needed sunlight. In addition, the defoliants sprayed by the American imperialists made it impossible for us to count on our harvests. (*Agent Orange really did work.*) With a tradition of steadfast resistance and with their common faith in the revolution and in Uncle Ho, the people of the mountains of Tri-Thien worked with the soldiers of our armed forces to overcome natural disasters and the savage schemes of the enemy to gradually, step by step, regain the initiative on the battlefield.

Implementing the resolution of the Tri-Thien Regional Committee on increasing self-sufficiency, the division joined the soldiers and civilians of Tri-Thien in working the fields, planting manioc and corn while keeping one hand on our machetes and the other on our guns. Dozens of black-smith forges were built to produce hand tools. The raw materials for making machetes and picks were the empty cartridge casings and bomb shards left behind by the Americans. Thousands of machetes and picks were produced to supply to our units, and some were given to the civilian population. The division rear services staff organized work-parties of hundreds of personnel who spent weeks on the road traveling to Laos and to Quang Binh to pick up seeds and breeding animals to bring back to plant and to raise in order to reach the target goal of five million manioc plants for the entire division and three kilograms of meat and 120 kilograms of green vegetables per man for the year 1969. (*That is about one half of one pound of meat per month per man.*) The manioc and corn grew thick and the harvest doubled and redoubled. The threat of starvation slowly receded.

The 18th Plenum of the Party Central Committee (*1969*) laid out a new course for the revolution in South Vietnam: "Step up our attacks in all areas...apply the formula of attacking in all three strategic areas [the mountain jungles, the rural lowlands, and the cities], and make the rural areas the primary focus of our attack. Working on the basis of our policy of protracted struggle, strive to gain a decisive victory in a relatively short period of time."[7]

(*At this time in 1969, they were talking "protracted struggle," the classic strategy of wars of liberation—but also offensive campaigns.*)

Planning for Operations in 1970—

Applying Central Committee Resolution 18 to the actual conditions on the battlefield, the Tri-Thien Regional Committee laid out guidance for PAVN operations during 1970: In addition to building up the strength of the revolution, step by step we will intensify our attacks against the enemy's "pacification" program in the lowlands and in the cities. The decisive issue will be for us to concentrate our efforts on gaining mastery of the mountain jungle region, and use that as the foundation for rebuilding our strategic posture in the three strategic areas."[8] In practical terms, this meant we would continue to work to defeat the enemy"s tactics of "garrisoning the high ground," "leap-frog tactics," and "helicopter assault tactics." "Launch a movement throughout the military region's armed forces to attack enemy aircraft."[9]

The operations plans was divided into two stages:

- From January to July we would build and create a new battlefield posture.

- From July onward we would expand our position and develop new strength.

On 28 January 1970 the Division Party Committee met at Co Trang to study Central Committee Resolution 18 and the resolution of the Tri-Thien Military Region Party Committee. After severely criticizing manifestations of negativism among our cadre and Party members, especially in such areas as fearing hardship, adversity, and sacrifice, ideological wavering and hesitancy, a decline in combat spirit, and sitting back to await the results of the peace talks in Paris,

(*Apparently some of the NVA thought like some Americans, they didn't want to be the last person to die in a war that was almost over.*)

The Division Party Committee set out four missions for the entire year of 1970:

- Seize the initiative by launching a continuous series of attacks to kill large numbers of enemy troops and destroy large quantities of enemy military equipment and to resolutely defeat the enemy's tactics of 'garrisoning the high ground,' leap-frog tactics,' and 'keeping our forces at arms length.' Our combat opponents in this effort would be the U.S. 101st Airborne Division and the puppet 1st Division. A Tuc, Cung Cap, the southern bank of the Ta Rut River, and the Western bank of the A Sap River would bound the area of operations. We would intensify the movement to shoot down enemy aircraft.

- Closely coordinate with our movement to disrupt pacification in the lowlands and the urban areas. Intensify operations in the foothills in an effort to link the three strategic areas.

- Ensure the flow of supplies along the supply route to the battlefield in the division's area of responsibility; build and protect supply warehouses and caches; increase production to ensure partial self-sufficiency in food; improve the living standards of the troops.

- Combine combat operations with force building and training in the units; hone the skills of our command and staff cadre; strive to grow in maturity and skill as we fight.

Our formulas for the year: determination, initiative, mobility, and flexibility. Our first task would be to organize elite units to penetrate to the enemy's intermediate line of defense in order to draw in, tie down, and erode the enemy's troop strength and prepare the way for battles which would progressively grow in scale and intensity.

The division decided to send its forces into the field early in order to carry out these four missions. Although the new year had already begun, the weather in western Thua Thien was still bitterly cold. 7th Battalion, reinforced by an element of 5th Regiment (the Hue City military unit) was the first unit in the entire Military Region to receive a deep penetration mission to the enemy's defense line on the Bo River. (*Gen Doi confirmed that this was the 7th Sapper Battalion and an exceptionally potent force.*)

This mission marked the beginning of our offensive against the enemy to expand our foothold on the Tri-Thien battlefield, the first such offensive since Tet 1968. To 7th Battalion's rear, 14 companies and division staff elements carried out transportation and logistics activities to support 7th Battalion's combat operations. (*Fourteen rear companies were also supporting other elements of the 324B Division according to Gen Doi.*) 7th Battalion received priority supplies of rice and salt to increase its daily rations. The division arranged for the battalion to celebrate the 1970 *Tet* lunar New Year one week early to enable the battalion to prepare for the offensive campaign. Comrades Duong Ba Nuoi, the Deputy Military Region Commander, and Nguyen Xuan Tra, the Division Political Commissar, attended a Tet party for the battalion to visit with and bolster the morale of the battalion's cadre and soldiers.

(*I interviewed Brigadier General (Retired) Duong Ba Nuoi in Hue in June 2001. At the time of this campaign, General Nuoi's headquarters was in Vinh in North Vietnam. Gen Doi told me that Gen Nuoi had previously been his assistant division commander.*)

(*In addition to the large and powerful 7th Sapper Battalion, the 324B Division employed the following units:*
29th Infantry Regiment with an artillery battalion and machine gun company
803rd Infantry Regiment with an artillery battalion and machine gun company
812th Infantry Regiment with an artillery battalion and machine gun company
(*It is not clear where the 812th was at this time. Gen Doi simply said it was up a little further north.*)

6th Tri-Thien Regional Forces Regiment OPCON (unconfirmed eight battalions)
33rd Artillery Battalion
16th Anti-Aircraft Battalion)

    (Gen Doi stated that he had four companies of 120mm mortars with six tubes in each company.)

Strategic Setting of the 304B Division in the Ripcord Area—

The North Vietnamese Army officers that I interviewed stressed that other units "would come and go," but the 304B and 324B Divisions always remained to conduct operations in Quang Tri and Thua Thien Provinces.

    Robert J. Destatte concludes from the official PAVN history, that: The 304B Division did not take part in direct combat for Ripcord; however, its operations in southern Quang Tri Province during that period were part of a coordinated plan of operations in B4 Front (Thua Thien Province and Quang Tri Province south of Highway 9). One intended objective, apparently, was to tie down forces that otherwise might have supported or reinforced US and ARVN troops in the Ripcord sector of operations.

    The 304B was located at its rear base in Quang Binh Province (in North Vietnam) at the beginning of 1970. Premier Pham Van Dong visited the unit at the beginning of the year. The Ministry of National Defense issued mission orders to the division on 13 January 1970. Its mission was to operate in southwestern Quang Tri Province under the command of B4 Front. The 304 Division is a much-celebrated unit for its victory at Dien Bien Phu.

    The 304B history states that:
    Southwestern Quang Tri was a very important area strategically. Here we could establish a staging area where we could expand our forces, receive agents and materiel, and strike deep in the enemy's rear in close cooperation with the lowlands in Trieu Phong—Hai Lang Districts, the lowlands of northern Thua Thien Province, and the B5 Front—Highway 9 Theater. Also from here, whenever we opened a large campaign we were in a position to cut the enemy's Highway 1 and Highway 9. Another factor was that this was an important rear area from which we could support battlefields deeper inside enemy territory.

    (It is believed that the area between FSB Barnett and FSB O'Reilly was the headquarters and base area for the 324B Division (as confirmed by Brigadier

General Bui Pham Ky in Hanoi in June 2001) and the support area for the 304 Division's assistance to the 324B Division. While the 324B Division's base was northwest of Ripcord, Gen Doi said that his forward division command post was southwest of Hill 902 co-located with the command post of the 803rd Regiment.)

The Ministry of Defense and B4 Front directed the 304 Division to prepare for long term operations in its assigned sector. The division's general missions were to wear the enemy down through attrition—particularly American and Republic of Vietnam mobile forces and local security forces, to support efforts by local forces to destroy the 'pacification' program in the lowlands, and to check the enemy in the western regions of Thua Thien and Quang Tri Provinces.

The division's specific missions were to:

• Draw out, tie down, attrite, and destroy the enemy to complement operations in other theaters.

• Organize the battlefield; transform southwestern Quang Tri Province into a solid rear base area, and the western region.

• Expand and protect stores of supplies and materiel, stockpile provisions, and produce enough foodstuffs to be self-sufficient.

• Simultaneously fight and build up the unit.

The division's advance elements set out on 3 February. The units arrived at their assembly area in the theater on 27 February 1970.

The division divided the mission into two phases. Phase one from April to June, would employ the 24th and 66th Regiments. During the second phase, from July to September, the division would bring the 9th Regiment down to take part in the fighting.

(How the 9th Regiment was detected and decimated in early July will be discussed later. The 3rd Brigade was indeed fighting the 324B Division and supporting elements of the 304B Division.)

The principle sector for operations would be Trieu Phong and Hai Lang Districts in the lowlands, while the areas north and south of the Ba Long River would be an important sector. *(Five miles south of the Ba Long is FSB Barnett, nine miles south is O'Reilly and 12 miles south is Ripcord.)* Here the division's goals were to initiate some good battles that could annihilate individual enemy companies or battalions. The standard for each phase was to destroy two battalion-sized clusters, destroy three-to-five separate companies, shoot down or destroy 30 airplanes, and destroy 10 armored vehicles.

With regard to the mission to organize the battlefield, the division would have to complete the road-building plan (paths for primitive transportation [porters, cargo bicycles, etc.], roads for motorized vehicles, routes that could provide support to tactical campaign operations, and a strategic road network), build supply storage areas, fortifications, battle positions, etc.

• Strive to build a base, in particular take part in building the local infrastructure and local armed forces. Help the populace produce crops, protect the crops, and stabilize the living conditions.

• Protect rice and ammunition for units operating in the area, keeping a sufficient reserve to support additional forces that might come in and long-term operations.

• Support expenditures by planting one million cassava shoots for Region Tri-Thien.

(The 304B Division employed the following units:
9th Infantry Regiment with an artillery battalion and machine gun company
24th Infantry Regiment with an artillery battalion and machine gun company
66th Infantry Regiment with an artillery battalion and machine gun company
68th Artillery Battalion
840th Pack Artillery Battalion)

II

The NVA Defend
Their Base Area

On 19 May 1970 the 4 [th] Military Region Headquarters, People's Army of Vietnam officially issued the following mission order:

"324B Division would concentrate its main forces to attack and destroy Operating Base 935 and block and attack enemy elements stationed around the hill and forces sent to relieve the base."

3

Operation TEXAS STAR Is Slow To Rise

From North Vietnamese Records[10]—

In coordination with 3rd Regiment's (*The 3rd Regiment of the 324B is AKA the 29th Infantry Regiment.*) operations along the Bo River, on 20 February 1970 the 324Bth Division Headquarters sent 3rd Battalion/1st Regiment (*The 1st Regiment of the 324B is AKA the 803rd Infantry Regiment.*) down with an element from 6th Regiment (Thua Thien Provincial Forces) to operate in a rectangular area bounded by Hill 935 (*Ripcord—935 is from the old French maps—927 meters elevation on US maps*), Doc May [Cloud Slope] (*southeast end of High Point 902*), Hill 350, and Tam Tanh. Using the lessons learned from 7th Sapper Battalion's operations, the regiment dispersed into individual platoons and companies and moved constantly, sneaking through the area to find enemy gaps and weaknesses. When the enemy moved his forces our troops launched small attacks and ambushes to erode his strength. The enemy troops were unable to eat or sleep. They were attacked wherever they went and our forces harassed and disrupted them at all hours of the day and night.

(*In late February and early March 1970, the 324B Division had elements of two of its regularly assigned regiments, a portion of the 6th Regional Force Regiment and numerous support units based in terrain that was to become known as the FSB Ripcord area. More PAVN units would soon join them.*)

Gen Doi explained to me that for simplicity and security, the 803ʳᵈ Regt, 812ᵗʰ Regt and the 29ᵗʰ Regt were referred to as the 1ˢᵗ, 2ⁿᵈ and 3ʳᵈ Regiments of the 324B Division. Their infantry battalions were: 1ˢᵗ, 2ⁿᵈ and 3ʳᵈ Battalions in the 1ˢᵗ Regt, 4ᵗʰ, 5ᵗʰ and 6ᵗʰ Battalions in the 2ⁿᵈ Regt and the 7ᵗʰ, 8ᵗʰ and 9ᵗʰ Battalions in the 3ʳᵈ Regiment.)

From US/ARVN Records[11]

Assaults by elements of the 3d Brigade, 101st Airborne Division (Airmobile) and the 1st Regiment, 1st Infantry Division (ARVN) into the Ripcord/ O'Reilly area were delayed by poor weather until mid-March, when the 2ⁿᵈ Battalion, 506th Infantry Currahees and the 4th Battalion, 1st Regiment (ARVN) conducted airmobile assaults into the area. On 12 March, Captain Albert P. Burckard's Company A, 2ⁿᵈ Battalion, 506th Infantry was to assault into an LZ on Hill 902, two and a half kilometers south of the old FSB Ripcord on Hill 927. The 1st Cavalry Division had first established the operational base on Hill 927 in 1968. When the 101ˢᵗ Airborne occupied Hill 927 in 1969, it was given the name FSB Ripcord. The NVA referred to the base as Hill 935 as that was the elevation shown on their old French maps.

The 3ʳᵈ Brigade Commander, at the time Colonel William J. Bradley, advised Brigadier General Hennessey, the 101ˢᵗ Assistant Division Commander, that operations in this area will likely meet heavy resistance and should not be undertaken unless considerable strength is to be employed—more strength than was currently being planned. General Hennessey said the operation will go as planned—no additional troops.

The brigade commander considered Hill 927, the old Ripcord FSB, indefensible terrain as it was dominated by the twin peaks of Hill 1000, just one kilometer to the west. He selected Hill 902, two and a half kilometers to the south as a better choice to open a new FSB Ripcord.

From North Vietnamese Records[12]—

On 11 March dozens of enemy helicopters landed the 2nd Airborne Battalion (*2/506ᵗʰ Infantry*) on Hill 884, two kilometers west of the enemy base on Hill 935 (*Ripcord was Hill 935 on the PAVN copied old French maps.*). With a firm understanding of the enemy plan, 1st Battalion, (*803ʳᵈ Regt*) and an attached element of 6th Regiment had already deployed in ambush positions. As soon as the enemy helicopters touched down, B-40 rocket launchers and 82mm mortars hit them setting two helicopters on fire in the middle of the landing zone. The other enemy helicopters flew away quickly. Enemy artillery and aircraft took turns bombarding the landing zone to permit the helicopters to land their troops.

As they tried to land our troops hit them again. Fighting throughout the day and night of 11 March, the enemy was still unable to capture Hill 884. On the morning of 12 March 3rd Airborne Brigade sent helicopters that picked up the enemy battalion and flew it back to *Dong Lam* (*FSB Jack*).

On 14 March two companies of 1st Battalion/506th Airborne from the enemy base on Hill 530 landed by helicopter on Doc May (*southeast end of High Point 902*) to conduct a 'sweep' against our forces. 2nd Battalion attacked them right after they landed, killing more than 30 Americans and damaging two helicopters. The next morning they were forced to withdraw back to Dong Lam. (*As detailed below, the landing was on 12 Mar, not the 11th, and it was on Hill 927, not 884. The PAVN were probably confused by the helicopters trying to go into Hill 902 then diverting to 927. One helicopter, not two was shot down and later extracted by Chinook on 5 Apr. Three men from A Co were killed on 12 Mar, not thirty.*)

From US/ARVN Records[13]

A little break in the weather came on 12 March favoring US/ARVN forces. Captain Carmelito (Sonny) Arkangel's B Co, 2/506th landed on the southeastern ridge down from the peak of Hill 902. Following B Co, two ARVN companies landed to the west on the ridge running north on Coc Muen Mountain.

As Captain Albert P. Burckard's A Co, 2/506th approached the planned Landing Zone on Hill 902 (to be the new FSB Ripcord); he discovered that the vegetation was too thick to land the troops. The newly arrived Battalion Commander, Lieutenant Colonel Andre Lucas, and Colonel Bradley decided to divert to old FSB Ripcord. After forty minutes in the air in the area, they approached the LZ. Heavy enemy resistance immediately met A Company's landing as it assaulted onto Hill 927, old Ripcord.

Captain Burckard (who was not interviewed by Keith Nolan for his book, RIPCORD) made the following notes in his daily field journal:

> The first platoon in, 2nd Platoon, Lt Kelly, got in OK. As soon as my CP landed and the first helicopter of the 4th Platoon, Lt Davis, we started receiving small arms fire from the west. SP4 McCoy, about five feet to my left, was shot through the chest and the door gunner of the 3rd helicopter in was shot, also bringing the helicopter down-just a few holes in it, not dam-

aged much. It was extracted by CH-47 about two hours later after we had stripped it of its two machine guns, ammo and medical gear.

After 4th Platoon got in, about twelve NVA 60mm mortar rounds landed 25 meters to the north. I moved Lt Davis to a small hill to the north to cover that direction and try to observe where the fire was coming from. Thirty minutes later, 15 more rounds of mortar came in killing Lt Davis and his RTO and wounding four others.

The first platoon landed and I moved and I moved him to the west about 400 meters. The 3rd Platoon came in and I kept him at the firebase. Each bird that came in was taking small arms fire from the north and west. I moved the 4th Platoon back up to my location and dug in for the night. About 1730 we took another ten rounds of mortar fire. No casualties except Sgt Ames, the Platoon Sergeant of the 3rd Platoon got shrapnel in his knee. The 1st Platoon actually observed the enemy mortar platoon firing. We called in the ARA gunships immediately and completely covered the area with rockets. The result was that we took no more mortar rounds, but had a sleepless night.

On Friday the Thirteenth, I moved 3rd Platoon off Ripcord and 1st Platoon returned to secure it. As soon as the 3rd Platoon reached their objective hill about 600 meters to the west, I moved out with 2nd Platoon to join them. At 1800, 1st Platoon observed an NVA mortar section setting up to fire about 600 meters to the west of Ripcord. We called in ARA and blasted the area. Received no more mortars from that location, but we kept tube artillery coming in all night. Towards dark, we got the biggest scare of all—the ARVN artillery on Firebase O'Reilly got their grids mixed up and fired four 155 rounds into my location. The only casualties, fortunately, were two sprained ankles and a badly bruised shin as everybody fell over rocks scrambling for cover.

The S3 called the morning of 14 Mar, saying that the ARVNs captured a document yesterday indicating that an NVA Battalion CP is about 1300 meters to our west. We were to air assault to that location with the entire company, but were socked in all day. A log bird flew in low and was able to re-supply by kick out. As it was hovering, an NVA fired an AK-47 at it.

On Sunday, 15 March, I moved the 2nd Platoon and CP down to join the 3rd Platoon. Disbanded the 4th Platoon because of lack of personnel. Company field strength is now 75. "Black Spade," Lt Col Lucas told me that an entire NVA regiment was in our area and we would be extracted so B52 Bombers could strike.

Captain Albert P. Burckard was awarded the Silver Star for his courageous actions in leading his company under intense enemy fire on 12 March 1970.

Captured enemy documents, discovered later, indicated the presence of the 6th Infantry Regiment, Independent Thua Thien Province Viet Cong Force in the Ripcord area. Not until research for this book, was it known that significantly more enemy units than the 6th Regt were in the area.

After three days of fighting and failing to secure Hill 927 (Ripcord), the troops of A Co, 2/506th were extracted. B Company and the two ARVN Companies continued to patrol and fight around Ripcord, Hill 902 and the Coc Muen.

B-52 bombing and extensive tactical air and artillery strikes were employed, a necessary tactic if a firebase was to be established. As Major Herb Koenigsbauer, the 2/506 S3 Operations Officer noted, it also told the enemy that the 101st probably would be coming back.

Regrouping into a company position to wait out the weather, Captain Burckard noted some interesting observations in his field journal on 18 and 19 March. He wrote, "Just looking around at my equipment and comparing what we have with WWII and Korean war equipment, some of the more important innovations are the Claymore mine, M79 Grenade Launcher, hand-illumination flares, the M16 rifle—the best in the world. The poncho liner, LRRP rations and secure radio sets. Things like personnel sensors, chemical defoliants, Rome Plows, COFRAM artillery rounds, 'Spooky' gunships, flare ships and mini-guns are also new. Perhaps the single most important weapon, however, which was proven early in the war is the helicopter—outgrowths of which are medevac, aerial rocket artillery and Cobra gunships. The twelve month service tour is also important." Albert went on to say, "I have noticed a change in my attitude towards the company recently. When I first took over, I cared more about looking for NVA and trying to get in contact to get a body count. Now I see things more in terms of saving the lives of these men rather than going after some illusive enemy who chooses his own place and time to hit you and usually comes off better psychologically, but far worse casualty wise. Our firepower and support are so great that an attacking force really has no chance. Because of this, the NVA chooses to hit and run."

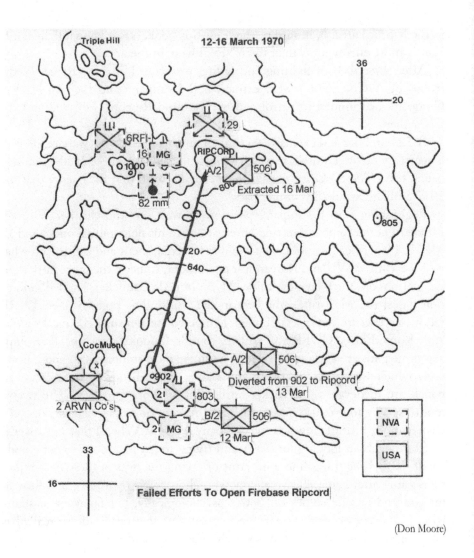

Triple Hill

12-16 March 1970

36

20

6RFI-

16 | MG

1000

82 mm

29

RIPCORD

A/2   506

800   Extracted 16 Mar

805

20

640

CocMuon

x

2 ARVN Co's

902

2   803

2 | MG

B/2   506

12 Mar

A/2   506

Diverted from 902 to Ripcord
13 Mar

NVA

USA

33

16

Failed Efforts To Open Firebase Ripcord

(Don Moore)

From North Vietnamese Records[14]—

In addition to its infantry attacks, the entire regiment launched a concerted movement to shoot down enemy aircraft. On 16 March, 1st Regiment's 16th 12.7mm Machine Gun Company shot down five enemy helicopters. On 18 March infantry soldiers of 2nd Company shot down four helicopters using light machine guns. On 25 March the entire regiment shot down or damaged a total of 14 helicopters, bringing the total number of aircraft shot down in a little less than one half month to almost 40. These losses reduced the mobility of American forces based in the mountains jungles of Tri-Thien. (*Only one UH-1 was shot down on 12 Mar and it was recovered. There were no major US operations in the area on 25 Mar and no US aircraft lost.*)

From US/ARVN Records[15]

On March 29th, C Co, 2/506 conducted an air assault seven kilometers to the northeast of Ripcord on Hill 316. After C Company secured the hill, Captain Dave Rich's B Battery, 2nd Battalion, 319th Field Artillery brought in their six 105mm howitzers. Thus, Hill 316 became FSB Gladiator and was ready to support the Ripcord area to their southwest.

The 3rd Brigade requested and received two Pink Teams from the C Troop "Condors" of the 2nd Squadron, 17th Cavalry. The two teams performed reconnaissance and surveillance in the Ripcord area from 0935 until 1516 on 1 April.

Captain Bill Williams, having replaced Sonny Arkangel, took B Co, 2/506th and air assaulted onto old Ripcord, Hill 927, on 1 April. Again, the enemy employed intense mortar, recoilless rifle, and small arms fire. Captain Williams said, "The fire was coming from every direction. The enemy knew every spot on that hill." The incoming fire was continuous. Lucas tried to go after the enemy mortars by inserting Captain Rembert Rollison's D Co, 2/506th on the northeast side of Ripcord. Lucas then reinserted A Co to the east of Ripcord. Lieutenant Colonel Lucas tried to reinforce Williams' B Co on the would-be firebase itself. Lucas dispatched the battalion Reconnaissance Platoon from Camp Evans. Only ten men from the recon platoon were able to exit the moving helicopters as they flew over Ripcord. Late in the evening as the enemy mortar fire slackened, B Co, the 2/506th advanced command post part and the Recon Platoon withdrew from the hill on foot with seven killed and twenty-one wounded to join A Co in their NDP.

B Co was ordered to move north from A Co's position on 2 April as the weather completely closed in.

The remnants of the 2/506 Command Post Advance Party stayed with A Co. This motley group included Major Laurence J. Law, 2/506 Executive Officer (wounded on Ripcord), Capt King, CO of C Btry, 2/319 FA Bn and his first sergeant, 1st Lt Joe Smith, Engineer Platoon Leader and eight engineers, the 2/506th Bn Commo Officer, 1st Lt John E. Darling, and one Pathfinder. A Co troops gave up some of their LRRP rations for the "guests."

On 5 April the division reserve or "swing" battalion, the 2nd Battalion, 501st Infantry, took over defense of FSB Gladiator. This freed up Lieutenant Chuck Hawkins, acting commander of C Co, 2/506th to move his company by helicopter to join A Co at their NDP east of Ripcord. C Co walked into a bunker complex on 6 April between Ripcord and Hill 1000. They killed an enemy soldier who had written a letter to his wife in which he stated that the "NVA winning in the south."

Captain Christopher Straub from the division reserve battalion, now under the operational control of the 2/506th, took his D Co, 2/501st into a hot LZ on Hill 902. The 1st Platoon of D Company went through an abandoned bunker complex and then met fierce resistance further down the ridgeline.

During the period 2—10 April, the 2d Battalion, 506th Infantry and the 2nd and 4th Battalions, 1st Regiment (ARVN) conducted combined reconnaissance in force operations in the Ripcord/O'Reilly area to locate and destroy enemy mortar and recoilless rifle positions.

On 11 April, acting commander First Lieutenant Chuck Hawkins' C Co, 2/506th conducted a ground assault on Ripcord and secured the firebase unopposed by 0800 hours. Very poor weather probably lulled the enemy into thinking an air assault unlikely and they were surprised by the ground attack. Notwithstanding the poor weather, a Chinook from the "Pachyderms" of A Co, 159th Assault Support Helicopter Battalion, piloted by Tom Hirschler, brought in two engineer bulldozers.

During the night of 14 April, "Playtex" Chinooks of C Co, 159th Aviation Battalion flew three re-supply missions into Ripcord beginning at 2230 hours.

Further inclement weather precluded insertion of artillery into Ripcord until 16 April. The re-positioning of Battery B, 2d Battalion, 319th Artillery (105mm howitzer) from FSB Gladiator was followed on 17 Apiril by the insertion of Battery C, 2nd Battalion, 11th Artillery (ARVN) (105 mm howitzer). The 159th Assault Support Battalion flew 110 Chinook sorties for this mission.

The Chinook is called an assault "support" helicopter. The word "support" is certainly a misnomer. These Chinook crews were brave and courageous as they routinely, directly faced the enemy as they hovered their giant, noisy whirly birds while picking up or dropping their cargo. These aircrews were *assault* soldiers. Their exposure could be thought of as an infantryman standing in one place for several seconds while walking point six feet above the ground with a six-by-eight foot shiny Plexiglas window drawing attention with great, very noisy blades beating the brush.

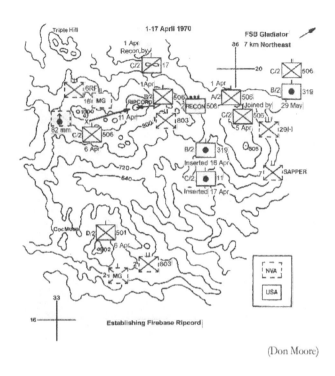

(Don Moore)

After punishing enemy fire forced A Co first, then B Co to withdraw from Hill 927 under punishing fires, it was a great stroke of luck for the Currahees that C Co finally gained the high ground and set about fortifying the firebase. Captain Isabelino Vazquez-Rodriquez returned from R&R and resumed command of C Co, taking over from 1`st Lt Chuck Hawkins. Captain Vazquez modeled the defenses of Ripcord after the border outposts where he earlier served with the Special Forces. LT Jim Campbell remembers him telling his troops in his harsh Puerto Rican accent, "There be no sandbagged bunkers on this firebase." He considered these above ground bunkers easy targets for the enemy.

Charlie company troops built L-shaped fighting positions dug deeply into the ground. They seemingly strung miles of triple layer concertina and hog wire. To this they added hundreds of trip flares, claymores and detonating wires connected to mines. Thickened fuel, known as phougas (Napalm), was placed in barrels, drums and canisters in and around the wire, all connected to trip flares. A bulldozer prepared a deep trench to receive steel conex containers, which served as the battalion headquarters and the medical aid station. The firebase itself provided a most exemplary model for the fortification of a hilltop. For the few nights in July that I stayed on Ripcord during almost continuous enemy attacks by fire, I was very grateful for these professional preparations.

In late May, the ARVN troops of the 1st Regiment, 1st Infantry Division were redeployed to FSB O'Reilly, about ten kilometers to the north. A Battery, 2nd Battalion, 11th Field Artillery with its 155mm howitzers replaced the ARVN 105mm howitzers

The Currahees of the 2nd Battalion, 506th Infantry continued security, patrol, and ambush operations in the vicinity of Ripcord and made frequent enemy contact.

4

The Fighting Spreads
And Intensifies

From North Vietnamese Records[16]—

By early June the network of defenses along the enemy's intermediate line had been subjected to constant attacks. The division had eliminated more than 2,000 enemy troops from the battlefield, and the majority of these troops were Americans. The division had inflicted heavy losses on two infantry companies, three artillery batteries, two battalion command posts, and 16 infantry platoons. The U.S. 2nd Battalion/501st Airborne had been eliminated from the battlefield. Almost 170 helicopters had been shot down or damaged, and we had captured four enemy flight crewmen. The division had tied down eight American battalions along the Bo River line, exceeding even the target goals set for it for Phase One by Regional Party Committee.

(The claim of 2000 American KIAs in the Ripcord area represents a modest 800 percent exaggeration by Communist's standards. During the period of the 12 March-31Aug Ripcord battle, the entire 101st Airborne Division lost 526 men KIA. The 3rd Brigade suffered losses of 250 soldiers KIA. The 2nd Battalion, 501st Infantry, the hardest hit unit, lost 61men KIA during the four months between 12 Mar and 18 Jul when they were withdrawn from the Ripcord area and placed on alert as the division reserve, ready reaction force. Three US/ARVN battalions operated near the Bo River—not eight. No air crewmen from the 101st became prisoners. The NVA destroyed twenty aircraft from the Division during the first six months of

1970—three at Ripcord. Note that both the numbers of KIAs and downed helicopters reflected in the NVA reports are exaggerated by about 800 percent.)

From US/ARVN Records[17]

The 2nd Battalion, 501st Infantry, now back in action around FSB Granite about ten kilometers southeast of Ripcord and seven kilometers north of FSB Maureen, conducted reconnaissance operations. Sappers attacked A Company's NDP the early hours of 24 April after destroying a bunker complex on 21 April. Sappers hit Firebase Granite at about 2200 hours on 29 April. Withering fire from Granite's defenders and massive artillery broke the sapper attack. A prisoner reported the NVA assault commander killed in the attack. The other two NVA infantry battalions broke off their planned attack.

Action in the 3rd Brigade AO dramatically shifted well to the north to FSB Henderson in Quang Tri Province. Henderson occupied the same parallel as Khe Sanh and Shepard. The 3rd Brigade provided 155mm artillery support to the ARVN troops operating to the west of Henderson. A company from another brigade occupied Henderson under the 3rd Brigade's operational control. (The company commander will go nameless.)

In addition to the US 155 battery, an ARVN 105 battery and a forward ARVN regimental tactical operations center supported operations from Henderson. The firebase received several loads of concertina wire, claymores and other fortification material. The OPCON company commander failed to use the fortification materials and secure the explosives. Large amounts of 105 artillery ammunition for the ARVN battery remained in their cargo helicopter delivery nets or stacked in the open on the base. Captain Fred Spaulding, then the brigade assistant S3 reported that Colonel William Bradley and his S3, Major Robert A. (Tex) Turner visited Henderson on 3 and 4 May and they were appalled at the lack of progress in organizing the firebase. Spaulding stated that the company commander simply failed to follow orders. Colonel Bradley specifically told the US company commander what had to be done on Henderson, but the location there of a forward ARVN Regimental Command Post there blurred the lines of responsibility.

On 5 May, Captain James E. Mitchell's battered A Co 2/501 landed on Henderson to get it organized, to get some "rest," and to absorb about sixty replacements. Lieutenant Richard E. Hawley, Jr.'s 2/501st Reconnaissance Platoon also arrived on Henderson late in the afternoon of the 5th. Now, although adequate manpower occupied Henderson, unfortunately, the fortifications still needed much work, the artillery ammo remained exposed and unprotected, fields of fire had not been adequately cleared, no patrols had been sent out, and no listening posts established before FSB Henderson suffered a devastating attack just before dawn the morning of 6 May.

Sappers, followed by assault troops equipped with AK-47s, RPGs, and a flamethrower, came through the heavy fog, quickly hitting the exposed ammo and fuel storage dump. The entire firebase seemed to explode. In Hawley's recon platoon, which had bunked down next to a large amount of recently delivered artillery ammunition; every man in the platoon suffered wounds or died in the attack.

Colonel Bradley, Major Turner, and Brigade Command Sergeant Major Raymond C. Long arrived by helicopter at about 6:45 AM in the morning of the attack on 6 May. As they exited the aircraft and headed for the command bunker, a mortar round hit just behind the group killing CSM Long. Major Turner moved through the intense incoming mortar fire to check each position of the firebase and helped to evacuate the wounded. Although he had been wounded himself, Turner continued to administer aid to injured soldiers. Once Colonel Bradley and Major Turner departed Henderson, Captain Fred Spaulding, 3rd Brigade Assistant S3, "took charge," where he performed triage and arranged medical evacuation for the wounded. He called in tactical air strikes and artillery based on crater analysis. As the situation stabilized somewhat, Spaulding flew to Mai Loc to brief Lieutenant Colonel Livingston and one of his company commanders. Spaulding then led the 2/501st "Drive On" Battalion command group and the replacement company onto Henderson at about 2000 hours that night, 6 May. It had been a long, bad day. Twenty-three US and three ARVN KIAs and a total of 55 WIA paid the price for the lack of proper preparedness.

While assigned to the Pentagon in 1971, Colonel Bradley learned, in shock, from his Officer Effectiveness Report written by Major General Hennessey subsequent to the fight at FSB Henderson that General Hennessey held Bradley accountable even though it was an ARVN firebase with an ARVN Regimental Command Post. Colonel Bradley immediately took early retirement.

(Fred Spaulding)

Fred Spaulding took this picture of FSB Henderson on 6 May after the early morning sapper attack. The ammo and fortification materials can be seen still in their cargo nets. Sappers hit similar stacks of uncared-for ammo on the other end of the firebase causing most of the casualties.

As if on dramatic cue, the North Vietnamese struck in the far south end of the 3rd Brigade's AO just before dawn the next day, 7 May. First Lieutenant Donald R. Workman's D Company, 1st Battalion, 506th Infantry, had air assaulted onto old FSB Maureen on 5 May. All three platoons moved off the old base to patrol in differing directions. Rather than set up an NDP, 1st Lt Lawrence E. Fletcher brought his 2nd Platoon back onto Maureen. He continued patrolling on 6 May, but again brought his platoon back to Maureen for the night. Sappers hit just before first light on 7 May killing six members of the platoon wounding twelve others. Fletcher, his radioman and his platoon sergeant became the first KIAs.

Well before the attacks on Henderson and Maureen, the ARVN reported on 27 Apr their readiness to proceed on foot into the A Shau and to reopen Firebase Bradley. Shortly following the significant losses at Henderson and

Maureen on 6 and 7 May, Major General Hennessey announced that the Division and particularly the 3rd Brigade, had become overextended and the plans to push further into the A Shau/Warehouse Area have been canceled. The ARVN forces withdrew back to O'Reilly and Barnett.

Apparently emboldened by their string of successes, the North Vietnamese decided to attack FSB O'Reilly the night of 28–29 May. Alerted by the springing of a trip flare in the wire, the ARVN on O'Reilly called for air support from the 101st Airborne Division. "Griffin" Cobra gunships from C Battery, 4/77th Artillery aided by a helicopter flare ship destroyed the attacking force. The official body count included 77 enemy KIA and two prisoners. The ARVN lost three KIA and fifteen WIA. This time, the good guys won.

Back to the Ripcord area—

Having just taken command of A Co, 2/506th Inf, Captain Chuck Hawkins pushed two of his platoons up the hill between Ripcord and Hill 1000 on 3 June. The point man of 1st Lt Lee E. Widjeskog's 2nd Platoon, the lead platoon, spotted an NVA soldier on the trail. The point man fired a shot and began to retreat to the rear when he turned and discovered that his slack man had already left. The point man refused to resume the lead and Widjeskog had difficulty finding another soldier to take point, when the newly arrived Pfc Wieland C. Norris volunteered to walk point. Norris had not gone very far when an NVA ambush opened fire and shot Norris through the heart instantly killing him. Pfc Norris's brother, the very famous, Chuck Norris, told us Wieland's death could have been avoided as a married man with a child really did not have to answer the draft for induction into the Army.

On 16 June, Captain Hawkins' A Co, 2/506th assumed control of FSB O'Reilly from the ARVN and Captain Rollison's D Co, 2/506th replaced B Co, 2/506th on Ripcord. Unlike most of the infantry units in the rest of Vietnam, it was common in the 101st to spend months in the field with the only "break" being rotated onto a firebase to provide security. I noted this to General Hennessey soon after my arrival in the Division. He responded that if he brought them back to the base camps or to Eagle Beach, they would just get in trouble. That policy still bugs me.

On several occasions enemy sappers attempted to infiltrate the defensive perimeter of Ripcord without success. A captured document stated that twenty-two members of sapper recon teams had died while attempting to

breach the Ripcord wire. The NVA incurred these losses before the 1 July
siege began.

On 21 June, Captain Bill Williams' B Co, 2/506th combat air assaulted into
the Triple Hill area about 1800 meters northwest of Ripcord. B Company
spotted a few men including a Caucasian wearing a US uniform walking with
five NVA soldiers. All scrambled away. Three days later, they saw another
NVA patrol, again wearing US uniforms, but could not establish contact. B
Company found and searched a complex of 75 bunkers. The complex not
bearing much reward, Lt Col Lucas ordered Williams' company over to Hill
805 with orders to shut down the enemy mortar fire from that area.

The aggressive patrols of the 2nd Battalion, 506th Infantry and the 2nd Battalion 501st Infantry had certainly stirred the pot for the enemy base area
around Ripcord as they destroyed bunker complexes, killed enemy soldiers and
disrupted the "orderly" flow of supplies and reinforcements down the Ho Chi
Minh Trail. Indeed, 3rd Brigade soldiers had a major impact on the enemy in
the Ripcord area. In addition to Ripcord's artillery firing into the Trail complex, the Air Force had placed a Directional Beacon on Ripcord and the Navy
and Marines had installed a Tactical Aircraft Antenna for "beacon bombing"
in the A Shau Valley, the Warehouse Area and other parts of the Ho Chi
Minh Trail. These electronic devices facilitated night and foul weather tactical
air strikes and provided the North Vietnamese with ample reason to want us
out of their neighborhood.

Right after assuming command of the 3rd Brigade on 23 Jun, I received an
order to open my alternate Command Post at Camp Carroll as things became
heated up near Khe Sanh. The 2nd Battalion, 502nd Infantry came under my
operational control. Lieutenant Colonel Chuck Shay's 2nd Battalion 502nd
Infantry "Strike Force" aggressively operated with 1st and 2nd Battalions, 3rd
Regiment, of the 1st Infantry Division, ARVN.

Elements of the 2nd Squadron, 17th Cavalry concentrated their efforts on
the reconnaissance and surveillance of the area between FSB Shepard and the
Laotian border where the Ho Chi Minh Trail entered South Vietnam and the
A Shau Valley. On 1 July the 2nd Squadron, 17th Cavalry moved north to
Quang Tri and I assumed operational control of the Squadron. I sent word to
the commander of the 2/17th Cav to meet me at Shepard. The commander of
the air cavalry squadron, Lt Col Robert F. Molinelli, call sign "Cheyenne
Phantom," and I had not yet met. I assigned him sectors of our AO and told
him what I wanted his squadron to do. Molinelli looked at me in disbelief. He

said, "Sir, I can't do that, I work for Division and already have a bunch of things I've got to do."

About that time, my boss, BG James C. Smith, Assistant Division Commander (Operations), (this of course was before BG Sid Berry replaced Smith) walked up to our spot on the peak of Shepard. Jim Smith and I had served together on the faculty at the Command and General Staff College years earlier. I asked General Smith if he would explain the meaning of "Operational Control" to Lt Col Molinelli. Jim did so with all the patience and thoroughness of a Leavenworth instructor. At the conclusion, I asked Molinelli if he had any questions. He replied, "No Sir," and moved out smartly.

Unknown to me, Molinelli had already become legend in air cavalry. He greatly added to his fame for his daring and brave leadership in Lam Son 719 in 1971. Working together in 719 and later at Ft Hood, Bob Molinelli and I became the best of friends. One of my favorite "Mo" stories happened when Bob was flying gunships in the Delta as a captain in the 114th Aviation Company "Cobras" in 1965, he answered a Tac E (tactical emergency) call by running from the shower and flying the entire mission stark naked.

Captain Mac Jones, Operations Officer, C Troop, 2/17th Cav recalled another Molinelli story:

> Lt Col Molinelli was in the Squadron Officer's Club with the B "Banshee" Troop Commander and Mo was wondering aloud it there was anybody there that could beat his ass. The B Troop commander said not me, but then, 1st Lt Bruce Pullen walks into the club and gets the invitation to fight the Squadron Commander. Well, Pullen cleaned the club with Mo's butt!! Molinelli says, hey, the best man won, no problem, have a beer.

From North Vietnamese Records[18]—

> Military Region Headquarters decided to continue the attack and apply strong pressure to the enemy's entire defense line in order to force him to respond in many different locations at the same time. Meanwhile we would gradually move our local force units down to operate in the lowland foothills to provide direct support to our grass-roots movement aimed at disrupting the enemy's pacification campaign. At the same time the Military Region would use its own main force units to attack and shatter a number of the important links in the enemy defensive network in order to cause it

to disintegrate and collapse. Building on this foundation we would open a gateway down to the lowlands.

Higher authority assigned responsibility for carrying out this mission to two units:

- 324B Division was responsible for attacking and destroying the enemy's operational base on Hill 935 (*FSB Ripcord*) in Thua Thien.

- 304B Division would attack and destroy the enemy base at Da Ban (*FSB Barnett*) in Quang Tri Province

(*During this period the North Vietnamese High Command assigned 304B Division to Military Region Tri Thien in order to be able to draw on its forces to work on the 324B strategic supply line—a very important factor in how the 324B Division could conduct its operations against Ripcord. The 304B Division would protect the 324B supply and services operations and provide porters for food, ammunition and other supplies and medical support. General Doi was reluctant to give the 304B Division much credit, but he did confirm that they were in support of his division.*)

Hill 935 (*FSB Ripcord*) was located in the mountain jungles of *Phong Dien* district. The top of the hill was approximately 350 meters wide by 550 meters long, and it was the key to opening our route back down to the lowlands.

(*Unequivocal statement of the strategic and tactical significance of FSB Ripcord.*)

In August 1969, after retaking the lowlands and the cities, the Americans and the puppet launched a counterattack up into the mountain jungles where they formed a defensive belt by building a number of 'operating bases' on top of a series of high points. The purpose of these bases was to 'sweep' the mountain jungle region and push our forces further away in order to maintain security in the lowlands and urban areas. Operating Base 935 was built during this time frame. It was an artillery firebase made up of one 85mm [sic] gun battery, one 105mm howitzer battery, and one battery of 106.7mm mortars [4.2 inch mortars]. The base was made up of three areas: the command post area, the logistics area, and the artillery firing positions and defensive fortifications. The artillery revetments and defensive fortifications area were built with wood and lead [sic—they must mean 'aluminum']. The positions were half-buried underground and were covered with sandbags. Between eight and ten barbed wire fences were built around the position. Minefields containing mines of all types were laid in the important sectors and along the slopes of the mountain.

(*The above is a North Vietnamese description of Ripcord before the 1970 TEXAS STAR Operation that reoccupied and rebuilt Ripcord. Ripcord was the base for a battalion headquarters (for a short time also an ARVN battalion head-*

quarters), a battalion medical aid station, one battery of six105mm howitzers, one battery of six155mm howitzers, a quad 50mm machine gun section, three platoons (twelve tubes) of 81mm mortars, two 90mm recoilless rifles, a platoon of engineers, supply and storage areas, and three helicopter landing pads controlled by Pathfinders.)

Fire Support Base 935 was one of the most effective firebases supporting the U.S. 3rd Brigade, 101st Airborne Division during its operations in the A Luoi and A Bia areas. (*Great testimony to the outstanding work of C Company, 2/506th under Captain Isabelino Vazquez-Rodriquez.*) As 1970 began, because of our increasing pressure in this area the Americans reinforced their presence by sending in reinforcements: 2nd Battalion/602nd (*502nd*) Airborne, 2nd Battalion/506th Airborne, and the U.S. 3rd Airborne Brigade. In addition to the forces assigned to defend the firebase, the enemy also spread troops out on a number of other hill positions in the vicinity of Hill 935. These positions included Hills 902, 884 (*High Point 891 on Coc Muen*), 805, 797 (*1000 meters southeast of O'Reilly*), and 550.

On 19 May 1970 the Military Region Headquarters officially issued the following mission order:

324B Division would concentrate its main forces to attack and destroy Operating Base 935 and block and attack enemy elements stationed around the hill and forces sent to relieve the base. The division's area of responsibility would cover four primary areas: Coc Muon; the Doc May-Coc Ba Lai-Hill 665-Co Va La Duc area; A Dam and Hill 1251; and Co Pung and Hill 1078 (*all key terrain in the Ripcord area*).

The second area listed would be the primary area in which we would focus our effort to destroy enemy relief forces. The supporting sector would be Tam Tanh, Cung Cap (south of Rakkasan), and the eastern and western banks of the Bo River.

The Division Party Committee, chaired by Secretary Nguyen Xuan Tra, held a meeting on 21 May 1970. The Party Committee decided the following: The specific assigned mission of each unit in the division's battle plan was intimately linked to the successful fulfillment of the vital mission of the entire Military Region. If our division could "uproot" Base 935 we would weaken the foundation of the enemy's defensive network in the foothills and open the way for our armed forces to return to the lowlands when the time was ripe. This would be the first battle in which most of the division's forces would be concentrated in one sector, and this concentration would allow us to properly carry out our mission. This battle would be very important in building up the combat traditions and the tradition of victory of our division. The division's party committees, party chapters, and all

units were ordered to study and digest the following requirements for the
mission:

Move quickly and make full use of time, be daring in moving forces in
close to Base 935, besiege, attack and destroy the enemy, and force the
enemy to send forces out to rescue the base. Resolutely cling to, attack,
inflict casualties on, and annihilate enemy reinforcements, and eventually
reach a point at which we could overrun and eliminate Base 935. (*Clearly a
major offensive undertaking.*) Emphasize a spirit of initiative in coordinating
combat operations, exploit our spirit of independent combat operations,
and carry out the mission in an outstanding manner in all our primary sectors. Maintain good cooperation between the different spearheads, the different troop columns, and the different units.

On the afternoon of 22 May Division Commander Chu Phuong Doi
issued the following mission orders to his units:

- 1st Regiment, *(803rd Regt)* reinforced by Sapper Battalion 7B, one
  12.7mm machine gun company from the 16th Anti-Aircraft Battalion,
  two mortar companies from the 33rd Artillery Battalion, and 2nd Bat-
  talion/6th Thua Thien Regiment, was assigned the mission of conducting the attack in the primary sector to surround and besiege Base 935

- 3rd Regiment *(29th Regt)* (minus one battalion), reinforced by one
  12.7mm machine gun company from 16th Battalion, was assigned the
  mission of annihilating enemy forces in Area 4: Co Phung and Hill
  1078

- 8th Battalion/3rd Regiment *(29th Regt)*, reinforced by one sapper company, would continue operations along the eastern and western banks of
  the Bo River. If the enemy launched an operation to attack our rear area
  in the mountains, 8th Battalion would be the first unit to be sent to up
  into the mountains to engage the enemy.

The combat guidance formula was to besiege the base and destroy any
relief troops and reinforcements. Primary focus would be on annihilating
relief forces, and after we made progress we would move on to overrunning
the base. How effective we were in besieging the base would be of decisive
significance to the enemy's decision to send in relief forces.

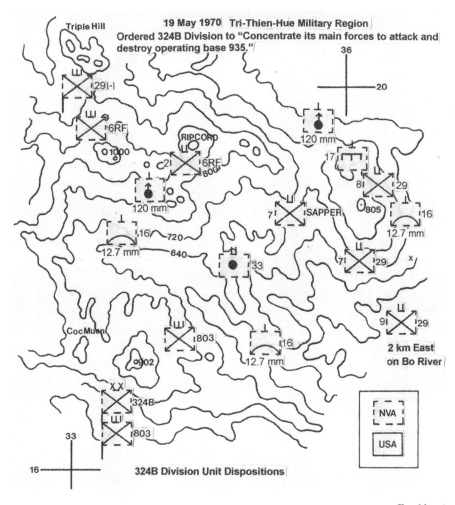

Anticipating the difficulties our forces would encounter in the coming battle, division headquarters ordered the division staff offices and division units to make their preparations as complete possible, especially with regard to provision of mortar ammunition. The division's Chief of Rear Services personally went down to the warehouses and supply caches to check on the quantities of food and ammunition the division had on hand. After conducting a reconnaissance of the battlefield accompanied by our reconnaissance teams, military cadre at all levels worked to update and perfect each unit's specific battle plan. Political staff personnel fanned out to each unit to help our grass roots organizations fully understand the mission and build battle resolve and a firm combat spirit. A vigorous, boisterous emulation movement to kill the enemy and score victories to celebrate the 15th anniversary of the formation of the division was launched. All units arranged for their troops to sign up to participate in emulation campaigns with specific targets goals to be met. (*An emulation program is where the unit selects the highly successful accomplishments of another PAVN unit and then strives to emulate it.*)

1st Regiment's action slogan at this time was "Seize mastery of the mountain jungles, maintain a firm grip on the foothills, and make a powerful advance into the lowlands." 3rd Regiment put forward the following resolution: "we will not be discouraged by the ferocity of combat or depressed by starvation and hardship. (*They were expecting the worst. We did not disappoint them.*) The Party has called on us to attack, and nothing can stop us."

On 20 June all preparations were basically completed. The soldiers set out on their approach march to their battle positions. Enemy activities at Operating Base 935 and on the surrounding positions continued as normal.

(*The poor and limited intelligence provided to the 3rd Brigade commander at this critical time is somewhere between disappointing and disgusting. As noted above, the NVA Military Region Commander on 19 May ordered the 324B to attack and destroy Hill 935 [Ripcord] and the 304B would protect 324B supply and services operations and provide porters. Col (Ret) Lewis Sorely, at my request, reviewed his extensive notes of the MACV Weekly Intelligence Estimate Updates (WIEU) for the period Jan–Aug 1970 and the only mention found of the 324B Div and the 304B Div was during the 11 Jul 70 WIEU which reported: 'In the A Shau Valley: Two divisions: 324B [which left South Vietnam in Mar–Apr 1969, returned in Nov 69 and the 304B[which went north in Nov 69 and began coming back in the last few days].' This was two months after these two divisions had been ordered to annihilate Ripcord. At the 16 May 1970 WIEU, General Abrams commented, "I Corps is the corps where we've really never been out on the border, so they've got a substantial infrastructure in terms of logistics and all that inside South Vietnam. It's been ten years, I guess, since anyone's been in the Do Xa." The fact that this is all MACV Weekly Intelligence Estimate Updates found with a direct connection to the Ripcord battle at the MACV level is pathetic.*)

III

The North Vietnamese Attack

"At exactly 6:00 A.M. on 1 July the 324B Division Command Post issued the 'open fire' order to all sectors."

The 324B Division. Published by the People's Army Publishing House (*Nha Xuat Ban Quan Doi Nhan Dan*), Hanoi, 1992.

5

Ripcord Comes Under Siege

From US Records—[19]

The sun rose just after 6 AM on 1 July, with clear skies above and a low lying fog that hung in the valleys until strong breezes cleared it away. At that hour, it looked as though it would be a beautiful day.

At 7:08 AM on 1 July, the 2nd Battalion, 506th Infantry Command Post and D Company on Ripcord received five 82mm mortar rounds and small arms fire from the southeast. At 8:50 AM, another 15 rounds of 82mm mortar fire impacted inside the firebase perimeter. At 1:45 PM, the enemy fired sixteen 75mm recoilless rifle rounds, six to eight of which impacted inside the perimeter. At 7:12 that evening, four 82mm mortar rounds landed on the firebase. The Americans responded with artillery, air strikes, and organic mortar fire that targeted suspected enemy locations throughout the day. Fifteen US personnel, all of them artillerymen assigned to Battery B, 2d Battalion, 319th Artillery, located on the highest point of the firebase, received minor wounds during the day. Most of the casualties occurred as the battery employed counter-battery fire under the daring leadership of Captain Dave Rich.

In reaction to these attacks, the aero-rifle platoon, Troop, C "Condors", 2d Squadron, 17th Cavalry, air assaulted west of Ripcord to search for and destroy enemy mortar and recoilless rifle positions. When the platoon received fire on the landing zone, Troop D, 2d Squadron, 17th Cavalry reinforced the aero-rifle platoon. Both elements passed to the operational control of the 2nd Battalion, 506th Infantry until extracted the following day.

Helicopters flying to and from Ripcord shared in the risk of injury from enemy ground and indirect fires. "Varsity" Chinook 103 took hits and landed on Ripcord on 1 July. "Pachyderm" 495 also took hits on Ripcord, but flew to fly to FSB Jack and extracted from there.

WO1 Fred Behrens had completed his round of "newbie" orientations while taking his check ride with B Co, 101st Aviation Battalion "Kingsmen" Instructor Pilot CWO2 Bob Kovalak by flying a re-supply mission to FSB Ripcord the afternoon of 1 Jul. Fred recounted the story:

> The Pathfinder on Ripcord cleared us in for a drop-off and warned about incoming mortar fire. My IP, Bob, told me to not touch the controls unless he took a hit. On short final, the Pathfinder told us to not land. We went back to Camp Eagle and the mission was rescheduled for that night. At night, Kovalak let me fly into Ripcord. We thought we took a hit and the Crew Chief, Sp4 Paul Danner, was anxious to get back to Eagle and check it out.
>
> I landed at Eagle and Danner finds the bullet hole. He goes ape and screams it was my FNG magnet ass that caused it. He had never before taken a hit and he blamed it all on me. The exciting flying continued at Ripcord and throughout the AO right up to the big extraction operation on 23 July. Flying with CWO2 Joe Chapados, we went to a staging field at Camp Evans very, very early on 23 July. We flew into Ripcord and field locations near there, but none of the "Kingsmen" took hits. Amazing, the bad guys fired from everywhere, but we never got hit.

Fred recalled that the flying had become fairly routine after Ripcord until he moved to the 326th Medical Battalion and started flying Dust Off medevac missions. His luck ran out on a medevac mission into the A Shau on 23 April 1971. His helicopter was shot down and he took a round through the ankle (eventually losing a foot). The Rangers he supported pulled him out of the wreckage. In the ensuing action one of the Rangers had been captured, one Ranger was reported missing and two pilots and two Rangers had been killed; a costly mission, indeed. On 25 April, Captain Dave Ohle, L Co, 75th Ranger Regiment, led a small rescue party in to bring them out. (Dave Ohle later retired from the Army in the grade of lieutenant general.)

From North Vietnamese Records[20]—

> At exactly 6:00 AM on 1 July the 324B Division Command Post issued the "open fire" order to all sectors. Three 75mm recoilless rifle positions and

five 82mm mortar positions fired a 30-minute barrage into Base 935. The initial volley hit the command post of the U.S. 2nd Battalion/506th Airborne. The American artillery firing position was hit; an observation tower collapsed as the result of mortar hits, a radar installation suffered heavy damage, and the logistics support area caught fire. More than 70 American troops were killed in our attack by fire. At the same time 1st Regiment's mortar positions also accurately shelled the command post of the puppet army's 3rd Company/2nd Battalion/505th Regiment [sic] (*There were no ARVN "puppet" troops in the Ripcord area at this time.*) on Hill 902.

(*The open fire order may have been issued at 6:00 AM, but the first rounds initiating the siege landed on Ripcord at 7:08 AM. No KIAs 1 July although 15 artillerymen received minor wounds while delivering counter-battery fire.*)

3rd Regiment's mortars shelled targets at Co Pung and on Hill 1078. Enemy artillery firing from Cung Cap (*FSB Rakkasan*), Hill 700, Cooc Bai (*O'Reilly*), and Hill 367 (*maybe FSB Barbara*) rained shells down all over the area around Base 935. Additional reconnaissance aircraft were sent to the area and AD-6 and F-5 aircraft dropped their bombs haphazardly all over the countryside. At 9:00 AM on 1 July the enemy began sending infantry to relieve Base 935. Helicopters picked up an American company from Hill 797 (*near O'Reilly*) and landed it on Hill 805 to cover Hill 935's southeastern flank.

(*Elements of the 2nd Sqdn, 17th Cavalry landed near Hill 805 on 1 July and came out on 2 July. The South Vietnamese VNAF flew AD-6 and F-5 attack aircraft, but not at Ripcord. The US Air Force, Navy and Marines who mostly flew F-4s, F-105s, A-4s and A-6s superbly supported us.*)

Understanding the enemy's intentions, 1st Company had dismantled a 12.7mm machine gun and carried it up the steep slopes on the side of Hill 805. There they built a firing position from which they could engage the enemy as he landed his troops from the air. As soon as the enemy helicopters landed fire from 1st Company left two of the helicopters burning in the middle of the landing zone, and three helicopters that were about to land troops right behind them suffered the same fate.

(*C Company 2/506th suffered eight KIAs on 2 July on Hill 902 from an enemy night attack led by sappers as described below; not from the air assault.*)

The enemy had lost one entire company and suffered heavy casualties in another company, and Base 935 was under heavy pressure, but the enemy still did not send in large forces to relieve the base.

From US Records—[21]

At 3:46 AM on 2 July, the night defensive position on Hill 902, approximately 2000 meters south of Ripcord, occupied by the CP and 1st and 2d Platoons, Company C, 2d Battalion, 506th Infantry received RPG, satchel charges, and small arms fire. A well-organized and executed attack by at least one enemy sapper company of the 7th Sapper Battalion penetrated the perimeter and occupied positions inside the NDP. Infantry, as always, supported the sappers. The enemy soldiers and elements of Company C exchanged satchel charges and fragmentation grenades in a fierce close-in battle killing the enemy soldiers within the perimeter and the remaining enemy forces withdrew at approximately 4:20 AM. Captain Thomas T. Hewitt, having replaced Captain Vasquez only two-weeks earlier, died in the initial firefight. The company aid man, Private First Class Gerald A. Cafferty, immediately organized the defense of the position. "Doc" Cafferty attended to the seriously wounded as he went about checking positions and returning enemy fire with his personal weapon. Assisted by the Company RTO, Sergeant Jack Dreher, Cafferty called in life-saving gun ships, mortar, and artillery fire. The dazed and shaken artillery forward observer finally took over calling in fire support. One example of the ferociousness of the night time engagement involved Specialist Four Michael K. "Alaska" Mueller. Although suffering from multiple wounds, "Alaska" fought alone from his foxhole and single-handedly killed seven enemy soldiers around his position. Sporadic contact and mortar fire continued until approximately 5:30 AM. The night long action resulted in twenty NVA killed, seven US KIA, six US WIA, and one US MIA-Presumed Dead. The MIA was PFC Stephen J. Harber. While policing up the position, soldiers from C Company found a boot with a foot in it and Harber's dog tag attached.

"Varsity" Chinook 868 was hit and shot down on Ripcord on 2 July while trying to recover "Varsity" 103 shot down the day before. "Varsity" 868 flew back to the 159th base at Hue-Phu Bai Airfield.

From North Vietnamese Records[22]—

> The enemy had lost one entire company and suffered heavy casualties in another company, and Base 935 was under heavy pressure, but the enemy still did not send in large forces to relieve the base.

324B Division decided to continue the shelling of Base 935. At 10:00 A.M. on 2 July the enemy airlifted 2nd Battalion/501st Airborne from Phu Bai onto Hill 884, Cooc Muon, Hill 902, and Doc May. (*Doc May, meaning "cloud slope," is a ridge running southeast down from the top of Hill 902.*) 1st Regiment had carefully deployed its forces to wait at each of these locations. As soon as the helicopters touched down our medium machine guns opened fire simultaneously, lacing the landing zones with long streams of bullets. In the first minutes ten enemy helicopters burst into flame. The newly landed enemy infantry hastily deployed for battle. They spread out quickly around each of the high points to stave off attacks by our infantry. After putting in a brief fight, however, our forces attacked their bivouac locations.

(*The 2/501ˢᵗ suffered no KIAs during these assaults on 2 July nor were any helicopters destroyed.*)

From US Records—

At 10:20 AM on 2 July, the "Drive On" 2d Battalion, 501st Infantry passed to the operational control of the 3d Brigade and combat assaulted with three companies into landing zones to the south and southwest of Ripcord. Company A, assaulted onto a landing zone in the vicinity of Hill 902 and immediately received 30 rounds of enemy 82mm mortar fire, which resulted in one soldier being wounded. Lt Col Otis Livingston's Battalion Command Post (CP) moved from Phu Bai Combat Base and collocated on Ripcord with the CP, 2nd Battalion, 506th Infantry.

"Pachyderm" 499 recovered "Varsity" 103 from Ripcord on 3 July marking the first time a "C" model Chinook had been recovered by another "C" model. (Recovery of Chinooks previously required a CH-54 "Flying Crane" or the partial disassembly of the damaged Chinook.) Unfortunately, in an apparent attempt to lighten 499 by reducing the fuel load, it ran out of fuel and crashed just short of Camp Evans. The helicopter crew escaped serious injuries, but both Chinooks were "totaled." Incidentally, these aircraft losses are considered accidents and not the result of enemy action.

At 9:50 AM on 4 July, while conducting a search and attack operation approximately four kilometers southeast of RIPCORD, an individual from Company C, 2d Battalion, 501ˢᵗ Infantry unintentionally detonated a booby trap consisting of five 82mm mortar rounds placed along the trail in a "daisy chain." This unfortunate ambush resulted in five men killed and another five wounded.

At 12:10 AM in the middle of the night, 5 July, and again at 12:50 AM, the enemy engaged the night defensive position of Company C, 2/501st Infantry with small arms fire and satchel charges, which resulted in three soldiers being wounded. A search of the contact area under illumination revealed no enemy casualties remained in the area. At 6:05 AM the enemy again attacked, employing rocket propelled grenades, small arms fire, and satchel charges. This time a search of the contact area yielded five confirmed NVA KIA. One US soldier died and 14 more were evacuated as a result of wounds.

From North Vietnamese Records[23]—

On 3 July 17th Engineer Company/1st Regiment sprung an ambush using a pre-laid mine field, inflicting significant losses on an American company at Doc May. The survivors fled to Peak Number Three of Hill 935, where they were hit by a second attack launched by 2nd Company/1st Battalion. Sixty American troops were annihilated. The enemy had to move a company by helicopter from Cooc Muon to reinforce their comrades on Doc May. The result of all this was that in the First Stage of the battle we achieved our intended goal of besieging Base 935 and forcing the enemy to send out troops to reinforce and relieve the base.

(Not 60 "annihilated", but a five-82mm mortar round booby trap detonated on 4 July killed five US soldiers and I received my first and only direct communication from General Creighton Abrams, Commander of US Military Assistance Command Vietnam, wanting to know why I was taking such large numbers of casualties. The above referenced NVA attack of Peak Number Three of Hill 935 did not happen. Hill 935 was Ripcord and the enemy never once penetrated the wire, much less "annihilating" 60 men.)

To relieve the pressure on Base 935, beginning on 3 July enemy B-52s began carpet-bombing the area, hitting pre-selected coordinates. C-130s [sic] fired heavy machine guns and dropped parachute bombs. Interspersed between the air strikes the enemy fired coordinated artillery barrages from seven different artillery firebases, all firing simultaneously at one single target.

(And General Berry thought we couldn't coordinate our supporting fires! Brigadier General Sidney B. Berry was the new Assistant Division Commander (Operations). He repeatedly lectured all battalion commanders and brigade commanders asserting that we did not make adequate use of supporting fires. The NVA saw it differently.)

To deal with the enemy reaction, 324B Division Headquarters decided to expand the area covered by our offensive, to attack the enemy even at night, and to resolutely strike daring, painful blows designed to kill his troops and crush their fighting spirit. On 5 July, 3rd Battalion maneuvered down from Doc May to Hill 902, where it attacked and inflicted heavy losses on one company of the U.S. 2nd Battalion. That same day 7th Battalion eliminated more than 80 enemy troops in an ambush as they were moving from Cooc Muon back to Doc May. 1st Company of the 7B Sapper Battalion attacked the enemy artillery base on Hill 700, destroying four guns and killing the gun crews. 2nd Battalion attacked an enemy troop concentration on Hill 1251 (*Cooc Muon aka Coc Muen*), killing more than 100 Americans.

(*This has to be the same incident described above with the mortar shell booby-trap killing five. Only one platoon from C Company 2/501st Infantry in that area took casualties. "Hill" 700 with artillery guns may have been in an area with ARVN troops, but certainly not our 3rd Brigade. We had no troops on Hill 1251.*)

Recollections of Cobra Pilots—

David Grubb, "Redskin 32," D Co, 158 Assault Helicopter Battalion, described some of the air action in and around Ripcord:

The thing I recall most about Ripcord was that our company was out of pilots, but we could put up one more aircraft if I used my crew chief in the front seat. The crew chief had a fixed wing license in civilian life and could fly the Cobra at least straight and level and could possibly get us back to base if I got hit. The CO agreed to the plan and my crew chief and I worked the mission hard all day. We never got out of the aircraft. We did hot refuel and rearms. The CO in effect closed the company area and everyone just stayed at the ammo pile and did hot rearms. At one point in a gun run the crew chief looked at me in a little rear view mirror the Cobra had and said "Sir there are tracers coming at us." I tried to be as calm as possible and said "just use the minigun on any area you see tracers coming from when I make our turn." I had given him a quick gunnery course on the way out to Ripcord so he did just as I asked and fired back long and hard every time we made our break. When the day was done for us the crew chief was real quite and I think for him the war got real in an instant. He was a hero with the other enlisted guys for awhile, but I am sure his view of things was never the same.

CWO Rick Freeman flew Cobras in the Aerial Rocket Artillery (ARA) role in C Battery "Griffins", 4th Battalion, 77th, Aerial Rocket Artillery. Technically, the fire support from the ARA was provided through artillery command/operational channels. The C/4/77 was based at Camp Evans and was in General Support Reinforcing the 3rd Brigade's Direct Support Artillery Battalion, the 2/319th Artillery. In actual day-to-day fighting, the Griffins did not wait for artillery fire support channels for clearance to fire. The Griffins responded directly and immediately to the grunts on the ground.

Aircraft Commander Freeman recalled:

> Several things come to mind. I think Ripcord was more of an event for us—C/4/77—than Lam Son 719. Lam Son was longer and much larger in scale but not nearly as intense as Ripcord.
>
> The day before the extraction we flew a lot, some cover for slicks and hooks, some for fire for A/2/506, an infantry company southeast of Ripcord. I had Lance McIlheney in my front seat, I had been in country sixteen months, Lance, maybe a week. Late in the day we were told by our operations people that we may have to provide cover all night. It had been a long hot day, we were tired, and the thought of flying all night didn't set well. Artillery was readily available, lots of TAC air had been put in, I had heard over fifty sets of F-4's. As a later Phantom driver I find that hard to believe. Anyway, about dark we were told we were going to fly cover all night—oh boy!
>
> As a rule we carried 1,000—1200 pounds of fuel. This allowed us to carry a decent load of ordnance. Two platoons rotated the cover. The fuel load gave us a little over an hour on station and we relieved each other over Ripcord so they were never without someone being able to shoot. The relieving Cobras then flew to Evans for fuel, then to our battery area go get a drink, latrine, sandwiches if the cooks had them, etc. That gave us 15–20 minutes on the ground before we had to leave to replace the platoon on station so they could leave to refuel.
>
> As the night wore on it got very sleepy, so Lance and I rotated sleeping while on cap. Lock your harness and sleep. We turned down the radios, left the intercom up. As the time wore on and we needed to head back we would wake up the other pilot and go to POL. I don't remember either of us shooting one round all night. My biggest concern was sleeping with a very serious FNG in my front seat. If we had to shoot we needed to be alert and sleep provided that, so I slept when I could.
>
> We flew through the morning, provided cover all day while the artillery tubes were lifted out, and covered A/2/506 as they walked to an extraction spot. We were roughly 30 hours straight on the rotation. The other platoon that was not on rotation was on alert for the rest of 3rd Brigade. (My log

book shows: 22 JUL 70 contact Raffles A/2/506 6+15 day 3+30 night 23 JUL 70 Ripcord mortar watch 3+15 night—13 actual flight hours.)

Several days later I was on alert and got a fire mission southwest of Evans. There was a low overcast. As I made radio contact, I could hear an intense firefight in process. The speaker on the other end was desperate, he said we were the fourth set of Cobras he had called that morning and none were able to get to him and he needed help really bad. He, Chuck Hawkins, CO A/2/506 was in a bad way. The NVA knew the weather was unusual, Tac Air out of the question, and so far no Cobras.

A Co was on the south side of the ridge that ran west from Helen, the biggest hill south of Evans. I was now on the north side of the ridge over the flats, the overcast covering the ridge tops. Every time Chuck spoke I could hear the screaming, yelling, automatic weapons firing, grenades going off, the whistles from the NVA. You could almost smell it. I don't know why artillery from Rakkasan was not going in, but I was all there was right now.

I considered going over the cloud top, momentary IFR, to get to the south side. I knew where I was, knew the terrain, but how low were the clouds in the valley on the south side? What was my wingman going to do? I knew he wouldn't be comfortable doing that, but A Co needed help now. I told Capt Hawkins to give me ten minutes, I'm not leaving you, but I have to get there.

I turned east, pulled max torque. I flew along the north side of the piedmont, past Helen to the Song Bo River. My wingman right behind, I briefed him on victor (VHF) what I had in mind. We turned right, down the river, been there many times. We flew to the crow's foot and took the right fork, the left fork went to firebase Veghel. I slowed down, told my wingman to get separation, I called Capt Hawkins, the firefight was still as intense as he responded. The valley narrowed and the ceiling was low. I could have gone over the top but it would have been close.

I asked if he could hear me, he responded affirmative. The valley floor was rising as the valley narrowed toward the upper end. I'm running out of room and I still don't know where the two valley sides are. I asked for his location, typical grunt response, "I'm not sure." He was on the south slope, to my right as I headed west, just below the clouds. I knew the NVA were close, I could hear them every time he keyed his mic. I just didn't know where exactly.

I'm running out of room and I need to shoot. I'm down to 40 knots or so. I said let me start at the bottom of the valley and you adjust my fire to where you need it. He said to start 100 meters up from the floor. After two pair of rockets, I was on target. I pressed as much as I could, I had to turn around. My wing was able to observe and he was in hot. The smoke from my rockets was very visible. There were minor adjustments, every time Capt Hawkins keyed his mic you could hear the impact of the rockets. The adrenalin was running fast for him, they were finally getting relief. I called for a replacement section when we were about half expended.

We ran four sections for A Co that morning. They were finally able to break contact.

A Co stayed out another 2–3 weeks. I flew by and called almost every day. Usually all was well, sometimes he asked for me to shoot in an area that had a sniper that bothered them or toward an area that they had been probed from.

One day I called to see how they were doing and the RTO answered the call. Where was the six? He couldn't talk; he had been hit in the throat by shrapnel. He refused to be med-evaced, tough guy. After a few days he could whisper, sounded like the recon teams we worked for from SOG (Special Operations Group-usually in Laos or North Vietnam). A few days later D/2/506 joined with A Co and a few days after that they came out. I still called every day for a sitrep, it had gotten quiet.

I was sitting in my hooch one night watching the movie Combat. Sarge and Little John were going through some ville in France when there was a knock at the door. Who knocks in Vietnam? At a Battery hooch? In walks Capt Chuck Hawkins, Capt Gabe Rollison (D Co CO), a platoon sergeant, and a private. They came to say thanks. What an honor. They took the time from their stand-down to come find me to say thank you personally. I'm just a GI like they are and was looking out for them with the weapon system that I had. I was happy to do it. It is a very fond memory.

A busy time. At one point in the summer of '70 we were down to 16 pilots, we had a lot of WO-1's. I went over 1,000 hours in country on 8 Jul 70, I had been to the SIP course and I was very busy with training "newbies" besides the cross-border SOG missions. We were working for CCN at Quang Tri and Delta Project at Mai Loc. I notice from my log that I flew with both of the other platoons, the battery commander Maj Bill Dick—great guy—and the maintenance officer George Shirilla. I logged several missions with crew chiefs in the front seat. I didn't record who my wingmen were, didn't seem necessary at the time.

1st Lt Michael L. Harvey, who flew a Cobra helicopter, call sign "Griffin" 19, in support of the 3rd Brigade, also flew cross-border operations to support Special Forces operations in Laos and North Vietnam. Mike's Cobra took hits with bullets striking his chest protector and injuring him in the throat and face and causing his Cobra to crash. He earned the Distinguished Flying Cross and the Purple Heart Medal. Mike and I reflect on those days (a lot!!) as we annually spend a week riding the horseback trails of the Texas Hill Country.

Action Elsewhere in the 3rd Brigade—

On 8 July my attention switched to our AO in northwest Quang Tri Province—about fifty-five kilometers from Ripcord. We received intelligence that the replacement-filled NVA 9th Infantry Regiment entered South Vietnam from Laos near Khe Sanh enroute to replace the badly mauled 66th Infantry Regiment. A Scout helicopter of the 2nd Squadron, 17th Cavalry, while flying reconnaissance in very poor weather, surprised the enemy column as they moved through tall elephant grass.

Immediately after discovering the large force near Khe Sanh on 8 July, we inserted Troop D "The Blues", 2nd Squadron, 17th Cavalry in the area to capture a prisoner. After capturing three prisoners and a large number of documents Troop D was extracted. The captured documents confirmed the enemy force to be the 9th Infantry Regiment. For its efforts, Troop D suffered six men killed and five more wounded.

With the help of the 4th Battalion (Aerial Rocket), 77th Artillery, 139 enemy soldiers were killed. CW2 Mike Allan described his part of the action:

On July 8, 1970, Charlie Troop 2/17th Cav was assisting in an operation and was rearming and refueling out of Quang Tri. I was in Quang Tri refueling, just about ready to call for taxi for take-off for my team, when I hear a call on Guard Radio. The call was coming from our Squadron Commander, LTC Molinelli (Cheyenne Phantom). "Any Cobra in the vicinity of Khe Sanh, come to Khe Sanh strip. We have multiple targets here for you." He did not sound like he or his people were in trouble. He sounded more like he was excited that he had found something significant. I was mission commander for myself in an AH-1, and for an OH-6 scout. We started out towards Khe Sanh and came up the frequencies Cheyenne Phantom (Lt Col Molinelli) had put out on his Guard Radio call. We could tell that something was going on and we picked up that a large number of troops had been caught out in the open just south of Khe Sanh. We reported in and received clearance to go in shooting. My scout picked out a trail and was soon giving spot reports and marking targets to shoot. It was almost like a gunnery range, literally like shooting fish in a barrel. Multiple targets all over the elephant grass plain. We would shoot up everything until we were expended and then go back to Quang Tri, refuel and rearm. The Blues were inserted to find and fix the stragglers on the Khe Sanh plain. We kept going until the sun went down. The Blues stayed out that night and the next day we were at it again. This time the targets were sporadic. The Blues policed up the enemy bodies and took prisoners. We had killed off a very large number of NVA. The prisoners were questioned. It was determined that the unit we had caught in the open was an NVA Anti-Aircraft Battalion that had just crossed over into Vietnam from Laos with the 9th NVA Infantry Regiment. The NVA backpacks had brand new uniforms, Ho Chi Minh sandals, and fresh food.

Captain Mac Jones, Operations Officer, C Troop, 2/17th Cav "Condors" provided a more colorful depiction of insertion of Delta Troop:

> I was on the flight line in Quang Tri with every slick in the Squadron lined up behind me. Delta Troop was ready to load, 90 guys to attack 750 NVA!!! On my PRC 25 radio, I hear a Scout call "'I've got five, no ten, fifty, damn I've got them all, launch the world!!!." I stepped out and swung my arm in a circle, all 16 slicks cranked, I didn't need orders, I knew we had those bastards caught in the open, and I knew what Molinelli was going to do. Their AA fire sucked that day, don't recall anybody taking a serious hit. Remember the body count—323 NVA confirmed dead, B-52's to strike later. (This was an update of the previously reported 139 KIA.)

Lieutenant Colonel Chuck Shay's 2nd Battalion 502nd Infantry "Strike Force" and the 1st and 2nd Battalions, 3rd Regiment, of the 1st Infantry Division, ARVN, joined the fight against the 9th NVA Regiment.

The piles of the enemy bodies along with weapons and other equipment provide ample evidence of the destruction of the NVA 9th Infantry Regiment. The highly effective 2/502 Infantry returned to Thua Tien Province 15 July. The 2nd Squadron, 17th Cavalry then left the 3rd Brigade and reverted to the Operational Control of Division as some of its elements continued to patrol the area.

This action fifty-five kilometers north-northwest of Ripcord occurred at exactly the same time that the battles for Hills 805 and 1000 had become more costly.

Back in the Ripcord Area—

The weather generally improved with higher ceilings and better visibility, but the winds always presented a major problem. In the mountainous area of Ripcord, O'Reilly, and Barnett, winds gusting to 40 to 75 knots were routine. I recall landing my Huey on FSB Barnett to visit our troops there in support of the ARVN on the firebase. The gusting wind completely turned me around 360 degrees on my approach and while sitting on the ground, my airspeed indicator recorded 65 knots. At that speed the helicopter could not be shut down without the flapping rotor blades possibly striking the tail boom, so my copilot held the controls while I delivered mail and visited with my troops. I could understand why a helicopter had not landed on Barnett in six days. Three soldiers, overdue to rotate off Barnett, happily climbed aboard for a ride to Evans with the Brigade Commander.

Enemy activity in the immediate area of FSB Ripcord increased dramatically in early July, which indicated a buildup of enemy combat and combat support forces. Increased enemy antiaircraft fire led the division commander to direct that beginning 16 July helicopter gunships must escort all Chinooks flying into FSB Ripcord. (This is consistent with General Hennessey's ever-present concern about calling attention to "un-necessary aircraft losses." It certainly made sense that if enemy anti-aircraft fire continued to increase, counter actions were necessary.)

Observation from FSB Ripcord revealed considerable enemy activity on Hill 1000, one kilometer to the west of the firebase. Extensive cannon and aerial rocket artillery and tactical air strikes concentrated on the hill to weaken enemy defenses in preparation for a ground assault by Captain Rembert Rollison's Company D, 2d Battalion, 506th Infantry on 7 July.

At 9:40 AM on 7 July, Company D made initial contact with a well fortified enemy position which engaged Company D with RPD machine guns, satchel charges, fragmentation grenades, and small arms fire. D Company employed organic weapons, tube artillery, ARA, and tactical air strikes on the enemy positions, but could not dislodge them from the hill. Company D terminated contact at approximately 3:00 PM and moved off the hill having suffered losses of three men killed and nineteen wounded. The company confirmed six enemy killed in the action.

Beginning with a tactical air strike at 8:00 AM on 8 July, a two and one-half hour artillery and air preparation pounded Hill 1000. In addition to the employment of all calibers of cannon artillery (105mm, 155mm, 8 inch and 175mm), high performance aircraft dropped 250 and 500 pound bombs, while helicopter gunships from the 4th Battalion (ARA), 77th Field Artillery pounded the hill with 2.75 rockets and CS (tear gas) munitions. The artillery on Ripcord, 1000 meters away, fired directly into Hill 1000. At 10:30 AM, artillery fires were shifted, and Companies C and D, 2nd Battalion, 506th Infantry began the second assault on Hill 1000.

At 10:50 AM, both companies reported being engaged by intense small arms and automatic weapons fire from enemy troops located in mutually supporting bunkers. Captain Jeff Wilcox's C Company neutralized one bunker as they reached the westernmost knoll and highest point on Hill 1000. The enemy not only survived the horrendous prep fires, but also came to the slits in their bunkers sending out withering fire on the attackers. C Company reached the high ground on the west ready to provide direct fire support to Captain Rollison's D Company for their attack on the easternmost knoll. D Company did not advance. Lieutenant Colonel Lucas ordered Wilcox to attack across the one hundred meters of open terrain to seize the eastern knoll. Lieutenant Jim Campbell told Wilcox that he would lead the attack on the other knoll, but Wilcox insisted that it was his responsibility as the company commander to lead the men in this assault. Captain Wilcox began at 11:40 AM to lead his grossly under-strength thirty-man company across the barren saddle when heavy fire killed one soldier and wounded three others. Private First Class Rickey L. Scott, an unarmed conscientious objector medical aidman, responded to the call for "Medic!" and was instantly killed. At this time, Captain Fred Spaulding, flying in a 3rd Brigade Aviation Section scout helicopter, called Captain Wilcox and warned him of a large enemy force moving quickly towards him from the west. Lieutenant Colonel Lucas monitored Wilcox's net and ordered both C and D companies to immediately break contact and withdraw down the hill.

Contact on Hill 1000 terminated at 1 PM. The two men killed and four wounded during the assault dealt an extremely severe blow to the morale of the remaining twenty-four, totally exhausted, men of Company C.

Lt Col Lucas ordered a second attack on Hill 1000 for the afternoon to which. Captain Wilcox strongly protested; his depleted company, exhausted as they were, could not possibly continue the attack. Lucas cancelled the order.

From North Vietnamese Records[24]—

The enemy forces in Base 935 were "pinned down and trapped" by the siege pressure applied by the cadre and soldiers of 2nd Battalion/6th Thua Thien Regiment. All enemy counterattacks designed to loosen our siege ring were beaten back by our troops. In a little over ten days of siege warfare the enemy in the area of Hill 935 had lost almost 700 men, seven enemy artillery pieces had been destroyed, and more than a dozen enemy aircraft were shot down. On 11 July the enemy was forced to use helicopters to transport 2nd Battalion/501st Airborne back to Phu Bai to regroup. 1st Battalion/501st Airborne, which was left behind, was forced to pull back onto the highest point on Hill 935 and call in artillery and air strikes all around its position in order to be able to hold the position.

(*Lieutenant Colonel Thomas E. Aaron's 1ˢᵗ Battalion, 501ˢᵗ Infantry did not arrive in the Ripcord area until 18 July when he opened and began patrolling around FSB Gladiator. There certainly was no battalion pulled back onto Ripcord. A single rifle company plus small supporting units occupied Ripcord. Lieutenant Colonel Otis Livingston's 2ⁿᵈ Battalion, 501ˢᵗ Infantry did not get pulled out until 18 July. D Company, 2ⁿᵈ Battalion, 501ˢᵗ Infantry resisted the fierce sapper and infantry attacks on Hill 805 five nights in a row.*)

324B Division headquarters decided to step up the pressure to force the enemy to send in relief forces. Only one day after arriving back at its base camp, 2nd Battalion/501st Airborne was hastily sent to Hill 935 to deploy its forces. Two companies covered the Cooc Muon sector and four companies were stationed in the area around Hill 935. Inside Base 935 the enemy had two infantry companies and two battalion command posts. Meanwhile Hill 805 was being developed into an outer perimeter strongpoint to block the approach of our forces from the east. The enemy intended to hold Hill 935 at any price.

(*The 2ⁿᵈ Battalion, 501ˢᵗ Infantry moved troops to the northwest of Ripcord and temporarily located its command post on Ripcord, but did not place any rifle companies on the firebase.*)

The altered disposition of enemy forces caused the 324B Division to send 3rd Battalion and Sapper Battalion 7B to attack the enemy force on Hill 805. 9th Battalion and 2nd Battalion/6th Regiment attacked the southwestern sector of Hill 935.

(*Two battalions of infantry and sappers attacked Hill 805 and two battalions attacked the southwest side of Ripcord. They failed to penetrate Ripcord defenses and paid a very high price at Hill 805*)

Meanwhile the 324B Division decided to use all its fire support assets to conduct powerful attacks by fire against the enemy strong points and increase the pressure on Base 935 in a determined effort to put the enemy completely on the defensive.

(*The North Vietnamese had pretty good intelligence. Much of it came from our US radio nets. Major Ho Van Thuoc, Operations Officer of the 6ᵗʰ Tri Thein Regiment at the time of the Ripcord battle, told me in my interview with him in Hue in June 2001, that they listened to our radio nets. The CIA confirmed that the enemy had over 200 radio listening posts in South Vietnam with English speaking operatives.*)

From US Records—[25]

On 10 July, FSB Ripcord received fire on eight separate occasions during the day from enemy 60mm, 82mm mortars, and 75mm recoilless rifles. The defenders suffered losses of two men killed and seventeen others wounded.

On the night of 12–13 July, the NVA launched an attack against the night defensive position established by Captain Straub's Company D, 2nd Battalion, 501st Infantry Hill 805, wounding sixteen of the defenders. The enemy employed 30–40 RPG rounds, satchel charges, and small arms fire. Company D countered with organic weapons, ARA, air strikes, and employed a helicopter flare ship to illuminate the attacking enemy soldiers.

Located only two kilometers east-southeast of Ripcord, Hill 805 constitutes a prominent terrain feature and affords excellent observation of Ripcord—very key terrain for the enemy and its occupation by American forces became critical for the security of FSB Ripcord. At 10:53 PM on 13 July, Company D, 2/501st again received enemy small arms fire, RPGs, and satchel charges. Once again, a determined enemy force attacked it at 2:03 AM, 14 July. A fierce battle raged for approximately one hour, as Company D adjusted M55 .50 caliber (Quad Fifties) machinegun fire directly from Ripcord. Artillery direct fire, and 81mm mortars also came from Ripcord as ARA gunships and tactical air joined the fight. A first light search of the contact area revealed five North Vietnamese soldiers had been killed and their bodies left behind, six US soldiers had died, and an additional nine men wounded in the attack. During the night of 14-15 July, the enemy again attacked Hill 805. At 1:59 AM, the NVA fired 35–40 rounds of 82mm mortar fire killing one US soldier. Prior to the night actions on Hill 805, Captain Straub had not lost a man KIA.

From North Vietnamese Records[26]—

On the 13th, 14th, and 15th of July we attacked enemy forces in the area around Hill 935, Hill 805, and Cooc Muon. The enemy was forced to send out reaction forces and enemy elements tried to rescue one another. Although we had not yet been able to annihilate entire American companies, the eight enemy companies stationed on the high ground in this area all suffered heavy losses.

(This marks an interesting change in tone. In one place above, the PAVN claimed to have killed over 2000 by the end of June. In separate engagements

detailed above, they have claimed to kill 310 Americans. And now they admit that they failed to eliminate even one US rifle company.)

On 17 July the division decided to mass its forces to launch powerful attacks in all sectors using every type of weapon at our disposal. At the same time an emulation program to shoot down enemy aircraft was launched. The division moved two 120mm mortars forward for the attack and shifted 7th Battalion over to Cooc Muon to replace 9th Battalion, which moved up to reinforce our units on the eastern side of Hill 935. On the night of 17 July all units moved forward to their targets.

(An emulation program is where the unit strives to match an earlier high standard of performance of another unit, e.g., shoot down x number of aircraft as was done by the x Division.)

From US Records—[27]

At my request, I was again given operational control of the 2nd Battalion, 501st Infantry "Drive On" for the purpose of attacking Hill 1000. On 14 July, the remainder of the 2/501st rejoined the fighting. This proved to be an especially frustrating time. Ripcord, which operations planned to serve as a fire support base for extended summer offensive operations into the A Shau Valley, the "Warehouse Area," and branches of the Ho Chi Minh Trail, found itself under almost continuous attack by fire and frequent probes by sappers. Most of the enemy fire came from the vicinity of Hills 805 and 1000. Captain Chris Straub's D Co, 2/501st Infantry occupied Hill 805, and took a nightly beating from enemy assault forces, sapper. Lt Col Lucas had tried to deny the enemy firing positions and observation from Hill 1000 by first sending his recon platoon to the hill for a short-lived, costly mission on 5 July (all seven members of the platoon took hits). Next, on 6 July, Lucas sent his D Company to assist the Recon Platoon withdraw. D Company attacked Hill 1000 on 7 July without success. Lucas tried a coordinated two-company assault on Hill 1000 with C and D Companies on 8 July, again, without success. After many, many fire missions into Hill 1000, the brigade tried to take Hill 1000 on 15 July by ground attack employing A and B Companies and the Reconnaissance Platoon of the 2nd Battalion, 501st Infantry being bravely led on the ground by Battalion Commander Lt Col Otis Livingston. The enemy fiercely defended using RPG, small arms, and mortar fire, which resulted in one US soldier killed and twenty wounded. US organic weapons, ARA, cannon artillery and air strikes were again employed against the heavily fortified hill. Partial sweeps of the contact area uncovered five dead North Vietnamese soldiers. The 2/ 501st Infantry Battalion (Minus) withdrew to a location southwest of Hill 1000, where, at 1715 hours it came under 82mm mortar fire. The 2/501 took no casualties from the mortar fire. The enemy force on Hill 1000 proved too strong, too determined, and too well-fortified to be dislodged without the cost in American lives becoming too great. The Brigade did not want to experience another Hamburger Hill and called off Livingston's planned attack.

The Ripcord firebase and units operating in the vicinity continued to receive daily attacks by fire from 82mm, 60mm mortars, and recoilless rifles. On 17 July, Ripcord received120mm mortar fire marking the first use of this weapon in the division AO in over 18 months. Fourteen US soldiers were wounded on Ripcord in these attacks on this date. The enemy deployed his forces in the Ripcord area to encircle the firebase, and employed 12.7mm machine gun and small arms fire against aircraft as they inserted and extracted troops, picked up casualties and delivered supplies. Ripcord itself did not receive a ground attack during the 1–17 July period; however, US units met determined enemy resistance on dominant terrain features around the fire-base—on Hill 1000 to the west, Hill 902 to the south, and Hill 805 to the east.

6

Workman's D Co Gets Battered

From North Vietnamese Records[28]—

At 6:00 A.M. on the morning of 18 July our heavy weapons opened up with massive barrages against Base 935, Base 805, and other enemy positions. The American battalion command post and the artillery firing position inside Base 935 were hit numerous times by 120mm mortar shells and sixty American troops were killed. Most of the American casualties were artillery gunners. Our guns rained shells down on the American company atop Hill 805, killing almost twenty enemy troops. The enemy was forced to send helicopters to Hill 805 to retrieve the troops stationed there. During the first few minutes of the battle our 12.7mm gun crews shot down three enemy helicopters, forcing the enemy to abandon his plan to evacuate the American company by helicopter. On the night of 18 July, 2nd Sapper Company launched a quick attack that cut the enemy force completely in two, inflicting more than 60 casualties. The enemy survivors fled through the jungle back to Cooc Muon under the cover of darkness.

(*Instead of the 140 claimed here, we lost three KIA on 18 July.*)

From US Records—

The 2d Battalion, 501st Infantry moved by air to Camp Evans from the Ripcord area on 18 July. With the 2/501st went Hill 805-battered D Co, 2/501st that had been OPCON directly to Lucas's 2/506th. Recognizing the continuing shortage of infantrymen in the bush with the 2/506th, I tasked Lt Col Bobby Porter, Commander of the 1st Bn, 506th Infantry to place one rifle

company of his battalion OPCON to the 2/506th. He detailed Captain Don
Workman's Company D, 1st Battalion, 506th Infantry, to the Brigade and I
further placed it OPCON to the 2d Battalion, 506th Infantry. The company
combat assaulted into a landing zone approximately 1200 meters northwest of
Ripcord to begin patrol operations in an easterly direction towards Hill 805.

Lt Col Lucas decided to reinforce the firebase with the deployment of his
Ready Reaction Platoon from Camp Evans. 1st Lt John Hall had commanded
the 1st Platoon of D Co, 2/506th until May and since had been serving as the
Executive Officer of D Co back in the rear at Camp Evans. Hall had the additional duty of commanding the Battalion Ready Reaction Platoon. Lt Hall
brought his platoon of about thirty cooks, clerks and other REMFs (an
endearing term of description for those who serve in the rear echelon) out to
FSB Ripcord where they remained until evacuation of the firebase on 23 July.

Ripcord continued to receive sporadic enemy mortar fire throughout the
day of 18 July. After spending the night on Ripcord, I spoke with a sergeant
that morning as we stood leaning on ammo crates filled with dirt that shielded
the command bunker entrance just when a 120mm mortar round hit in front
of the crates and blew the sergeant and me eight feet back into the bunker.
(Unlike a certain US Senator, I did not collect a purple heart for my combat
wound.) The sergeant, who bled from both ears as a result of the blast, had to
be evacuated. The same 120mm round instantly killed Specialist 4 William D.
Rollason who stood in a similar position to my right at the next bunker opening. Shrapnel from the round also wounded four other soldiers.

With a splitting headache and barely able to hear after taking the blast of
the 120mm mortar, I left Ripcord to visit other units of the brigade. I was
advised over the secure radio net that at about 1:30 PM, on the fourth Chinook sortie of the day to Ripcord, a CH-47 helicopter, "Pachyderm" 810,
from Company A, 159th Aviation Battalion, which carried a sling load of
105mm howitzer ammunition to Ripcord, took enemy 12.7mm machine gun
fire as it came to a hover. The aircraft crashed directly onto the ammo bunker
of B Battery, 2nd Battalion, 319th Field Artillery and spilled burning JP-4 aviation fuel down into the ammo dump, setting off over 400 rounds of artillery.
The fire and explosions continued for over eight hours and rendered the battery's six tubes of 105mm artillery as destroyed or unusable. The fire also
resulted in extensive damage in, and to the Medical Aid Station bunker and
tactical operations center on the southern portion of the firebase. An AN/
MPQ-4A Counter Mortar Radar, two 106mm recoilless rifles, and an AN/
GRC-163 VHF radio set took hits from the explosions. One CH-47 crew-

member, Specialist 4 Michael A. Walker, died, and five crewmembers wounded in the helicopter crash. In spite of the fire and exploding 105mm ammunition, the firebase perimeter remained intact. By late afternoon, the fires came under control and cleanup operations began.

As a result of the massive damage caused on Ripcord in the early afternoon of 18 July, we now had troops engaged with a well-fortified, determined enemy without the capability of providing them105mm direct artillery support. Only the 105mm can deliver rapid, close-in fire support. It remains a fundamental dictum of infantry combat that you do not commit infantry to direct engagement without supporting close-in artillery notwithstanding what happened in this same brigade during recent combat operations in Afghanistan. (The 3rd Brigade, 101st Airborne Division was deployed to Afghanistan in 2002 without any artillery to support their operations. Precision weapons are great, but there are and always will be, well dug-in and/or concealed troops that cannot be detected for precision weapons. For these, you need artillery or area-weapon suppressive fires from fixed or rotary wing aircraft that cover a large area and deny observation and movement to the enemy.)

From my helicopter, after retuning to the Ripcord area, I asked Brigadier General Sidney B. Berry for additional troops and appropriate support to immediately open old FSB Gladiator and insert a 105mm artillery battery to cover the Ripcord area. About three hours later, the 1st Battalion, 501st Infantry passed to my operational control while enroute in the air on the way to Gladiator. Immediately following the Infantry and an Engineer Platoon that I had requested to clear the old firebase, B Battery, 320th Field Artillery landed. The battery was laid and ready to fire at 6:37 PM on that same day, 18 July. Having inserted the artillery battery, the Chinook battalion's day was far from over; they continued to fly 29 sorties into Gladiator that night. A rather busy day for me after being blasted into action and near deafness earlier in the morning by a 120mm mortar round detonating three feet in front of me.

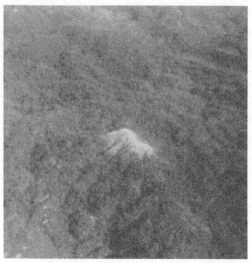

(Mac Jones)

Hill 316—Before it again became FSB Gladiator on 18 July.

From North Vietnamese Records[29]—

The next morning, 19 July, our heavy weapons continued to pound Base 935, starting a large fire in the logistics area. The enemy artillery ammunition stockpile caught fire and exploded for three hours straight.

(The North Vietnamese missed claiming the CH-47 shoot down. Instead, they seem to think the explosions and fires occurred a day later caused by their mortar and recoilless rifle fire into Ripcord.)

On 20 July the enemy sent a company from 1st Battalion/506th Airborne from the northern sector of Hill 935 down to Hill 605 to cooperate with a company from 2nd Battalion/506th Airborne in recapturing Hill 805 and retrieving the bodies of the American dead from the battle of 18 July. The enemy force ran into determined resistance from 1st Company/3rd Battalion. During our first counterattack 10th Company gunned down almost 30 enemy troops in front of our fortified positions, and four enemy helicopters were shot down. On the night of 20 July the enemy was forced to send in another company from Cooc Bai as reinforcements. The enemy strength on Hill 935 and in the surrounding area rose to 11 companies.

(The 2/501st Infantry was withdrawn from the Ripcord area on 18 July. We had one rifle company on the firebase and four companies in the bush making their estimate/claim exaggerated by six companies. Airmobile tactics really do confuse the enemy about our dispositions. It is interesting to note that the other "bookend" major battle of the Vietnam War, the 1st Cavalry Division in the Ia Drang Valley in November 1965, had also greatly confused the North Vietnamese Army with its airmobile tactics. The 1st Brigade replaced the 3rd Brigade. Thinking the 3rd Brigade rapidly withdrawing, the NVA launched an attack in the open against what they thought was a much smaller and much weaker American force—a mistake that cost the NVA more than 600 lives.)

From US Records—[30]

Ripcord continued to receive sporadic mortar fire throughout the period 19–22 July. The enemy launched a total of 34 standoff attacks during these four days, which resulted in seven US soldiers KIA and 35 WIA. During this same period, a total of fifty-one tactical air strikes were directed against enemy targets in the Ripcord area. With a ceiling less than 200 feet and visibility less than $1/8^{th}$ of a mile, Chinooks flew two re-supply sorties into Ripcord on the night of the 19th.

On 19 July, the last of the 105mm artillerymen of B Battery, 2nd Battalion, 319th Field Artillery withdrew from Ripcord. The NVA now concentrated much of its 82mm mortar fire on the remaining artillery at Ripcord, the 155mm howitzers of A Battery, 2nd Battalion, 11th Field Artillery. Sgt Daniel F. Esposito, the Ammo Chief, instructed the Chinooks by PRC-25 radio to drop their sling loads of ammo directly into the battery's firing position instead of at the ammo supply point. Frequently braving incoming mortar and recoilless rifle fire, Esposito was twice wounded. On 21 July, a heavy salvo of 82s on the A Battery position wounded seven and killed Sp4 Roberto C. Flores, Sp4 David E. Johnson, and 1st Lt J. Robert Kalsu, the acting battery commander. Bob Kalsu was the 1969 Buffalo Bills Rookie of the Year and could have avoided Vietnam, but chose to honor his commissioning oath from the University of Oklahoma ROTC program. Bob was the only professional athlete killed in Vietnam. Sgt Alfred Martin described Kalsu as a well liked and inspiring combat leader. Captain Thomas M. Austin, a self-confessed certified REMF, rushed out to Ripcord to take command of A Battery after Lt Kalsu's death. Short, round, and weighing well over 200 pounds, Austin became an easy target for the incoming enemy fire and soon took hits from shrapnel and required medical evacuation.

On 20 July, enemy contact by Captain Don Workman's Company D, 1st Battalion, 506th Infantry and Captain Chuck Hawkins' Company A, 2d Battalion, 506th Infantry, east and south of Hill 805, respectively, resulted in six NVA KIA, four US KIA and five US WIA in heavy contact at 5:30 PM. 1st Platoon, Company D, 1st Battalion, 506th Infantry met an enemy force employing 60mm mortar and small arms fire 1500 meters east of Hill 805. The contact terminated at 6:20 PM.

At 7:12 AM on 21 July, three kilometers east of Ripcord, Captain Workman's Company D, 1st Battalion, 506th Infantry, while preparing to leave its night defensive position, received approximately eighty devastating 82mm mortar rounds and small arms fire from an enemy force that surrounded their position. As the company returned fire with organic weapons and employed cannon artillery and ARA against the enemy, Captain Rollison's Company D, 2d Battalion, 506th Infantry air assaulted at 10:55 AM from a pickup zone five kilometers northwest of Ripcord to an LZ just north of Workman's contact area (about two kilometers east of Hill 805). Rollison attacked to the south to reinforce the beleaguered unit making light contact with the enemy enroute and suffering four WIA. Rollison captured a 12.7mm machine gun, and discovered a large bunker complex. Captain Kenneth R. Lamb, who had replaced Jeff Wilcox as commander of Company C, 2nd Battalion, 506th Infantry while the company was on FSB O'Reilly, brought Company C in to destroy the recently discovered bunker complex.

Captain Rembert "Gabe" Rollison's Company D, 2nd Battalion, 506th Infantry linked up with Workman's Company D, 1st Battalion, 506th Infantry at 12:23 AM on 21 July as sporadic mortar fire continued to impact in the area until 4:15 PM. Air strikes and helicopter gunships supported both companies. Company D, 1st Battalion, 506th Infantry suffered five killed and 31 wounded, while accounting for eight confirmed enemy killed.

Early in the morning of 21 July, First Lieutenant Laurence Rosen, "Dust Off" 91, a Medevac pilot flying from Camp Evans, began evacuation of the wounded. After two trips, Rosen called his headquarters at Camp Eagle to request assistance. A UH1H helicopter from Company C, 326th Medical Battalion, piloted by First Lieutenant Allen Schwartz, responded. Schwartz arrived just as Rosen returned for his third evacuation. Rosen told Schwartz to hold to the east so he could observe as Rosen made his pickup. While attempting to extract casualties from the Company D, 1st Battalion, 506th Infantry area of contact, an RPG round hit Schwartz' aircraft in the tail boom and caused it to crash to the ground. At 9:47 AM, Medevac pilot, First Lieutenant Laurence Rosen, returned for his fourth extraction after his earlier pickup of six critically wounded at 8:20 AM and was surprised to see the crashed helicopter wildly thrashing on the LZ. Rosen could see Lieutenant Schwartz and his crew hunkered down on the north side of the western half of the LZ. Lieutenant Rosen, now an Anesthesiologist practicing medicine in San Antonio, described the action:

> When we touched down for the fourth time Brent Law sprinted to Schwartz's ship and shut off the fuel and ran back to our ship and helped load more wounded. (He was a great soldier and brave beyond belief but had he asked me for permission to go to Schwartz's ship I would have denied it because: our mission was to evacuate the wounded, I was not afraid of being hit by pieces of it and I hoped someone would blow it up in an attempt to block the avenue of approach from the eastern portion of the saddle.)
>
> When we returned for the fifth trip Specialist Law was killed by a bullet that came through the pilot's side of the front upper windscreen just above the crossbar support member. The round hit the co-pilot (Warrant Officer Doug Rupert was up for AC and had been flying in the left seat all day for "orientation". I spoke to him a few years ago and he told me that he has never seen a nickel of compensation for his injury, he was from Canada and lives there now) on the lateral side of his upper arm lateral to the humerus. It passed through his arm, between the side and back pieces of the armored seat and entered Law's chest between the front and rear pieces of his chicken plate. He had already returned to the ship and connected to the floor by his tether strap and vest. The impact threw him back towards the bulkhead but we had already loaded the ship so his impact was softened by the other wounded. He started to fall out the door and the crew chief, Sp4 Malenfont, grabbed his tether strap and pulled him in. I made a pedal turn and dove off the side of the LZ to get out of the line of fire. We returned to Evans (Charlie Med) and Law was taken into the aid station. A few minutes later the doctor came out and told us he was dead. (I later learned that when I dove the ship into the trees I dragged one of the ground troops to his death. Unknown to me, he jumped up and grabbed onto our skids when I exited the LZ.)

Thus ended the tale of a most harrowing day as experienced by Dust Off 91, Dr. Laurence Rosen. Larry, a highly skilled pilot and brave and courageous soldier, received the Silver Star for his five daring evacuation missions, but in my book, it should have been the Medal of Honor.

A third aircraft, from Company A, "Ghost Riders", 158th Aviation Battalion, was hit by small arms and .51 cal machine gun fire at 4:58 PM, while attempting to extract elements of Company D, 1st Battalion, 506th Infantry. The aircraft caught on fire and crashed onto the pickup zone. I saw Captain Workman as the blades of the crashing Huey decapitated him. At approximately 5 PM on 21 July, Companies C and D, 2nd Battalion, 506th Infantry and Company D, 1st Battalion, 506th Infantry were extracted and returned to Camp Evans.

Six other aircraft received ground fire in the Ripcord area on 21 July, with three of them having been hit by machine gun and small arms fire. All returned to Camp Evans, and one was found to be non-flyable.

In telling some of the key events of the battle for Ripcord, I sought out the details of what aviation crewmen were doing which were not available to Keith Nolan when he wrote about Ripcord. The rather bland paragraph above is the official record of the extraction on 21 July. Through the Vietnam Helicopter Pilots Association, I found the aircraft commander whose shot-down Huey decapitated Captain Don Workman. The aviator was WO1 Larry Kern, "Ghostriders", A Company, 158th Assault Helicopter Battalion. He was shot down and his helicopter shot-up so many times on his first several missions in our AO, his buddies gave him the call sign, "Magnet Ass." Wanting to try and improve his luck somewhat, they had changed his call sign to something modestly more acceptable—"Crash." Warrant Officer Kern flew in the Ripcord area from the beginning of TEXAS STAR starting in April.

A great soldier, Larry Kern, told of his grim tale:

> Ripcord came under a very heavy siege for weeks in July and on the 18th of July, the downing of a CH 47 over an ammunition dump turned the Firebase into what looked like an active volcano. We faced some very dangerous rescue missions that day. The damage to the base was devastating, and its ability to defend its own perimeter was severely compromised. This made the base extremely vulnerable, turning the situation into a full-blown emergency. Early the morning of the July 21, 1970, my company, the "Ghostriders" flew in support of what we were told was to be a rescue mission just off Firebase Ripcord to the east. My co-pilot was WO1 James ("WEASEL ") Saunders, an active duty Navy Admiral's son, and one of my best friends; Door Gunner was Specialist 5, ("MAC") William McFarland. I had not flown with McFarland but a few times before that day. I believe he was in the second platoon and I was in the first. He struck me as nice a quiet guy who was always reading when we were on the ground. The

Crew Chief was Specialist 5 Ned Epps, a really nice kid who was always upbeat and seemed to be very good at his job.

Flying was voluntary, even for pilots. You could quit if you wanted to. I was very grateful to the guys who crewed the aircraft. Their jobs didn't end when we touched down at the end of the day. They had numerous duties to the aircraft and often flew more than the pilots because the pilots were limited to certain numbers of hours in time periods for safety reasons. I guess we all did not have good judgment or we would have said, "Do what you want with me. I am done." True as that was, the fact is that our pride and dedication to each other told us that was not an option. We had our job and you soon become so attached to the other young men we flew with and supported on the ground that if you quit, the guilt of leaving the others before your turn was the same as abandoning them. We had to do it, we were young and being loyal to each other was more important than being safe.

That morning of July 21st, I did not know which ground unit we were supporting, just why, where and when. This was not unusual, because as an assault helicopter company, we flew in many areas of I Corps. On any given day, we found ourselves doing Combat Assaults in one place, then re-supply in another and rescues, Medevac, taxi service. You name it, we did it. We rarely knew the details of the guys we had on board. We were told our missions and we did our jobs. All I knew at that time was that we were supporting a mission involving troops around Ripcord who needed immediate aid. I now know, that we were supporting the troops of D Co, 1st Bn, 506th Inf, and C and D Co, 2nd Bn, 506th. D Co, 1st Bn, 506th had been pined down overnight. They had suffered heavy losses.

We flew Troops onto Hill 605, above and to the north of the saddle back ridgeline on which the troops of D/1/506 were still trapped. We brought those reinforcements from two hot LZs approximately two to three klicks to the northeast of Hill 605. Our company made about three trips to and from the pick up LZs to load the reinforcements and transport them to Hill 605. We had close and strong fire support from our Snakes (Cobra Gunships) from Company D/158th the "Redskins." That morning I flew in Chalk 2 position (second in line) we received heavy fire going into and leaving LZ 605. The LZ was small and very difficult to get into and out of. Because of the heavy enemy concentration to our north and west, and trees that prohibited a straight-in-and-out flight path, we flew in with our crew firing their weapons non-stop. Dropped off the troops, performed a pedal turn and flew out under the next aircraft coming in. Very dangerous, even without enemy fire.

The "Ghostriders" were lifting in Captain Rollison's D Co, 2/506th to assist in the extraction of the badly hurt Captain Workman's D Co, 1/506th.

Larry Kern's story continues:

We waited at our staging area in our aircraft, ready to return when called. We ate our C rations. Our aircraft was originally Chalk 2, but before we departed Camp Evans my position was switched with Chalk 4. I was a relatively new pilot in command, and no experience in leading missions. The battalion commander's aircraft had been having mechanical problems. "Irish" (Capt. William Glennon) our first platoon leader was chalk one. "Irish" had just been called by the Battalion Commander, Lieutenant Colonel Robert Gerard, to come in his aircraft to pick him up. Me, being in the position of chalk two, would then become the lead aircraft. We had just cranked up our aircraft when the word came down for me to fly lead. I keyed my mic and said 'Hey guys I don't think I'm ready to lead a mission. What say you?' "Irish" agreed. 'Yes, "Crash" it's too soon. Bixby you and crash swap positions.' I picked up the aircraft hovered to the left then back to their position as Bixby hovered forward to my spot. (A definite violation of superstition. You never switch your luck.). We became Chalk 4, meaning we were now the 4th in the line of what I believe was about 10 aircraft. Within seconds of accomplishing this switch we got word from the colonel that his aircraft had been repaired. He did not need to take "Irish" and his aircraft from our flight. We were instructed to lift off and head west back to the 605 area. Well the deed was done, I was now flying chalk four, and I had switched positions. Lucky for me I was not a superstitious person. That would change later that day. Actually sooner than later.

All of our aircraft rose to a hover creating a large cloud of dust due to the dry staging field that we were on. I started having feelings of uneasiness already. "Irish" nosed his aircraft over followed by Bixby, then Sandy in chalk three, then me fourth with the rest of the flight in trail. After we reached altitude I tuned my FM radio to the proper frequency of the ground troops that were on the LZ. Within seconds, it became apparent that things were not going well. The young man on the radio was a victim of high anxiety. He was definitely in a pile of shit. 'We can't hold out, we're surrounded we can't hold on much longer. We need help now.' He was almost crying from fear and he also seemed to be untrained at his job as an RTO. The individual he was talking to may have been Lieutenant Colonel Lucas, the commander of Firebase Ripcord. He went by the call sign "Black Spade", and he was trying his best to calm the young man down. "Hang on Son. Help is on the way. Just try to stay focused now." We could hear gunfire in the background when the young man keyed his mic. This was not a good sign.

Our 158 Battalion Commander began to give us instructions over our radio frequency. "Ghostrider 16 (Irish) you need to fly the aircraft into the

LZ straight west. There is intense enemy fire on the western side of the LZ. Be advised there is a medevac already down, blocking the north side of the LZ. Do not, I repeat, do not cross over that LZ. Your aircraft needs to go in relatively low pick up the troops, do a pedal turn fly out east under the next aircraft going in. The men on the ground are surrounded. Our men are on the LZ or close to it."

A chill went up the back of my neck, this was not good. "Irish" came up on our frequency and said. 'OK guys did you catch that?' Sandy said. 'I think we caught that "Irish". Should we check our weapons?' "Irish" replied 'Roger that.' "Weasel" had heard the message, because like me, he was listening to all the radios as co-pilot. McFarland and Epps on the other hand may not have because it was possible their headsets may not have been on that radio. Because of the terrible noise that came from all the radios that we listened to, the crews usually would only have their radio switches turned onto the intercom and maybe to one or two other radios depending on the situation. Because of that, I needed to inform them of our situation. I gave them the green light to check their weapons. That meant that they were able to fire a number of rounds from their M60s to confirm that they were in firing order. Both McFarland and Epps opened up for about five to ten seconds. Sound of the weapons clattering stopped, but the increasing of our heartbeats began as we approached the mountain ridgelines.

As we neared the LZ. I remember looking at the aircraft in line in front of me and thinking of how beautiful the sight was. The green mountains in the distance framing the Hueys in a way that was very peaceful. We came in with approximately a little over two hundred yards of spacing. As "Irish" approached the opening on the ridge, which was the LZ, he radioed "Chalk 1 LZ Cold!" As he said that, I saw large green tracers coming at him from his twelve o'clock, originating from the ridgeline to the west of the landing zone midway up the slope of Hill 805. I radioed to him "No Chalk 1, you're taking fire from your 12!" At that time he did his pedal turn and radioed that he was taking fire. I could also see that mortar rounds were hitting the LZ as well. Chalk 1, flew east underneath Chalk 2 as instructed.

I could see that Sandy in Chalk 3, on his approach, was receiving fire from the green tracers of .51 Cal. enemy fire from those two positions on Hill 805 mountain slope to the west. The aircraft escaped damage and pedal turned out as did the first two. The noise now was getting serious. My crew was firing their weapons and I could hear enemy fire. The distinct sound of AK 47 was not only evident from outside the aircraft; I could also hear the enemy fire over the radio while Chalk 2 and Chalk 3 talked. Their crews were not firing while on the LZ. They were busy helping the troops get on and they would not fire until they got out because they could hit our guys by accident. My aircraft started receiving heavy small arms fire from left, right, and below. My crew began firing their M60s furiously. The noise was deafening. "Weasel" said, "Shit "Crash" this is bad." I looked at him and said, "Lets get in and out fast, shadow the controls. OK?" He clicked his mic twice meaning yes and I tried to get into a numbing zone.

Approximately 100 yards from landing, we received multiple hits to our aircraft. Chalk 3 was delayed on the LZ because the ground troops were panicking and too many men tried to jump on board his ship making it too heavy to lift off. I think they were trying to get some of the troops off of their aircraft as my aircraft came closer. I was forced to slow down, which was not a good thing to do at this particular time. We were receiving heavy fire now. I heard some rounds strike the aircraft. Chalk 3 was from still on the LZ. I began to fear that we had become sitting ducks and I knew something had to happen fast. I keyed my mike and said "I am almost at a hover should I break to the end of the flight?" "Irish" said, "No Crash, hang in there." Just as "Irish" finished speaking, Chalk 3 was able to lift off, turn and leave the LZ.

I saw the guys on the ground in trouble and knew I had to nose the aircraft toward the landing zone, which was very close by this time. It seems like it all happened in slow motion. Time is sometimes only in the mind, not in reality. I know people say this but the truth is that it seemed like hours. Just as I nosed forward we were hit with a barrage of many rounds. It sounded like someone had thrown handfuls of stones on a tin roof. Only it wasn't a roof, my Gunner "Mac" started screaming "Oh God I'm hit! Oh God I'm hit!" repeatedly. Things got worse very quickly. I felt the hits and suddenly we took a hail of hits all at once. I turned to see McFarland in the right-hand side crew well. He had stopped firing his M60 (It was gone. Totally blown off by an RPG.) He looked like he was in shock with his hands in front of his face, covered with blood, His helmet was badly damaged and obviously in great pain. I knew we were in bad shape. We were too slow, too high and now the enemy had us zeroed in. I still had no place to move forward to on the LZ because of the men on the ground were all clustered were my aircraft needed to land. We were still receiving hits to the aircraft from all sides and if I didn't move we couldn't survive.

The LZ; was within 100 feet. I saw the troops crouched, and lying on the ground, on the place where I was about to land. Some were firing into the trees. The Medevac that had been shot down previously was to the right of my landing spot and there were mortars landing to the left. While this was going on, we simultaneously received another volley of hits to the aircraft on both sides. The .51 Cals. to our twelve o'clock started hitting our aircraft with the force of sledgehammers. McFarland was still screaming. I knew we were badly damaged and the aircraft was being pounded and could not take any more hits. We needed to move out of the kill zone. I had to abort.

I keyed my mic and said, "Fuck this shit, Chalk 4. We are hit bad and taking more, have wounded crew, I'm peeling off!" I turned the aircraft to the left to get out of the kill zone and head back to Camp Evans. As we were in the left bank we received more .51Cal. hits. The aircraft was shuddering from the impacts. I leveled off heading away from the LZ. "Irish" came over the radio and yelled my call sign "Crash". "You're on fire; you're on fire "Crash"! Your 3 o'clock!" I looked to my right rear and saw my worst fear. FIRE!

By that time in my tour I had actually accepted the fact that I would die. I felt that I would not make it home. But my greatest fear was of burning to death after seeing some chard NVA bodies and in my mind the more unfortunate ones, the burned survivors. This was my worse fear. I looked and could see McFarland (who was still in great pain), and right behind him coming from the right side of the engine well, was a steady flow of flames and smoke coming from the right side in the area of the engine. Other pilots in my flight were then yelling the same thing, "Crash" you're on fire, go back to the LZ!

That was the last thing that I wanted to do. I looked forward (east) towards Camp Evans, miles away and saw nothing but mountains and thick jungle. Believing that the fire was fuel generated. I knew the only way to stop it would be to turn off the engine. Bad things happen to a helicopter over mountainous jungle when you turn off the fuel. And I knew that there was other damage to the aircraft as well. I left the LZ because I thought we could only survive by getting out of the kill zone we had been in. Our only chance was to get out and try to get to the lowlands. Now with fire involved, our only chance was to get down as fast as possible. I had no choice but to return to the only LZ that was within reach. So I kept turning to the left making a circle, to return to the LZ. As we turned we were approximately 200 yards out and started receiving exactly the same type of enemy fire as on our first run. Rounds started to hit my windshield spraying us with Plexiglas and many of the instruments on my control panel actually began to explode popping in little bursts of fire. I heard "Weasel" in the background of all this chaos key his mic and say "Crash," we're loosing power. "Crash" we're loosing power." I could feel the aircraft begin to respond in a way I had never felt before. Centrifugal force is what keeps the rotor blades from snapping. As they slow down at a certain point they flex (called coning) snap like a twig and ruin your day.

As we closed in on the LZ. I instructed "Weasel" to turn the fuel and battery switches off just as we touched down in the hopes of stopping the fire as quickly as possible, fearing that as soon as we stopped moving the fire would engulf the aircraft. We were still being hit by machinegun fire and I flared the aircraft to slow down, which also built up some of our rotor rpm.

We were shocked to see the troops on the ground, not realizing our situation and frantic, they were still waiting to be rescued on the spot where we had to land. They started to scramble as we approached. By this time I would not have been able to stop if I tried, we were too close, and would have crashed for sure on that LZ even if I tried to abort. My hands were full. "Weasel," by this time, seeing that the troops were in danger started waving his hands trying to get them to move away. It was too late for some of them. Approximately ten feet off the ground while in the flare position nose up I told "Weasel," when we are down, cut the fuel and switch the battery off. That, hopefully, would stop the fire. Then, just as we touched down, we were just short of the apex of the hill and the aircraft started to slide backwards in the air. I tried to pull pitch and there was nothing there. The aircraft nosed forward and there was a loud explosion over our heads. I don't know for sure to this day but either the blades flexed down due to the low RPM, or as WO1, Wayne "Andy" Capps, who was two aircraft back told me, he saw an RPG hit our rotor system taking off one of our two main rotor blades. What ever happened the fact was that we lost a rotor blade.

After the blade came off, the aircraft, now just barely touching the ground with one rotor blade, immediately hurled itself on its right side and dropped like a rock to the LZ surface. What was left of the rotor system continued to spin like a saw killing some of the men on the ground in the process. One of them, the only officer left on the LZ, Capt. Donald Workman the Commander of D Co, 1/506th. [Author's Note: the falling aircraft killed only Workman.] I was thrown violently in my seat because my shoulder harness was not locked. I felt massive shuddering of the aircraft and smoke and dust filled the cockpit. For a second, as we shook, I looked toward my co-pilot and could not see him. I thought he had disappeared, vaporized or been thrown out somehow.

I immediately noticed the difference in the sounds. Now on the ground and the engine stopped because "Weasel" had turned off the fuel to extinguish the fire, as I had hoped he would. The sounds had changed from the loud radio noises, and screaming of McFarland and enemy fire from all around, to new sounds. Now, through my helmet, I could hear firing and explosions, I looked out of what was left of my windshield and noticed that we were still being fired at by the same .51 Cal's. I glanced down and the co-pilot miraculously was back in his seat. I yelled to him "Get out "Weasel," now!"

I still heard AK47 fire striking the aircraft I thought we would soon be on fire or hit by a mortar or an RPG. I had to wait until he had vacated his seat because I was hanging over him. I released my seatbelt and fell into Weasel's seat. The small of my back was hurting and as I climbed up the floor, which was now a wall, I thought I must have been shot in the back. I got out of the top of the aircraft or what was really the left side of the aircraft, and found that I was perched in the open on top in plain sight of everyone in Northern I Corps with a weapon. I felt naked and at that moment I was probably the answer to a number of NVA soldiers fondest wishes. Firing and explosions were still happening all around. My back was in extreme pain. I had to get off that aircraft.

I scrambled over the skids of the Huey and dropped to the ground approximately 7–8 feet. My legs collapsed and I fell to the ground in a Yoga position. My chicken plate (chest armor) was forced up into my chin from my waist, and I was knocked into a dazed state.

It was surreal. I could hear muffled sounds and could see things around me but I could not feel anything below my neck and all sounds were very muffled. At that time I thought I was paralyzed and possibly dying from what I thought was a back wound. I was propped bolt upright like a rag doll, by my chest protector, sitting on the apex of the rise of the LZ, facing the same direction as the nose of my aircraft which was directly towards the .51 Cal. positions. They were still firing at me, hitting the ground and passing over my head, the green tracers looked like they were in slow motion.

I was in a dazed fog. I have no idea how long I sat there in that condition. I remember two mortars hit to the right front side of my aircraft about thirty or more feet and one about thirty yards to my left. I was sitting there like a rag doll propped upright by my Chicken Plate waiting to be hit again. I just felt tired and helpless, unable to do anything, and was rather serene and ready to die. I could still see the green .51 Cal. tracers coming at me and knew I would die at any second and had accepted that as my fate. It was very peaceful. I was ready. I was at peace. It felt good. It was over. Then something broke the trance.

I heard a muffled yell from someone. The calls soon became clear. "Crash", "Crash!" Get down Crash!" This pulled me out of my daze and I realized I was still alive and sounds became louder and I could start to move again. I fell forward on my face to the ground and began to feel my body again. I checked my back for blood and found none and knew I was not shot. (I would find out when I got home in March 1971,during out-processing that I had broken two vertebrae in my back and one in my neck. I was young enough to think for months that I had just sprained my back.) The voice yelling "Crash" belonged to "Weasel" who was below me on the hill and he yelled at me "Get off the top of the rise, they're shooting at you!" This much I knew.

Where is Mac? I asked Weasel then Epps. They shrugged their shoulders. We started to crawl back to the aircraft. We heard a voice to our left. It was a soldier, who had crawled out to us from the tree line on the south end of the LZ. He yelled, "Follow me we have to get away from the aircraft they'll hit it with an RPG!" McFarland wasn't with us and I said, "We need to find our gunner." "I am sorry Sir but he died. The men on the other side of the LZ told us he is dead." He said, "Follow me, grab a weapon and a steal pot." I started shaking. McFarland was dead. This was the first guy I had lost. He was my responsibility. I failed. I felt like I was supposed to do something but had no idea what that could be.

The grunt was crawling and now we too were infantry and in deep shit. This guy was our leader. We were like fish out of water. Just minutes before we were in an aircraft in a completely different environment. Now we instantly found ourselves totally disoriented. This Grunt was our lifeline and we were in shock. We followed him crawling nose to heal. Saunders following his heals, I following Saunders, and Epps following me. We started crawling toward the tree line to the left. On the way Saunders took an M16 and helmet from a body and I looked next to where I was lying and there was a body with an M16, and one clip of ammo which I took. I couldn't take his helmet; I didn't want to see his face. I could not look at the dead. It was too much for me to absorb. I felt odd taking his weapon and was trying to keep from looking directly at the dead. It all was so overwhelming to me. I was flying minutes before and now I was crawling among the dead and knew I was probably soon to be dead as well.

We crawled to the tree line and immediately inside of the tree line I saw approximately 8–10 men in holes. Two of them frantically waved their hands motioning us to hurry. The guy leading us took us into one of the holes, We crouched down into the bottom of it and he worked on my face. "You were shot down Sir. You have some wounds but your gonna be fine." He was trying to comfort me. "I am sorry you got shot down trying to get us Sir, we appreciate it." This kid was sorry we got shot down. I felt like shit.

I asked him how bad our situation was and he told me, "Very bad, we lost a lot of guys since yesterday and we probably won't get out, we could be overrun at any time." He told me we were hiding in the openings of NVA bunkers. At the bottom of the holes were crawl holes that led to underground systems. He left the hole and told us to wait. While we waited the three of us started to cry because of McFarland dying and regained our control as the soldier, who had helped us, returned.

He gave me a steal pot and I realized I still was wearing my flight helmet. He asked me to follow him and I left the hole and crawled with him towards another hole on the edge of the tree line facing the west. As we moved to the position I began to notice my surroundings. Two Cobras circled our area firing constantly. There was smoke in the air and a smell that was a mix of explosives and the smell of blood. There was small arms fire just below us in the trees. The mortars had stopped. I looked at the kid and said, "It seems to have gotten quieter?" He said, "Yea. It gets hot while you guys come in. They start really hitting us when the choppers come in. You guys get the hell shot out of you. We really thank you Sir." He did it again.

As we approached the bunker a guy pulled me inside. He was a Specialist 5, he said he was the highest-ranking soldier left on that side of the LZ. He had a radio and he told me that the command and control wanted to speak to me. I got on the radio and was asked by the person on the other end, "Who are you?" I told him I was Ghost Rider 549, which was my aircraft's call sign. He asked me what my MOS was, I told him, Aircraft Commander. As we were talking I was looking at what was left of my aircraft, 549. That was my favorite ship in the company. I just recently got to fly it and had hoped to claim it as mine. There it was laying on the LZ, a total mess. McFarland under it and we probably were not going to get out of this trap. He paused, then he said, "Good, we were told you men were dead." I said, "We lost one of our crew." He said "Sorry son, but we have to get you people out now." Then he asked, "Do you know the location of the .51s that brought you down?" I told him, "Affirmative." He then told me, "You get the coordinates. And we will send them some airmail." With the help of the Specialist, I pointed out the locations and he found the coordinates and radioed them up. He gave me the radio back. On the radio was a spotter plane for the Air Force, a Skymaster Cessna. Next an Air force jet fell out of the sky and dropped napalm on the targets, lighting them up with huge balls of fire. Then a second jet did the same, followed by a third. For a few seconds I was delighted at the thought of killing the bastards that had played a big part in shooting us down and killing my gunner. I hoped they didn't die. I hoped they were wandering around burned to a crisp but not dead.

I did not have much time to feel good. Immediately following the air strike, the Sergeant had received instructions. He relayed to us that we would within minutes; be fired upon by our own aircraft. The only way off the south side of the LZ was to cross to the north side and team up with the others and get to the only other LZ left to us for escape. The minute the strike ended, we would cross the LZ. We scrambled to the bunkers; I was in a small one alone. I covered my neck and within seconds, all hell broke loose as we were fired upon by our own aircraft. I could hear Cobra fired mini guns and rockets, as well as explosions from the fixed wing's bombs. After a very long time of constant explosions the firing stopped.

Within seconds the Sergeant called to us, "Get out! NOW!" We scrambled out of the holes and ran to him at the edge of the LZ and he formed us up in a single file, and hit us on the back one at a time. We ran across the LZ as fast a possible. We were not fired on as we crossed. I remember seeing the dead from a new perspective, upright. I ran in front of my aircraft and behind the medevac into the trees on the other side. The small number of troops on the other side were waiting for us. I saw my Gunner, McFarland on a stretcher badly wounded but alive. My aircraft had fallen on him. The men on the other side had dug him out from under the aircraft had him on a poncho litter ready to move. Also "Weasel" had already gotten to that side with another Specialist 5. In an attempt to check on McFarland, they crawled unnoticed below the hill line while the air strike on the .51 cals, was happening. I was busy calling the strike and had no idea that "Weasel" had left. I thought he was in one of the holes.

I was told by the ground troops that my aircraft had killed an officer who was rushing to get on my aircraft, not knowing we were crashing. He was about to go home in days. His name was Captain "Ranger" Workman. With its one remaining rotor blade, my aircraft decapitated him, as it flung on its side killing the captain instantly. He was going to leave the unit in six days and go home in three weeks. To this day I am haunted by that fact. I don't know what I could have done differently but that still doesn't make it go away.

We were formed up quickly; I would estimate our total number to be around 15 to 20 men counting my crew. At least a half dozen times during the ordeal some of the guys thanked me for coming into the LZ to try to pull them out and two of them actually said they were sorry we had to try to get them and apologized. The men knew we were fish out of water and did their best to take care of us. The same parental feeling I felt for them as a pilot. I always felt a responsibility for the Grunts because we could either save them or in the case of Captain Workman, fail and do them harm.

The helicopters that rescued us were from my company. They had thought we were killed, so when "CW" the pilot of the first aircraft saw me as he was on approach he was ecstatic. He radioed the good news. I could see his face grinning from ear to ear. I could tell he was yelling over the radio, "It's Crash! He's alive! It's Crash! The seriously wounded were placed on the first two aircraft. While I was waiting a young soldier came up to me and asked me if I wanted my armor plate and handed it to me. "Thanks for trying to help us Sir. I'm sorry your pilot got hurt." (Meaning Mac) He had carried that 20-pound object, all the way from the saddleback LZ, while we were under attack and in danger of being killed. I was overwhelmed that he would do that for me. I was not about to tell him that it wasn't necessary. I thanked him and said, "These things are really hard to fit well. Thank you."

I was humbled by the number of times that the soldiers individually through the ordeal thanked us for trying to save them and how sorry they were that we got shot down trying to rescue them…But I just felt guilty; I *felt* I had failed. I remember crawling on the aircraft to leave, very sore and frightened that we would be shot down again. We were then taken to the medevac area. McFarland was sent to the hospital ship and than later to Japan with serious injuries I never saw him again. Epps was injured, but not seriously. Saunders and I were the least injured with minor shrapnel wounds. I had what I would later be diagnosed as a serious back injury. My neck was re-injured from a previous crash in April 1970. I also had numerous minor shrapnel and Plexiglas wounds to my legs, arms, and face and eye. The shrapnel was removed at the medical center. Tiny wounds to the body, major damage to the mind.

On 23 July, the "Ghostriders" as a unit helped evacuate Fire Base Ripcord under intense enemy fire. Of the fifteen aircraft our company flew that day only four were still flyable. The rest were shot down or damaged so badly they could not fly. These along with the aircraft I was shot down in two days earlier, aircraft #549, meant that twelve of our twenty aircraft were lost or needed major repairs.

The tale of Larry Kern's fateful day is ended, but not likely the end of his thirty-four years of agony and remorse.

Major General Bobby Porter, then Lieutenant Colonel Porter, Commanding Officer, 1st Battalion, 506thInfantry, tells how he reacted to news of the extraction of his D Company:

> I was advised by the Battalion XO that our Delta Company had been overrun during the battle and that several (probably seven) of our KIAs bodies remained on a ridgeline just east of Ripcord. Upon receiving the report, I proceeded to the Brigade CP. There, I requested Colonel Harrison to permit me to assemble a force of about thirty volunteers to CA with me onto the ridgeline and recover the bodies of our KIAs. Probably I uttered some unkind words about leaving the bodies of American soldiers on the battlefield.
>
> This was the only time that I can recall Colonel Harrison becoming upset. Further, it was the only mention I can recall of anyone saying anything about having taken too many casualties already and that we simply can't afford to risk taking more. Colonel Harrison went on to assure me that a recovery plan was in progress and that the bodies of our KIAs would be recovered. I'm confident that he told me at the time, but do not recall if the recovery forces were being organized by the Brigade or Division.

I remember Bobby Porter coming to me quite distressed about his men being abandoned on the battlefield. A major part of the frustration he felt at the time concerned the fact that his Delta Company, had not been under his control, but had been placed under the OPCON of the 2nd Battalion, 506th Infantry and that he had no input into the extraction operation.

There is no doubt in my mind that I grew increasingly concerned about the number of casualties we experienced and there certainly was no doubt in my mind that he proposed a high risk operation in a known hot area. Having just learned from a communications wiretap of enemy filed phones that an NVA division, with perhaps four regiments, commenced operation s in our immediate area, that I would launch yet another small force into the enemy's lap on 21 July. The decision to withdraw from Ripcord had not yet been made.

Our brigade aerial scouts made frequent recons of the area to verify that the body bags were still there and to look for signs of enemy activity. We also targeted the area for H&I fires day and night to discourage the NVA from seeking to exploit the bodies.

Two weeks later after the evacuation of Ripcord, I ordered the Brigade Reconnaissance Platoon to go in and recover the bodies of D Company, 1/ 506th. Early on the morning of the planned recovery operation, the Brigade Intelligence Section Sergeant Major came to see me saying, "Sir, we have a problem. Sergeant First Class John Doe told me that he would not go on this operation." I asked why. The sergeant major said, "The platoon sergeant told me that he was not going out into bad 'Indian Country' with a cherry LT. He said he had been around too long to risk his ass on a suicide mission with an FNG." I said tell the Platoon Sergeant to meet me at my helicopter in thirty minutes.

The sergeant was waiting at my helicopter and I said nothing but, "Get in." I took off and flew to the area of the bodies. I made a slow, high circle of the area pointing out the planned LZs near the bodies. I then made a steep, rapid approach to a high point overlooking the area. I landed and told my copilot to hold the controls and took the platoon sergeant over to look at the LZs from that angle. I told him, "The plan is to put two Hueys into each of the LZs with the LT taking half the men and you take the other half. When you have all the bodies accounted for, give me a call and we will pick you up."

We flew back to Evans in silence. When we landed, I asked when he and his men would be ready. . He replied that they would be ready in two hours.

We took off with the platoon and were joined in the air by a pair of Cobra gunships. We did not fire a prep, but went straight into the two LZs. They quickly located the bodies and put Captain Workman into one of the spare body bags that they had taken along and called us in for the pick up. The insertion and pickup were made without a shot being fired. I had most of the bodies in my ship and the smell was absolutely horrible. All of us had great difficulty not throwing up while trying to fly back to Evans.

I never said anything to the platoon sergeant about his initial alleged refusal to go into combat. He was one of many great non-commissioned officers who did their very best to lead our soldiers.

Nor did my stalwart door gunner, Leonard Moore, comment on this rather bizarre mission of going out and landing on an unsecured hilltop in "Indian Country." Leonard provided security as my door gunner many, many times and became accustomed to being in firefights as he regularly flew with the 3rd Brigade's MiniCav.

Flying Chinooks in Support of Ripcord—

Chinooks flying into Ripcord almost always drew fire. We attempted to limit the sorties, but a Huey shot down on the main pad on 22 July required extraction. Tom Hirschler, the Aircraft Commander of Pachyderm 507 and his co-pilot, Curtis H. Downs, III (22 July was his birthday) got the mission. Tom Taylor was the CE, Flight Engineer. They were successful with the extraction and made a total of eleven trips in and out of Ripcord that day drawing fire each time.

Downs described how they flew the sorties:

> We initially flew to it like any firebase. As it got hotter we flew re-supply missions though artillery boxes to the firebase. Rounds planned and fired all around a "Tube" into the base and then out. When it really got hot we literally drug the sling loads in the trees and made a cyclic climb to the firebase. We actually used one route over the other on the 22d because we had approximately 3 seconds more time before the rounds started impacting on the hill. The wind gust and thermals around Ripcord were unreal—climbing at over 500 feet per minute with an eight ton load under the aircraft and the thrust control all the way down." (This "thrust control down" means trying to descend, not climb.)

Late in the afternoon 507 became non-flyable. Hirschler and Downs had been recommended for impact Distinguished Flying Cross (DFC) medals and as a result of existent policy, were temporarily grounded for the 23rd of July. Pachyderm 507 was flyable on the day of the extraction and became the only Chinook shot down on that day. A total of seven Chinooks took hits on the 23rd and three aircrew members were wounded.

Any Vietnam veteran will tell you of the brave and heroic actions of helicopter aircrewmen who he witnessed. And indeed the aircrewmen did perform actions that sometimes made them look fearless. All were brave and dedicated, but many were far from fearless. Captain Mac Jones, the Operations Officer of C "Condor" Troop, 2/17th Cavalry offered this explanation by way of comparison:

I'll tell you about taking hits to the inside. Regular folks just don't understand what fear is, especially when it becomes an institution, as in sentencing you to death row for 365 days and promising you a pardon if you get to the end. The fear of day one expands geometrically for the whole tour. Must have been the same for the bomber pilots of World War II. What's your pucker factor on the 25th mission?

Captain Rich Parris was the Liaison Officer from the 159th "Liftmaster" Battalion positioned on Ripcord recalled:

> Looking at the airspeed indicator as we hovered over Ripcord we saw 65 or 70 knots registering. The wind at times was incredible. I believe it was CW2 Jeff Brockmeier who lifted the hook off of Ripcord. His control touch was unmatched—he was one of those rare pilots who literally turned the helicopter into extensions of his hands and feet. The last clear memory of Ripcord was arriving there on the morning of 7–22–70, planning the mission, spending the night on the hill and directing the extraction the following day.
>
> My first tour in Vietnam was an infantryman on the ground with the 25th Division and I don't have memories of anything worse than what I experienced in the two days on Ripcord. It was absolute madness. There were lots of unsung heroes on the hill and in the air that day.

Rarely do we get a chance to hear from a helicopter crew chief about life on the forward edge of our battles in the Tri-Thien area. Specialist 5 Rick Miller described the living conditions for the enlisted crews in a forward deployed area:

> Well, all the chiefs and gunners were sleeping in one big tent at first, and if someone cut a fart, Lord help us if five or six more joined in. One night we had to leave the tent, the odor was so bad! Then came the underground bunkers. One night while playing spades with four others with one more on the fourth bunk up reading, there was this blood curdling scream and this guy jumped down four bunks yelling at the top of his lungs, "Snake, snake, big fucking snake!" We all looked up thinking he was full of it when to our surprise; a big "Boa" came out of the earth! All jumped up at the same time, everyone fighting for position going out first and at the same time and even without saying a word to each other, begin popping pins on mini-frags as we departed. The next day the Engineers asked if we wanted them to dig the bunker back out as one of the crew chiefs blew a Claymore at the top and caved in the bunker. "HELL NO" was our reply!!! After

that, we slept in the trenches at night with the Blues[Infantry]. We didn't get to plan out the ops for the next day, but we did have a system on who was to contact our parents or wives if one of us got killed. We would all tell our stories at the end of each day about the missions we went on and I think that everyone felt that the other's story was worse than our own. When in reality, we were really just trying to calm ourselves down by telling ourselves that the mission wasn't that bad......bullshit!

IV

Time to Leave Fire Support Base Ripcord?

Could there really be a North Vietnamese division with four regiments surrounding Ripcord on the north, south, east and west?

7

Intelligence from the Battlefield

A Co, 2/506th continued deeper into enemy territory southeast of Ripcord as they noticed the size of the bunkers becoming larger. By midmorning on the 20th, they reached the base of Hill 805. Captain Chuck Hawkins moved part of his company across the river that ran south of Hill 805. The remainder of his company set an ambush on the bank above the stream. The alert troopers of 1st Platoon, A Co, 2/506th made a startlingly discovery in the afternoon of 21 July. They found a field telephone (commo) line along a four-foot wide trail. Lieutenant Pahissa reported that they knew it was not a US line. He took a Sony transistor radio earplug from one of his soldiers and tapped the line with his Kit Carson Scout listening. Captain Hawkins rushed to the scene with his ARVN Interpreter, Sgt Long. The Interpreter, using a PRC 25 handset to tap the line also, excitedly reported that the line belonged to a mortar unit firing on Ripcord from the reverse slope of Hill 805 talking with someone in a division headquarters. Five hours of listening revealed, according to the Interpreter, that the enemy division headquarters had four regiments surrounding Ripcord on the north, south, east, and west. The NVA sent out a line repair team as the taps apparently had degraded the transmissions. A Co ambushed the repair team. Other smaller engagements occurred in A Company's area around the wiretap that indicated the presence of several different enemy units.

Although not verifiable intelligence, it certainly got everyone's attention, up to and including Brigadier General Berry, the acting division commander.

Indeed, the identification of the exact enemy units in the Ripcord area first became known during our research for this book. We now know the Division headquarters to be that of the 324B Division, with its normal three infantry regiments: 29th, 303rd, 812th and, the 6th Tri-Thien Regional Force Regiment, attached to the 324B Division for this special offensive. From General Doi's interview, we also know that they had four 120mm mortar companies, each with six tubes. Had they been able to concentrate that much mortar fire on Ripcord, the firebase indeed would have been destroyed with terrible personnel casualties among the defenders.

At 1300 hours on 22 July, 1.5 kilometers southeast of FSB Ripcord, Captain Chuck Hawkins" Company A, 2nd Battalion, 506th Infantry received rifle grenades, mortar, and small arms fire from a large enemy force attacking from the north, east, and southeast. Cannon artillery, ARA, and tactical air support engaged the enemy. A Co maintained contact until dark when the company consolidated its position and formed a defensive perimeter. Extraction of the wounded could not be attempted during the night because of the close proximity of the estimated three-company size enemy force. Most of the fifty-one personnel wounded in the company had minor wounds. Those who had more severe wounds were made as comfortable as possible until they could be extracted on the morning of the 23d. The company accounted for 61 NVA KIA with 12 US KIA.

(Instead of the estimated three-company size enemy force, more recent NVA source documents now lead us to believe that elements of two or three enemy battalions operated in A Co's area.)

The pivotal point on the US side in Operation TEXAS STAR centered on intelligence information gleaned from the wiretap established by Chuck Hawkins' A Company.

Pile on or pullout, this remained a hotly contested issue among the various commanders. At 5:15 AM on 22 July 1970, General Sidney B. Berry, acting Commanding General, 101st Airborne Division at Camp Eagle, wrote in a letter to his wife:

> We've now reached a point when we must question the continued use of RIPCORD. Is it worth the casualties for the purpose it is serving? If we decide "no," how do we get out of RIPCORD? If we vacate RIPCORD, then what do we do? Where will we place our artillery to support the attack we want to make into the NVA base camp and cache area?
>
> Today we must decide on a course of action that differs from what we are now doing. Now we are taking constant casualties on RIPCORD from incoming mortar rounds, particularly among our artillerymen on top of the hill. We are taking constant casualties among the rifle companies operating

in the mountains and jungles around RIPCORD trying to locate and destroy the enemy mortars and AA machine guns that attack our helicopters and people. Daily our artillery fire from RIPCORD grows less effective as enemy mortar rounds make it more difficult for the artillerymen to fire their howitzers.

There are plenty of NVA in those hills. More of them are moving in from North Vietnam via Laos. They are well equipped and supplied. The mountains seem loaded with 12.7 mm AA machine guns. Yesterday, we had two more helicopters shot down in the same area where a rifle company was in a tough fight. The NVA want very badly to inflict a major defeat on US forces.

MACV's hopes for some kind of successful summer 1970 offensive depend on the Screaming Eagles, but we cannot afford to take heavy casualties.[31]

General Berry later wrote at 9:30 PM on 22 July 1970:

Must get some rest, get up at 4 AM, and be in the air by 5 tomorrow to oversee tomorrow's operation—extraction from RIPCORD. This morning I made the most difficult professional decision of my life: to get out of RIPCORD as quickly as possible. Easier said than done.[32]

8

Time to go!!

On 22 July, Brigadier General Berry made the decision to evacuate our forces on FSB Ripcord and extract the remaining A Company 2/506th riflemen on the ground.

At a planning session held at the brigade headquarters at Camp Evans, General Berry asked what requirements were necessary for the brigade to conduct the extraction operation the next day. I requested and received operational control of the 2nd Squadron, 17th Cavalry, direct support of the 4th Battalion, 77th Artillery (ARA), direct support of the 101st Aviation Group, top priority for all Division and 24th Corps Artillery, and 48 sets (one set every 15 minutes) of close air support. Major Jim King, 3rd Bde S-3 and his great S-3 Air, Capt Fred Spaulding, put together a brilliant plan for the extraction.

Throughout the night of 22–23 July, massive artillery and air strikes were employed in the Ripcord area against known and suspected enemy locations.

From North Vietnamese Records[33]—

At 6:00 A.M. on the morning of 23 July the 324B Division Command Post received reports from our observation posts that many fires and large explosions could be seen all over the top of Hill 935. Meanwhile enemy artillery barrages blanketed the perimeter of the enemy base. The chief of division artillery reported that enemy artillery was firing heavily toward the east, but the fire was haphazard and uncoordinated. There did not seem to be any rhyme or reason in the direction of the enemy fire. One gun was even firing shells with different charges and settings, one right after another. Our cadre in the division command post huddled around the operations map. After analyzing the situation, the division commander decided that this might be an enemy deception operation, and that the enemy was firing off all his remaining artillery shells as part of a plan to evacuate Base 935.

The division commander sent a cable to Military Region Headquarters to report the enemy activities and the division's preliminary assessment of the situation. The Military Region commander responded with an order: "Overrun Base 935 and do not allow the enemy troops to escape!" (*In this mission, the 324B Division clearly failed.*)

The division concentrated its heavy weapons to fire heavy barrages into Base 935 using all the ammunition it had (we fired a total of 344 rounds of all calibers). Ten enemy helicopters trying to land to pick up the troops from Base 935 were hit and set on fire. Taking advantage of the blinding smoke that covered the base, two helicopters daringly landed on Hill 935 and picked up the remaining survivors. In their haste to leave, the enemy left behind all their weapons and equipment. (*The NVA shot down one CH-47 Chinook during the extraction. All personnel and equipment, including the heavy Chinook loads of six 155mm howitzers flew out in orderly fashion. The six 105mm howitzers that were damaged by the CH-47 crashing and burning on top of them on 18 July remained on Ripcord. Our artillerymen had already rendered these tubes completely useless.*)

From US Records—

The extraction of the remainder of 2d Battalion, 506th Infantry from FSB Ripcord and vicinity commenced early in the morning of 23 July. Brigadier General Berry flew overhead in his Command and Control helicopter ready to assist as needed. Lt Col Lucas and his new S3, Major Kenneth P. Tanner, directed the withdrawal under fire of his battalion from his CP on Ripcord, but mostly from his OH-6 C&C helicopter. Near the break of dawn, Lucas inserted his D Company to go in and help with the extraction of A Company. Withdrawal from the firebase began with the first airlift by Chinooks at 5:45 AM. It continued despite a heavy barrage of incoming mortar rounds and 12.7mm machine gun fire delivered from multiple locations and ended at 12:14 PM. From various locations, artillery units fired more than 2200 rounds of mixed caliber ammunition in support of the extraction of the battalion and supporting elements on Ripcord. Fourteen CH-47 aircraft provided critical lift in 22 sorties, which included six 155mm howitzers, two M450 Bulldozers, large quantities of communication equipment, and one M55 (Quad 50) machine gun. The heavy lift extraction operation proceeded smoothly until 7:40 AM, when enemy 12.7mm machine gun fire shot down one CH-47 on the firebase. The aircraft made a forced landing amidst the 105mm howitzers that had been destroyed on 18 July. This prevented the extraction of the unusable 105mm artillery pieces and two damaged 106mm recoilless rifles. After being downed by machine gun fire, the CH-47 received a direct hit by an enemy mortar round, which caused the aircraft to burn and explode.

Eight additional CH-47 aircraft received hits during the extraction with four of them later declared non-flyable. Captain Benjamin F. Peters' Company B, 2nd Battalion, 506th Infantry commenced their extraction from Ripcord at 7:45 AM by UH-1H. Heavy enemy 60mm and 82mm mortar fire delayed the continuation of their lift-out until 9:35. Captain Randy House, 1st Platoon Leader, C Company, 158th Aviation Battalion, flew "Lead" for all the Phoenix aircraft. With heavy damage to the Chinooks while trying to extract the 155mmm howitzers and other equipment being shifted about the Firebase by the Pathfinders the radio frequencies became somewhat of a blaring blur. The Hueys of the 158th and 101st Aviation Battalions made holding orbits around Ripcord. Recognizing that the Hueys needed to get on with the job of extraction and in the absence of the Commander of the 158th Assault Helicopter Battalion who had gone to refuel, Captain House, Phoenix 16, assumed the role of the Air Mission Commander. With Pathfinder help, Captain House worked the Hueys onto Ripcord, one bird at a time, in between incoming mortar rounds and through 12.7mm antiaircraft machine gun fire. (Ironically, Randy House, now Lieutenant General, Retired, piloted the first Huey to land on Ripcord on April Fools day, four months earlier. It was also House who earlier on the day of 23 July that flew the lead aircraft which inserted Captain Rollison's D Co, 2/506th into the jungle at 6:36 AM to assist in the rescue of A Co, 2/506th. For Randy House, flying "Phoenix" 16, 23 July would become an incredible day of heroism, quick thinking, and flying skill.)

Captain Thomas M. Austin, who replaced the fallen Bob Kalsu as commander of A Battery, 2/11th FA, went about checking the crew bunkers to insure that everyone would be evacuated and when he stopped by the entrance to the Fire Direction Center, an incoming mortar round blew him up the side of the hill. The explosion shredded his right calf and his left Achilles tendon. As Austin passed out, Sgt Dan Esposito organized the battery medics, Sp4 Lanny W. Savoie, Sp4 Dominec Inninico and Sp4 Sam Craft to administer aid to Austin as Esposito and Pfc Robert Weber tried to lift the very weighty Austin on a stretcher into a Huey. After banging Austin's head several times against the side of the helicopter, they finally shoved him aboard and ended his forty hours of combat duty for the Vietnam War. For his many acts of initiative and bravery under intense fire, Sgt Esposito was awarded two Bronze Stars.

Seventy-four USAF, Marine and Navy tactical air sorties, as well as, continuous ARA and cannon artillery fires supported this extraction. (At our planning session on 22 July, I requested 48 sets of jet attack aircraft, one set of two to four aircraft, every fifteen minutes. The Marine Major General commanding the Marine Air Wing said it would be impossible to properly employ that much air support. Major "Skip" Little, my Air Force Liaison Officer, assured him that we could and since we actually put in 44 sets, obviously, Major Little proved correct.

Captain Rembert G. ("Gabe") Rollison's Company D, 2nd Battalion, 506th Infantry air assaulted approximately two and one half kilometers southeast of Ripcord at 6:36 AM on the fateful day of 23 July to assist the extraction of Hawkins' very battered Company A, 2nd Battalion, 506th Infantry. Rollison had earlier fought in this area but the heavy fighting by Chuck Hawkins' A Company and the surrounding NVA had put a new and confusing look on the jungle. "Gabe" radioed Chuck to make some noise so they could find them. Hawkins replied that he could just follow the trail of bodies. A company had counted 61enemy KIA.

Captain Fred Spaulding along with his faithful and very brave scout helicopter pilot, Warrant Officer Steven M. Wandland, left their position around Ripcord where they had assisted in the coordination of the Air Cavalry, the Aerial Rocket Artillery and Tac Air and came over to assist in the extractions of the last troops in the area. Pickup from the newly blown LZ of Companies A and D began at 1:05 PM and completed without helicopter damage or personnel casualties at 2:01 PM.

Throughout the morning, FSB Ripcord came under incessant enemy mortar fire, with several hundred rounds impacting throughout the firebase. Air, artillery, and ARA destroyed a number of enemy mortar and machine gun positions. In addition, numerous enemy troops, who had been driven into the open by tactical CS gas, fell victim to US firepower.

Typical of the heroism of the aviation soldiers that day was the Phoenix crew of Warrant Officer 1 Kenneth Mayberry. Counting multiple 82mm and 120mm mortar rounds exploding around their intended pickup spot, Warrant Officer David Rayburn, the copilot, heard the Pathfinder radio "Go around!" Mayberry pressed on as he saw infantry troops standing in the open mentally urging him to land. A mortar round between the Huey and the troops

knocked the soldiers onto the ground. Crew Chief Specialist 5 John Acker-
man and Door Gunner Specialist 4 Wayne Wasilk rushed 20 yards through
the incoming fire and helped the wounded infantrymen on board the chopper.
With smoke billowing from the Huey and pieces falling off during flight,
Mayberry took the soldiers directly to the 187th Mobile Army Surgical Hospital landing pad. Warrant Officer Mayberry noticed blood covering his boot as
he took the crew to pick up a replacement helicopter. They flew many more
hairy extractions, but not until that night did Mayberry discover that the
blood came from shrapnel embedded in the calf of his leg.

Lieutenant Colonel Andre Lucas, "Black Spade", Commanding Officer 2d
Battalion, 506th Infantry and his S3, Major Kenneth P. Tanner, came back to
Ripcord after inserting Rollison's D Co for yet another check of his firebase
and the progress of the extraction. Lucas stood in the open urging on 1st Lt
Gary Watrous in the direction of air and artillery strikes against enemy mortar
positions just as a 120mm mortar round struck the base. Tanner and Pfc Gus
Allen of A/2/506, who just happened to be moving by at the time, died
instantly. Lucas absorbed a large part of the blast, shattering both legs. After
being pulled into the bunker and treated by Captain James D. Harris, the Battalion Surgeon, the ever-present, courageous Captain Randy House picked up
Lt Col Lucas and flew him back to Charlie Med at Camp Evans. Andre Lucas
died on the Medevac pad. The same mortar attack wounded twenty-seven
others.

I immediately placed Major James King, my Brigade S3 Operations
Officer, in temporary command of the 2/506th on Ripcord (one week before
he was due to rotate home). Spaulding and Wandlland took King from Camp
Evans out to the smoky, exploding Ripcord. On the brief helicopter ride from
Evans to Ripcord, Jim King made a hast\y estimate of the situation and con-
cluded that he had to do four things:

1. Keep the helicopter extraction going.

2. Keep up the fire support from "all available."

3. Make sure that every single soldier was evacuated from the hill.

4. Develop a course of action for withdrawal from Ripcord by ground
    should the helicopters not be able to continue air extraction.

(Major James M. King had been the S3 Operations Officer for six months
of tough combat with the 1st Battalion, 501st Infantry from December 1969

through May 1970 under the hard charging leadership of Lt Col William E. (Bill) Dyke (later Lt Gen). He was brought up to 3rd Brigade Headquarters in late May as the S1 in preparation to succeed Major Robert (Tex) Turner as the Brigade S3. During Keith Nolan's research for RIPCORD, no one could locate Jim King, partly because we were all looking for James E. King, not James M. King. Fred Spaulding located him in July 2004 by retrieving his SSN from a set of orders which awarded him the Silver Star. We are glad some of his story can now be told.)

Captain Ben Peters, Commanding Officer of B Company, 2/506th, the base security force, and Major King both walked the base and the perimeter to insure that all soldiers had been taken off the hill. Peters rode the last helicopter out. Or so we thought. An Air Cavalry Scout pilot called on my frequency telling me there was a man in jungle fatigues still on Ripcord wildly waving his arms. I flew in for a very close look to verify and pick up the man. A small shot of wisdom hit me on final approach saying it might be a ruse by an NVA soldier. I directed the Air Cav Team to give cover as CW2 Leslie R. Rush; an artillery spotter picked him up using his LOH. I followed Rush back for the drop-off at Camp Evans. The man was a non-English speaking Kit Carson Scout who had had been taking cover deep, deep in one of the bunkers.

*From North Vietnamese Records*³⁴—

At 12:30 P.M. on 23 July there were no more enemy troops left on Hill 935. At 1400 hours that same day U.S. B-52 bombers bombed and destroyed Base 935. 324B Division's campaign to besiege Operating Base 935 and attack enemy forces in the field was over. During twenty-three days and nights of continuous combat 324Bth Division had killed more than 1,700 American troops, shot down 97 helicopters, and captured or destroyed sixteen 105mm and 155mm howitzers together with large quantities of weapons, military equipment, and supplies. Our attacks had inflicted serious losses on five battalions of the U.S. 3rd Brigade, and three battalion command posts had been destroyed. For the first time in the history of the *Tri-Thien* battlefield a heavily fortified U.S. battalion-sized base camp located on high ground had been attacked and destroyed by one of our divisions.

(Once again, gross, gross exaggerations. The NVA attacked by fire, but never penetrated the defensive wire of Ripcord. From 1 to 23 July, we lost 75 KIA, six tubes of 105 howitzers, three helicopters, no battalion command posts and the

base not destroyed until we did it ourselves with artillery, close air support and
B-52 bombing—and later, persistent CS gas.)

From US/ARVN Records[35]

With the extraction of all friendly units from the Ripcord area, the division
began an extensive artillery and aerial bombardment plan directed against the
NVA forces massed in the area. During the period 24 to 31 July, 12,305
rounds of mixed caliber artillery, 135 forward air controlled missions for 226
sorties, 168 drums of persistent CS agent, and 130 barrels of thickened fuel
and numerous B-52 strikes were directed against known and suspected enemy
locations.

As an extension of the battle for Ripcord, the next major operation in the
3rd Brigade AO was launched on 13 August as Lieutenant Colonel Chuck
Shay and his Shillelagh returned to 3rd Brigade control. Major Vince
McNamara (who had replaced the departed Jim King as the 3rd Brigade S3)
put together the plan for this highly successful operation. The troopers of the
2nd Battalion, 502nd Infantry combat air assaulted into the area of the Khe Ta
Laou River Valley. The area, near FSB Barnett, lay about fourteen kilometers
northwest of FSB O'Reilly and had been a major support area for the NVA
forces in the Ripcord area. The "Strike Force" engaged the enemy forces from
the minute it hit the ground. The "O Deuce" found several large bunker complexes, some of which had been support headquarters. They had numerous
firefights. The battalion lost five KIA and sixty-four WIA. The 2/502nd took
two prisoners and killed eighty-four NVA. The Strike Force helicoptered
back to Thua Thien Province 30 August.

Grey clouds hid the sun; rain seemed ever-present as the monsoon season
dampened operations of friend and foe alike. The Battle for Fire Support Base
Ripcord, the aborted last major US ground offensive of the Vietnam War,
now past into history.

*   *   *

As stated in the Preface: "I still had one battalion left. I had used only two
battalions from my 3rd Regiment. One battalion had been operating east of
the Bo River," responded Major General Chu Phuong Doi, whose entire
324B Division had been committed since 19 May 1970 to "concentrate its
main forces to attack and destroy Operating Base 935." After three hours of

questioning, General Doi had been asked by the author while visiting Doi in Cao Bang, Vietnam 26 May 2004, "What would you have done if we had not evacuated Firebase Ripcord on 23 July?" His response seemed like a most uncharacteristic admission that his division, which had once consisted of nine infantry battalions, had been ground down to only one fully combat capable battalion.

General Doi went on to say that he would continue with the strategy that he learned at Dien Bien Phu and later practiced at Khe Sanh along Route 9 in 1968. He would have his troops continue to move closer and closer to the besieged enemy digging tunnels like they did at Dien Bien Phu. Just before the time of my discussions with General Doi in May 2004, General Doi had been honored at the 50th Anniversary of the history turning victory of the Viet Minh over the French colonialists at Dien Bien Phu in 1954. The memory of that glorious battle had been emotionally refreshed. I am not sure those were his true thoughts in July 1970 after losing thousands of his soldiers to our troopers and our truly superb air and artillery support.

9

The Siege of FSB O'Reilly

Because the 101st Airborne Division proved unwilling to pay the high price in human lives that it would have taken to sustain this forward base, this allowed the NVA 324B Division to force the closing of FSB Ripcord. Understandably, Hanoi declared it a great victory over the Americans and ordered the 324B Division to press on with the attack and to now eliminate FSB O'Reilly.

FSB O'Reilly served as home base for our sister regiment, the 1st Regiment, 1st Infantry Division, ARVN, who had primary responsibility for the base and the area immediately around it. 3rd Brigade maintained a liaison party on O'Reilly to work with the MACV advisors and the ARVN commanders. From time to time we would temporarily relieve the ARVN infantry company on the base with one of our rifle companies, but the AO would remain ARVN. Also, we would sometimes rotate with the ARVN artillery battery on O'Reilly. We were proud to fight with and support the 1st Infantry Division, ARVN. They were well-trained and dedicated troops. The 1st Regiment and my brigade routinely conducted joint officer training programs. The ARVN knew our fighting doctrine and tactical procedures as well as we did and they had the discipline to operate in the field correctly and proficiently.

After a two-week respite following the closing of Ripcord on 23 July, the B4 Front ordered the 324B Division to attack O'Reilly. In May, the B4 Front had directed the 324B Division to commit all of its assets in the offensive against Ripcord, which proved to be the first time that 324B Division had a single mission for which it would employ all division assets. After Ripcord, the 324B received another single division mission—the destruction of FSB O'Reilly.

From North Vietnamese Records—

Excerpts of Merle Pribbenow's translation of the 324B history regarding the siege of FSB O'Reilly, are provided below.

After the victory on Hill 935, the division was ordered to expand its offensive and destroy the enemy Cooc Bai (*FSB O'Reilly*) base to support operations being conducted by other sectors of the Military Region.

Cooc Bai Hill was located along the border between Quang Tri and Thua Thien provinces, about nine kilometers northeast of Base 935. The top of the hill was small and the sides of the hill were sheer slopes, so the base could not accommodate as many enemy troops as Hill 935 had. Cooc Bai was squeezed in between the O Lau and My Chanh Rivers. It was both an artillery firebase and a forward operating base of 1st Regiment, 1st Division of the Saigon puppet government. The base was built at the same time as Base 935 (Ripcord). Base 935 had covered Cooc Bai's forward flank, so the loss of Base 935 made Cooc Bai the outer defensive outpost of the enemy's Bo River defense line. Stationed atop Cooc Bai were the puppet 3rd Battalion/54th Regiment (*OPCON to 1ˢᵗ Regt*), 1st Battalion/1st Regiment, and artillery unit. (*The two infantry battalions were not on O'Reilly at the same time.*) Other units in the Cooc Bai area included the U.S. 1st Airborne Battalion on Hill 316 (*This was the 1ˢᵗ Inf Bn, 501ˢᵗ Inf on and around FSB Gladiator,*) the U.S. 3rd Airborne Battalion at Cung Cap (*This was the 3ʳᵈ Bn, 187ᵗʰ Inf on and around FSB Rakkasan.*), and 2nd and 3rd Battalions/1st ARVN Regiment in the area of Dong Ngai, Co Pung, and Co Va La Dut.

Artillery support for the Cooc Bai base was provided by artillery firebases at Chiem Dong (Hill 367), Cung Cap (*FSB Rakkasan*), Hills 316 (*FSB Gladiator*) and 700, and long-range artillery based in the lowlands. If Cooc Bai was attacked the enemy was able to send in forces quickly to relieve the base. The enemy defense network was built on a line of hills along the banks of two rivers, with Cooc Bai and Hill 935 serving as the central points. From this line the enemy could push forward to any piece of terrain along the entire western side of Route 12.

We will slowly isolate Cooc Bai and gradually work towards using heavy shelling attacks combined with infantry attacks to overrun Cooc Bai. Forces participating in this battle consisted of:

1st Battalion/6th Thua-Thien Regiment and 9th Battalion/3rd Regiment, assigned to conduct siege operations from the southeast to the southwestern approaches to Cooc Bai.

7th Battalion/29ᵗʰ Regiment and Sapper Battalion 7B deployed at Cooc Muon and Hill 1314. These units were to be prepared to advance forward to Hills 787, 884, and Cooc Pe Lai and to attack enemy forces landing by air in our rear area.

8th Battalion/29th Regiment was to be prepared to attack enemy counterattack forces moving down from Quang Tri.

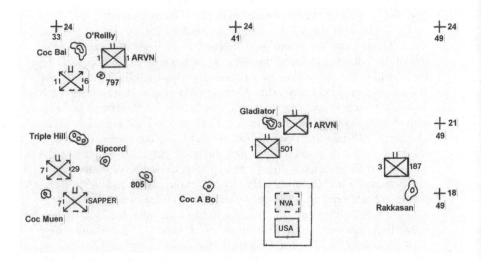

3rd Battalion/803rd Regiment was to conduct a 'diversionary attack' against Hill 316 (*Gladiator*) to draw in enemy forces and pin down the two American battalions in the Tam Tanh-Co Tien area.

Combat guidance for this operation was as follows: surround the enemy position and annihilate enemy relief forces, making the annihilation of enemy forces in the field [i.e., not occupying fortified positions] our primary focus.

(*The 324B mustered (according to their official history) eleven infantry battalions, four artillery battalions, one anti-aircraft battalion, one sapper battalion (reinforced), three machine gun companies, and support troops from their own 324B plus thousands of porters and support troops from the 304B Division for their attack on Ripcord. According to the above historical quote, the 324B Division had been reduced in strength and could now commit to the attack of O'Reilly, only five infantry battalions and the remnants of a sapper battalion. I am most pleased to conclude on behalf of my 3rd Brigade troopers, the artillerymen, the aerial rocket artillerymen, the air cavalrymen, the aircrewmen of the 101st Avia-*

*tion Group, and the Air Force, Navy and Marine jet attack support aircrewmen,
that we blew the Hell out of the 324B Division during their "victory" at Ripcord!!!)*

At 1600 hours on 6 August, under the blazing summer sun and at a
time when the Americans and their puppets were under the maximum psy-
chological and emotional tension, the division commander issued the order
to attack.

Eight heavy weapons firing positions opened fire simultaneously, rain-
ing shells down onto Cooc Bai and hitting dozens of puppet soldiers fighting for water next to a helicopter delivering water rations. Four 105mm
howitzers were blown out of their firing revetments and a number of combat fortifications and bunkers were destroyed. The initial attack by fire,
which lasted 30 minutes, inflicted heavy losses on one puppet company and
the headquarters of the puppet 1st Battalion/54th Regiment. One enemy
artillery position was destroyed.

Fifteen minutes after our artillery opened fire the enemy artillery firebases on Hills 367, 316, 700, and at Cung Cap turned their guns and began
firing. They fired all night into the green jungle canopy surrounding Cooc
Bai. Between 7 and 12 August the enemy sent in a continuous stream of
troops to relieve the siege of Cooc Bai. The 6th Thua Thien Regiment
attacked the enemy troop landings, inflicting heavy casualties on the reinforcements. On 13 August the enemy was forced to send in his last two
battalions. The entire puppet 1st Regiment plus the puppet 3rd Battalion/
54th Regiment were now located at Cooc Bai.

In addition to the reinforcement troops, enemy B-52s carpet-bombed
Cooc Muon, Xa Kut, and other areas where they suspected our troops were
operating. Every day the enemy fired more than 1,000 artillery shells into
the area west of Cooc Bai. (*The official history "explains" the progress or lack
thereof of destroying O'Reilly, as follows.*)

In this changing situation the division issued the following policy
guidelines: reinforce existing fortifications and build additional bunkers
and fortifications at all blocking positions; continue heavy attacks by fire
against the enemy bases; make flexible use of various tactics to engage
enemy troops in the field, combining quick raids with tactics designed to
inflict casualties and erode the enemy's manpower strength; stand ready to
move quickly to engage the enemy in the appropriate sectors; resolutely
defeat enemy efforts to land forces by air; shoot down or damage even
larger numbers of enemy aircraft.

(*The desperation of the situation is brought into focus by the following quotes:*)

If 1st Regiment was sent into battle at this time we had no rice with
which to feed it. The division decided all units currently engaged in combat
operations would continue combat operations. Meanwhile 1st Regiment
and 8th Battalion/3rd Regiment were assigned the mission of transporting

rice. They would also serve as the campaign's reserve force. (*Four infantry battalions committed to carrying rice!!*)

On 20 August 1970 the Military Region Headquarters decided to transform the attack on *Cooc Bai* into a campaign lasting through the end of September, taking us into the rainy season.

With the 324B Division forced to admit failure in their mission to destroy FSB O'Reilly, major engagements in the immediate area ended and FSB O'Reilly closed with an orderly withdrawal to the piedmont area on 7 October in accordance with the original ARVN plan for the onset of the monsoon season.

The Monsoon Season and Other Command Distractions—

The monsoon season made it prudent to move our firebases from the Annamite Mountains further east to the rolling terrain of the piedmont to effectively secure the highly populated littoral area. As no roads served the bases in the Annamite Chain and deteriorating weather conditions made flying air support difficult to impossible on occasion, this had been an annual transition for ARVN and US forces. Traditionally, the NVA and Viet Cong significantly curtailed their operations during the Monsoon. (I found it interesting that most Vietnamese did not know how to swim and men drowned with regularity during stream crossings.) The 3rd Brigade continued to operate with the 2/506th Currahees from and around FSB *Rakkasan*. The 3rd Bn, 187th Inf "*Rakkasans*" had been tasked to reopen, occupy, and patrol from Fire Support Base Jack, located between FSB *Rakkasan* and Camp Evans.

Trouble in the Rakkasans—

It was a Sunday. The grunts in the bush probably didn't know what day of the week it was or even what month, but every GI in the jungle knew exactly how many days were remaining before he caught the Freedom Bird back to the World. It was easy to tell when it was Sunday in the base camps of the 101st Airborne Division. For reasons I never knew, the daily morning briefing at division headquarters started at 0730 on Sunday; one hour later than normal. My staff was obliged to brief me an hour before the division meeting so I would be aware of what would be said about the 3d Brigade. Our briefing over, I was coming out of the command bunker at Camp Evans when my executive officer greeted me.

A cheery "Good morning, Sir," came from Lieutenant Colonel Bryan Sutton. Bryan was a great infantryman, ranger, airborne trooper and trusted combat leader who earlier had worked for me on the Army staff in the Pentagon in my Doctrine Division.

"Why the silly smirk?" I said.

"We've got a bit of a problem," the brigade executive officer reported, "one of your battalion commanders has been accused of being queer."

"Oh, no," I said in a most unenthusiastic response. This was not the sort of problem I needed. An allegation of homosexuality, founded or unfounded always came as bad news.

Bryan said, "Would you care to guess which one of your commanders has been accused of being homosexual?"

"John Doe," I said. (This was not his real name of course.)

This obviously surprised Sutton as he asked why I thought it was John.

I had an instant flashback to the previous day. On that day, I had held a "Come to Jesus" meeting with John. Over thirty-three years ago, but I remember it vividly.

John Doe came to the brigade in his third year in Vietnam. He was a perfect picture of a soldier. Strong chin, sharp features, brush haircut, muscular build, airborne, ranger! John's previous job was Senior Advisor to Colonel Gia Vu, the fabled commander of 1st Division Forward of the Army of Vietnam with three regiments deployed along the North Vietnam-South Vietnam border. The senior South Vietnamese officers spoke very highly of John. The top leaders at 24th Corps Headquarters in Danang wanted to recognize John's achievements and apparent potential by giving him battalion command in the prestigious 101st Airborne Division.

Just the day before, John and I half sat, half leaned on a waist high row of sandbags on Firebase Jack. I took out my stack of 3x5 card notes and began, "John, you recall that I told you when you assumed command that my style is to assume you will do very well and I will not comment when things are going well. On the other hand, if I'm not happy with your performance, I'll let you know about it so you will have opportunities to improve and will not hear of my displeasure for the first time when you read about it on your efficiency report. You will also recall that I have mentioned quite a few negative things to you and that I did not believe that you were up to the high standards expected in this great division.

"Today is a milestone. You have completed 30 days in command. That means that if either of us get wounded, or fall in a hole or whatever, that causes either of us to be evacuated, I must complete an efficiency report covering your command in combat." (In non-combat situations, the minimum is 90 days for an efficiency report.)

I then reviewed some of the things that had concerned me. Like finding a substantial number of his men of Firebase Jack without flak jackets immediately available and finding no gas masks at all on Firebase Jack in spite of the fact that the enemy had on several occasions used tear gas while attacking other firebases. "My chief concern," I went on, "is your style of leadership. I have told you and had my deputy brigade commander formally remind you, that I expect my battalion commanders to frequently hump the hills on foot with a rucksack on their backs with their troops for all sorts of reasons." (I named a few.)

"John," I said, "you have not done this a single time. You have not led your men on the ground. You fly over them in a helicopter and talk on the radio. I have walked with your men with a ruck on my back, an M-16 in my hand, spent the night on the wet floor of triple canopy jungle with your men, but you have not. It is my understanding that you prefer to send a Huey out to the bush, pick up one of your company commanders, bring him back to Camp Evans where you review his operations and issue new guidance. I find that unacceptable!"

John stated, "Sir, that's not a fair picture. I stay in close touch with my men. I find that bringing them back to base camp, they get the benefit of briefings by my staff; actually it's a two-way exchange. It's good for the staff too. Besides, the company commander gets a well deserved break, a good meal and a hot shower."

"Bringing them back for a break is one thing; failing to lead them on the ground is another," I replied. "Nonetheless," I went on, "Here is a pencil draft of your efficiency report if I were forced to write it today." It was not good. His career progression would have been terminated. John read the report and was visibly shocked. He promised an all out effort to do his best to justify the trust placed in him as a battalion commander. After my instant flashback, I returned to the current Sunday morning crisis.

"OK, Bryan, what do you mean about John being queer," I asked.

Bryan, now all business, said, "Sir, two of John's captains ran into each other on R&R leave in Bangkok. They, quite naturally, got to talking about the battalion, the officers, the men and their commander, John Doe. The two concluded he was really strange, in Army terminology, he exhibited homosexual tendencies." Bryan told me the captains' story about what allegedly had happened with their battalion commander.

Bryan continued his report. "The two captains vowed that when they returned to Camp Evans, they would jointly go see the battalion executive officer to report their concern about their battalion commander. The battalion executive officer just called me. He said the captains told him they thought Doe was queer and they wanted an immediate transfer out of the battalion. They said no way would they go back to the field under his command. Sir, we've got to do something right away."

"Right," I said, "I've got it." Bryan was genuinely concerned as he recognized the potential problems if the captains and John all remained in the same unit. Bryan had a keen feel for soldiering. It was a tragic, heartbreaking loss when Bryan was killed four months later near Khe Sanh leading his battalion in support of Operation *Lam Son* 719.

I asked the duty officer in my Tactical Operations Center to call the division operations bunker to find out the location of the commanding general. Major General Jack Hennessey had just departed Camp Eagle in his Command and Control helicopter for the 2d Brigade Area of Operations along the coast south of Hue. This was in the opposite direction of my area. I fired up my own command bird and headed south. I called the CG on the secure radio. Jack Hennessey was one of the Army's finest, later promoted to four-star general. We had served together when he had commanded the Army's first air assault infantry battalion during the test of new air assault concepts in Georgia and the Carolinas seven years earlier. The very same battalion John Doe now commanded. Jack had an unusual style of command in that he used a "directed net." This meant that the dozen or so stations on his command net were not allowed to talk unless he called them first. Kind of an electronic "closed door policy." So I knew I was already in trouble just calling him.

I told the general that I had to have a personal session with him, that it was not a tactical emergency, but still quite urgent. General Hennessey instructed me to meet him at Camp Eagle at lunch time (three and a half hours away). I replied that I needed to see him right away. He reluctantly agreed to return to Camp Eagle. I tactfully allowed him to touch down just ahead of me on the VIP pad at Camp "Starchy", as the troops called Eagle because the division staff officers all wore crisply ironed and starched jungle fatigues and spit-shined paratrooper boots.

Hennessey waited at the pad for me to get out of my helicopter and inquired as I walked up and saluted, "OK, Ben, what's so Goddamn important that it couldn't wait 'til noon?" I stated, "Two captains in John Doe's battalion have accused him of homosexual tendencies." After a few choice expletives, he invited me into his office.

The CG asked for the whole story. I told him that I had not personally interviewed the two captains, but they had made sworn statements and expected to be called as witnesses in any proceedings if necessary.

The captains found that they had had almost identical experiences with Doe. He sent a helicopter out to the jungle to bring the company commander back to Camp Evans. After briefings and discussions, John suggested that he and the company commander go to the chow hall. They would first go by the "officer's club" next door for a beer. After dinner, John suggested that the captain spend the night in camp. He could get a shower and than they could talk some more and maybe have another beer or two. John said his TOC could inform the company in the field and a helicopter would take him out at first light in the morning.

After a lot of talk and more beer in the battalion commander's hootch, John would talk about the great outfit and the long, proud tradition of the battalion's airborne service in three wars. The battalion's symbol was an Asian language character for Rakkasan meaning "paratrooper." John, at some point in the evening, would use a felt tip pin to draw the intricate character on his penis. He would then offer to draw one on the captain's penis. Both captains said they declined this kind offer.

John insisted the captain spend the night in his hootch because he had an extra bunk and they could continue to talk. After the lights were out, the captains said Lt Col Doe came over and kneeled by the bunk, put his hand under the cover and fondled the captain's genitals.

General Hennessey stated, "I'll have my Inspector General personally conduct the investigation. In the meantime, this is just an allegation and we need to keep it as quite as possible."

"Sir, I request that Lieutenant Colonel Doe be relieved of his command pending the outcome of the investigation," I proposed.

"We must presume he is innocent until we prove otherwise," the CG responded.

My position was, "Innocent or guilty, it doesn't matter to the officers and men of the battalion. Doe's credibility as a combat commander has been destroyed. He may recover credibility, but it will take a very long time. I strongly recommend that Doe be replaced before nightfall."

"Do you really think that is necessary?" Hennessey asked.

"Yes, I do. It may not be completely fair to Doe, but the welfare of the men and the integrity of the battalion as a fighting team has to take priority," I replied.

The general agreed. I told General Hennessey that I would tell Doe and then place his executive officer in temporary command until I heard further from him.

I went to Doe, who appeared terribly shaken upon hearing the accusations and he strongly maintained that he had never done anything that could be considered homosexual behavior. I said, "John, as far as I am concerned, you are innocent. I will give you a private office in my headquarters and my entire staff is at your disposal to help you prepare your defense. If you need any help getting papers or testimony from anyone outside the brigade just let me know and I'll do my very best to help. If I were in your shoes, I would fight this thing all the way." John didn't say much; he just thanked me for the offer of help.

A few days later we recognized that a major investigation would be required, so a new lieutenant colonel took command of the battalion. I left the brigade three months later, with the investigation still underway and the hope that John would get a fair shake.

Returning to "the world," I did not give much thought to John Doe and his problem until President William J. Clinton announced that he wanted to open our Armed Forces to homosexuals. The policy change managed to peak my curiosity about what happened to John Doe. I found him and talked on the phone with him. He informed me that the case dragged on as succeeding investigating officers rotated out of Vietnam and the Army finally just dropped the case. John served another eighteen months and retired.

An interesting distraction, but a distraction nonetheless as the battle with a persistent and determined North Vietnamese enemy continued.

V

Hanoi's View of the Battlefield

"1. An alien army is incapable of pacifying South Vietnam.

2. The NLF armed forces can bring about the disintegration of the Saigon army and thus leave military action wholly in the hands of the United States forces, exposing once and for all the foreign 'imperialist' nature of the war and strengthening the NLF appeal for a popularly-backed united front.

3. The widespread United States bombing of North Vietnam is ineffectual against a war effort based on a primarily agricultural economy.

4. The NLF can inflict an increasingly heavy toll of casualties on the American forces, thereby strengthening American domestic pressure for a settlement.

5. The number of American troops actively fighting in South Vietnam will never be sufficiently large to reach the ten-to-one (or greater) ratio required to defeat a guerilla force."

Lieutenant General Nguyen Van Vinh (a Southerner), Deputy Chief of Staff of the People's Army of Vietnam

10

Hanoi's Military Forces

Serving The Communist Party—

We have reviewed how the North Vietnamese military recorded the battle for Ripcord in their historical publications. Now we will seek to understand how they developed their military strategy for the "American War" and the Ripcord battle.

Whether we call the enemy of US forces in Vietnam the North Vietnamese Army (NVA) or the name they prefer, the People's Army of Vietnam (PAVN), the bottom line is that the true enemy of South Vietnam was the Lao Dong Party, the Vietnamese Communist Party. A secret document captured by the French in 1952 stated, "The ultimate aim of the Vietnamese Communist leadership is to install Communist regimes in the whole of Vietnam, in Laos and in Cambodia."[36] It is fair to say that many, many Americans do not realize that the Vietnamese Communist Party goal has been achieved. Vietnam and Laos currently are under Communist control and for a while, Cambodia was Communist controlled. The dominos really did fall.

Vietnamese Culture and Military Tradition—

Usually the first thing one learns about Vietnam is their ancient tradition of resistance to foreign domination. Many of us recall the pride with which Army briefers prepared us for tours in Vietnam by their pseudo—eloquent explanation of Vietnamese xenophobia.

The Vietnamese dynasty of Hong Bang can be traced back to 2879 BC. The Hong Bang kings ruled for 2,622 years. The Chinese first conquered the

Vietnamese in 111 BC. The first successful Vietnamese rebellion was led by two sisters in 39 AD, but they were able maintain independence for only four years. Rather than submit to Chinese rule, the sisters committed suicide and have been inspirational symbols of national resistance every since—even to the Communists.[37]

The Chinese ruled Vietnam for the next nine hundred years in spite of five periods of significant revolts. With the fall of the T'ang dynasty in China, the Vietnamese were successful in overthrowing the Chinese in 938 AD. This period was marked by many battles within the country and with neighboring kingdoms.

French domination started in Danang in 1858 and the country was completely consolidated under French colonial rule in 1883 when the last independent Vietnamese King, Ham Nghi, fled to the mountains rather than surrender to the French. The next half-century to 1933 was marked by riots, resistance and rebellions. Lanning and Cragg wrote that in mid 20th Century, the Vietnamese began to once again expel their invaders by, "Combining the political radicalism of the French Revolution and the dogma of Karl Marx and Friedrich Engels with their ancient tradition of resistance to foreign domination."[38] This began in earnest in 1941 with Ho Chi Minh's return to Vietnam and Vo Nguyen Giap's formation of the beginning of the Viet Minh—People's Army of Vietnam (PAVN).

The cost of doing battle in terms of North Vietnamese lives—

The lesson that America should have learned from the Vietnamese struggle with the French was that the Vietnamese Communists were willing to fight a long war—eight years against the French; and take heavy casualties—23,000 dead at the strategically decisive battle of Dien Binh Phu alone.[39]

General Vo Nguyen Giap in an interview with Italian journalist, Oriana Fallaci, admitted that from 1964 to 1968 the North Vietnamese had lost over 500,000 soldiers killed in action on the battlefield. As a percentage of their population, University of Rochester Professor John Mueller has pointed out; this was a casualty rate "probably twice as high as those suffered by the fanatical, often suicidal Japanese in World War II."[40]

Another take on this interview with Giap appeared in the Outlook Section of the 6 April 1969 *Washington Post*. In the course of the interview, Oriana Fallacci said: "General, the Americans say you've lost a million men." Giap replied: "That's quite exact." Fallacci added that Giap "let this drop as casually as if it were quite unimportant, as hurriedly as if, perhaps, the real number was even larger." Giap added another thought in this same interview. Giap said: "The U.S. has a strategy based on arithmetic. They question the computers, add and subtract, extract square roots, and then go into action. But arithmetical strategy doesn't work here. If it did, they would have already exterminated us."[41]

Stanley Karnow reports Giap saying in this Fallaci interview that the Vietnamese communists would continue to fight "as long as necessary—ten, fifteen, twenty, fifty years." Referring to their struggle against the French, Giap said: "Every minute, hundreds of thousands of people die on this earth. The life or death of a hundred, a thousand, tens of thousands of human beings, even our compatriots, means little."[42]

Giap's bitterness, at least in part, derived from the death of his wife and infant child in a French jail in 1941. At about the same time in 1941, the French in Saigon guillotined his wife's sister for being a terrorist.[43]

The Communist rulers seemed to actually take comfort and pride in their human losses. Maybe they learned this from the French. Guglielmo Ferrero wrote in his book, *Principles of Power*, that the leaders of the French Revolution seemed to believe, "The more blood they shed the more they needed to believe in their principles as absolutes. Only the absolutes might still absolve them in their own eyes and sustain their desperate energy."

In a message to Secretary of Defense Melvin Laird, General Creighton Abrams concluded, "Enemy staying power is his most effective battlefield characteristic. It is based first on his complete disregard for the expenditure of resources, both men and material, and second on discipline through fear, intimidation and brutality. An enemy decision to attack carries an inherent acceptance that the forces involved may be expended totally."

Troop Strength and Strategy—

Of all of the profundities uttered by Sun Tzu, probably the most profound was, "Know your enemy." Sun Tzu said over 2,500 years ago, in *The Art of War,* "if you know the enemy and know yourself, you need not fear the result of a hundred battles. If you know yourself but not the enemy, for every victory gained you will also suffer a defeat. If you know neither the enemy nor yourself you will succumb in every battle." We must conclude that we did not know our enemy in North Vietnam.

Sam Adams was an intelligence analyst with the CIA from 1963 to 1973. In the introduction to his fascinating book, *War of Numbers*, Sam Adams said, "I discovered that the issue of actual enemy numbers was peripheral to the real strengths and weaknesses of the *Viet Cong*. The main enemy strength lay not in the number of troops deployed but in the other areas that U. S. intelligence had hardly considered."

American strategy for the war in Vietnam was first formally stated in a Top Secret document drafted by a deputy to Secretary of Defense Robert McNamara, dated 8 February 1966, and approved by President Lyndon Johnson. The orders concluded: "Attrite, by year's end, [the communist] forces at a rate as high as their ability to put men in the field."[44] This strategy was presented on that date at the Commander in Chief Pacific (CINCPAC) Headquarters, Camp H. M. Smith, Hawaii. (I was present at that 8 February 1966 meeting as a Lieutenant Colonel on the CINCPAC staff and briefed the President, the Secretary of Defense and the Chairman of the Joint Chiefs on proposed plans for increased force deployments to Southeast Asia.)

The die was cast. We were to fight a war of attrition *based on our estimates of enemy troop strength*. General William C. Westmoreland, Commander US Military Assistance Command (COMUSMACV) maintained this under-standing of the US strategy into his retirement and during his libel suit against CBS.[45]

The order to "attrite forces at a rate as high as their ability to put men in the field," was allegedly interpreted by General Westmoreland as being able to accept the loss of one American fighter for every ten enemy killed. My reading of Westmoreland's book did not locate this precise statement.[46] Westmore-land did describe the battle for Dong Ap Bia (Hamburger Hill) as a victory. He considered it of strategic and tactical importance, a battle properly and well fought. Pointing out that the North Vietnamese suffered 597 killed com-pared to 50 American deaths, Westmoreland said: "a sharp defeat by any stan-dards." (Just over the "magic" 10 to 1.)

Obviously Westmoreland did not believe Ho Chi Minh when he said, "You can kill ten of my men for every one I kill of yours. But even at those odds, you will lose and I will win."[47] In sharp contrast, General Creighton Abrams, having replaced Westmoreland as COMUSMACV, said on numer-ous occasions that it did not matter how many enemy soldiers were killed, the only way to win the war was to provide security for the South Vietnamese peo-ple and give them a stable, responsible government.

Westmoreland and Abrams also sharply disagreed on the need for increased US troop strength in Vietnam. In the four years of Westmoreland in command in Vietnam, each year he asked for more troops to be deployed to Vietnam. In Abrams' four years in command, he never once asked for additional troops to be sent to Vietnam.

The frequently hostile disagreement on enemy strength present in South Vietnam is well covered in Westmoreland's book as he defends the Order of Battle calculated/estimated by his Military Assistance Command (MACV) intelligence staff and in Sam Adam's book that presents the CIA's calculated/estimated enemy strength in South Vietnam. A major impasse was reached between the CIA and MACV in mid 1967—well before the massive enemy offensive of Tet 1968.

The MACV Enemy Order of Battle listed four categories in 1966:

Regulars
Service troops
Guerrilla-militia
Political cadres

The primary area of disagreement was in the numbers for the guerrilla-militia. The guerrillas were Viet Cong whose mission was to defend the villages against South Vietnam government troops. The militia were Viet Cong who defended the smaller hamlets. These enemy "troops" rarely wore uniforms and consisted largely of women, old men and kids. In addition to defending their villages and hamlets, they set booby traps and placed mines. Sam Adams, the CIA analyst, and some of his bosses thought they were particularly important as it was learned that about 20 percent of friendly casualties were caused from mines and booby traps. This percentage was probably quite low. Also of great significance to the CIA's Adams, was the rapidity with which Viet Cong regular units were reconstituted after being "virtually wiped out." These fillers were immediately available and came from the ranks of the guerrilla-militia. This transition was made smoother because by 1967, Hanoi had found it necessary to shore up the guerilla-militia forces with men and women sent down from the North.

Another interesting statistic dredged up by Sam Adams was the Desertion-Defection rates. There were frequent departures from the ranks of the Viet Cong for a variety of reasons. Desertion was common on both sides for the Vietnamese. The desertion rate in the South Vietnamese Army (ARVN) was about twenty-five percent. The numbers were large on both sides. Defections to the other side, however, were rare. I have no numbers for the ARVN side, but the VC defections, the *Chieu Hoi* program where the defectors joined the cause of the Republic of South Vietnam and some became Kit Carson Scouts with US Forces, were only one in fifteen or twenty depending on the province. So much for winning the hearts and minds. Not wanting to fight and then deserting did not very often lead to joining the other side to fight for their cause.

James Webb has pointed out that terrorism was an early and important strategy of North Vietnam. "*Viet Cong* assassination squads were a key element from the very inception of the war. By the early 1960's the *Viet Cong* were killing an average of eleven government officials a day. Their approach was brutally simple. Those who showed allegiance to the South Vietnamese government would be killed, and those who stayed away would be left alone. By contrast, the United States used firepower massively and randomly, considering it to be purely a military, rather than a political, tool. In the process, James Webb contends that we drove a lot of people into the open arms of the Viet Cong."[48] The guerrilla-militia forces facilitated the terrorism of assassinations.

From this CIA-MACV disagreement evolved a colossal conundrum. Westmoreland got personally into the arguments as it presented him with a double dilemma. If the enemy numbers got "too" high they might contradict the image of success being promoted by MACV in 1967 or, on the other hand, give the appearance that MACV was trying to justify requests for more troop deployments to South Vietnam.

The CIA analysts used some of the thousands of captured documents (provided to them and other government agencies by MACV) and Vietnam field visits to arrive at enemy numbers much larger than agreed to by MACV. The MACV position was that the Enemy Order of Battle in South Vietnam total was about 300,000 and the CIA estimated it to be about 600,000.[49]

In addition to the considerable enemy troop strength in the South, there was an extensive and highly effective espionage effort by the communists. Enemy documentation cells produced thousands of fake ID cards to permit VC agents to pass the screening for South Vietnam government sensitive jobs, such as cryptographers, officer candidates, special branch policemen, and even staffers in the office of the South Vietnamese President.[50] The ID cards had fingerprints, but these were useless because there was no central system for checking fingerprints. The MACV provided intelligence bulletins that contained mentions of VC agents in after-action reports helping with VC attacks.

There were citing of good enemy agents and records of proselytizing sections. The CIA did not make a serious effort at trying to identify enemy agents in the South until late 1968. In a short period of time they identified over 400 agents and estimated that there were at least one thousand enemy agents in the South. Before the Tet Offensive of 1968, the CIA had identified only one enemy spy.[51]

MACV won its fight with the CIA and carried the guerrilla strength (minus the militia) at 80,000 in November 1967. The CIA had estimated the guerilla-militia strength at 250,000 to 300,000. MACV had dropped the militia as not important enough to count.

In early December 1967 the CIA was evaluating captured enemy documents that dealt with the Winter-Spring campaign's next phase planned for "January to March 1968." The campaign called for occupying and holding some of the urban centers in South Vietnam, and isolating many others." The campaign was to commit all communist forces in South Vietnam and their object was "to inflict unacceptable military and political losses on the Allies regardless of VC casualties during a U. S. election year, in the hopes that the United States will be forced to yield to resulting domestic and international pressure and withdraw from South Vietnam." It concluded "the war is probably nearing a turning point…The outcome of the…campaign will in all likelihood determine the future direction of the war."[52]

The initial plan for this massive offensive throughout the South was presented to the Politburo in January 1967, one year before the planned start date. General Nguyen Chi Thanh, Hanoi's senior commander in the South, left his COSVN headquarters and went to Phnom Penh, Cambodia. He flew by commercial aircraft to Hong Kong and then on to Hanoi. Thanh was concerned that President Johnson might allow General Westmoreland to go into Laos and Cambodia to locate and destroy the North Vietnamese bases there and seal off the Ho Chi Minh Trail. Giap did not support the plan for a massive offensive. He favored reverting to guerilla warfare in the South for the long haul. Le Duan seemed to think the Americans somewhat vulnerable in the South, but respected Giap's position and long-term contributions. As the only general equal in rank to Giap, Thanh continued to push for his plan for a major offensive to be followed by a general uprising in the South in early 1968. With Le Duan's support, the Politburo decided to give Thanh's plan further consideration. In July of 1967 the Politburo gave the go ahead for the General Offensive, General Uprising (*Tong Cong Tich, Tong Khia Nghia*) to begin on January 31, 1968.[53] General Thanh did not live to learn of the approval of his plan. He died of wounds received during a B-52 bombing before the July 1967 decision.

The CIA paper about the January to March 1968 VC campaign plan was sent to the White House. Since the front office of the CIA caved in to MACV on the strength of the guerrillas (80,000 instead of 300,000), the official position of the CIA was that the VC were not strong enough for such a major offensive and the White House should recognize that this is a report from a field station and not the position of the CIA. As the world now knows the massive VC countrywide offensive came off on schedule executed by a VC force more than four times the size recognized by MACV. The campaign was accurately predicted and reported from Saigon on Thanksgiving Day 1967 by CIA analyst Joe Hovey to apparently deaf Washington ears.[54]

Having decided to conduct the 1968 Tet Offensive "regardless of VC casualties," Hanoi found it necessary to send more than 250,000 North Vietnamese soldiers to the south in 1968.[55] General Westmoreland chose to explain Tet 1968 as a desperate "go-for-broke" effort by the enemy to avert inevitable defeat. The scope of the Tet general offensive was massive indeed. The offensive called for all National Liberation Forces/Viet Cong to attack district and provincial capitals of South Vietnam and to occupy all the major cities to ignite a general countrywide uprising against the Saigon government. They were successful in occupying the city of Hue for 26 days and executing three-thousand to five-thousand of its citizens loyal to the Republic of Vietnam.

The Tet 1968 strategy revisited by the North Vietnamese—

In a post war interview in Hanoi, General Vo Nguyen Giap offered this explanation: "For us, you know, there is no such thing as a single strategy. Ours is always a synthesis, simultaneously military, political, diplomatic—which is why, quite clearly, the Tet offensive had multiple objectives."[56] Both the Democratic and Republican political parties in Washington would be happy to employ Giap as chairman of their "spin" committees. My 3rd Brigade troopers would probably say, "What a load of bullshit." A military history published in 1982 in Hanoi relates that General Tran Van Tra, senior officer in the South at the time, said the offensive was misconceived from the very start. "During Tet of 1968, he wrote, "we did not correctly evaluate the specific balance of forces between ourselves and the enemy, did not fully realize that the enemy still had considerable capabilities and that our capabilities were limited."

General Tra lost much of his influence following Tet. Some believe that there was serious concern by the elite in Hanoi that the puppet NLF remain a true puppet and the Tet 68 offensive was an overt act by the North to destroy the hegemony of the NLF over the war in the south. It is clear that the NLF never regained its pre Tet 68 influence.

More pointedly critical, Dr. Duong Quynh Hoa "denounced the venture as a 'grievous miscalculation' by the Hanoi hierarchy, which in her view had wantonly squandered the southern insurgent movement." Dr. Hoa at the time of Tet "68 was a secret Viet Cong agent in Saigon and joined the commandos invading the capital.[57]

General Tran Do explained to Stanley Karnow that the Tet campaign went in an unexpected direction. General Tran Do said: "In all honesty, we didn't achieve our main objective, which was to spur uprisings throughout the South. Still, we inflicted heavy casualties on the Americans and their puppets, and that was a big gain for us. As for making an impact in the United States, it had not been our intention—but it turned out to be a fortunate result."[58]

Colonel Bui Tin, the PAVN officer who received the unconditional surrender of South Vietnam in Saigon April 30, 1975, assessed the Tet 1968 Offensive as follows: "Our losses were staggering and a complete surprise. Giap later told me that Tet had been a military defeat, though we gained the planned political advantages when Johnson agreed to negotiate and did not run for re-election. The second and third waves in May and September were, in retrospect, mistakes. Our forces in the South were nearly wiped out by all the fighting in 1968. It took us until 1971 to re-establish our presence, but we had to use North Vietnamese troops as local guerillas. If the American forces had not begun to withdraw under Nixon in 1969, they could have punished us severely. We suffered badly in 1969 and 1970 as it was."[59]

The assessment from Col Bui Tin is far more negative than one would expect from a senior officer of the PAVN. The reason is simple. Bui Tin's statement came from an interview in Paris by Stephen Young, a Minnesota attorney and human rights activist. The former PAVN officer moved to France after becoming disillusioned with the results of the communist takeover of the South. After interviewing six North Vietnamese officers while in Vietnam in June 2001, I think it safe to say that the only way you will get criticism of their government from North Vietnamese officers is to talk with them while they are no longer in Vietnam under the total domination of the Ministry of Defense and under the ever-watchful eyes of the secret police of the Ministry of the Interior.

More troops from the North—

The traditional Communist concept of long and vast guerrilla warfare that anticipated that the Viet Cong in South Vietnam would eventually emerge victorious was modified in 1959–60 when North Vietnam began to send cadre to the south and in 1964 when regular NVA forces were introduced. There are two likely reasons for this. First, the Politburo in Hanoi was greatly encouraged by the problems and political unrest in South Vietnam attendant to the assassination of South Vietnamese President Diem. Second, the conviction of the Party Central Committee that the planned and expected uprising of the population of South Vietnam must be controlled and carefully orchestrated by trustworthy cadre from the North.

One must understand what happened in the South in the mid 1950's. I do not believe that it was ever the intention of the North to let the southern cadres fulfill the "plan." Indeed it was President Ngo Dinh Diem's anti-communist denunciation campaign (best estimates are that well over 100,000 "denounced" VC were executed), which was in full swing in 1957 that propelled Pham Van Dong's tour of the South in 1958. Dong's findings resulted in the Politburo's decision in early 1959 to establish the two transportation groups on the DMZ in mid 1959. The anger in the South was that they had followed the *Viet Minh* directives to bury their arms and go underground after the Geneva Accords, and now they were being decimated by Diem's anti-communist denunciation campaign. The north feared loosing their entire infrastructure in the South. It was also in 1959 that about 60,000 of the 90,000 cadre who had gone north during 1954–55 under the repartition provisions of the Geneva Accords began returning south. The North knew as early as 1958 (Dong's inspection tour) that the South would require not only logistical support but also reinforcements from the North. It was in the plan all along. That they introduced them (formal configurations) in 1963 was long anticipated as demonstrated by the infrastructure, which had previously been built.[60]

Late in 1965 Ho Chi Minh, who by now, was a 75-year-old emphysema laden old man, was backing away from actively developing and executing strategy for the Politburo. Power was being shared principally between:

- Pham Van Dong, who became the Premier of the Socialist Republic of Vietnam in 1955. (Dong was a Southerner.)

- Le Duan who became the General Secretary of the Politburo in 1956 replacing Troung Chin (the party ideologue) who was demoted because of the excess of the land re-distribution program of 1956. He was quite strong willed and openly anti-China. As Ho withdrew, Le Duan became more powerful in policy making in the Politburo.

- Vo Nguyen Giap, who led all the military actions against the French, culminating with the decisive siege against the French at Dien Bien Phu. Giap was the founder of the People's Army of Vietnam and served as its commander until 1972.

- Van Tien Dung, who commanded the PAVN forces' devastating counteroffensive against Lam Son 719 in 1971. After leading the forces of the North in the Easter Offensive of 1972, Dung replaced Giap as the commander of all PAVN forces and led the campaign to defeat the South Vietnamese forces in 1975.

- Nguyen Duy Trinh, who was from the South and became the first Foreign Minister to also be a member of the Politburo.

At this time, mid 1965, Hanoi evolved a three-point strategy:

1. Endure the American led air strikes against the North.

2. Exhaust the American troops in the South. And,

3. Erode the will of the American people to continue the war.[61]

Although there had been major attacks on the Pleiku airfield and the Qui Neon barracks, the new strategy ordered by the Party Central Committee in Hanoi was announced to the world when the NVA launched its first offensive operation with large troop formations in South Vietnam.[62] This offensive was against the 1st Cavalry Division in the Ia Drang Valley in November 1965. Who makes this kind of a strategic decision?

The People's Army of Vietnam—

The General Staff of the People's Army of Vietnam makes recommendations to the Central Military Committee. The Central Military Committee makes recommendations to the Party Central Committee. Administratively above the Party Central Committee are the Political Bureau (Politburo) and the Party Secretariat. Decisions/Resolutions made by the Political Bureau are passed down through the Central Military Committee to the National Defense Supreme Council to the Minister of Defense and the Chief of the General Staff of the People's Army of Vietnam and the Central Office for South Vietnam (COSVN).[63]

Decision making through these multiple layers is sometimes facilitated by the fact that some key personnel are members of two or more of these governing bodies. The Chief of the General Staff of the PAVN like Senior General Vo Nguyen Giap and later, Senior General Van Tien Dung, were concurrently members of the Central Military Committee, the National Defense Supreme Council, the Party Central Committee and the Political Bureau.

It was this Hanoi decision-making group that ordered in June 1970, the reinforcement and strengthening of forces in the critical southern Laos northwest South Vietnam Khe Sanh-A Shau Valley-Ripcord area.[64] Related to this build-up of forces, was a change in strategy for this area. The criticality of this area for North Vietnam cannot be overestimated. It was at this juncture that the relative safety of movement of personnel, supplies and equipment down through North Vietnam to the DMZ ended and the Ho Chi Minh Trail in Laos and the A Shau Valley became vulnerable to US and South Vietnamese interdiction. With the loss of Sihanoukville and the corridor through Cambodia to the southern portion of South Vietnam, the security of the HCM Trail became paramount.

The most unequivocal statement as to the importance of the Ho Chi Minh Trail came from Colonel Bui Tin, former member of the North Vietnamese Army General Staff. Colonel Bui Tin was the officer who officially received the surrender of the Republic of Vietnam on 30 April 1975 in Saigon. During an interview published in the Wall Street Journal August 3, 1995, Col Bui Tin:

"Question: How could the Americans have won the war?

Answer: Cut the Ho Chi Minh Trail inside Laos. If Johnson had granted Westmoreland's request to enter Laos and block the Ho Chi Minh Trail, Hanoi could not have won the war."[65]

It is probably true that Hanoi could not have won the war without the Ho Chi Minh Trail, but on the other hand, much more than shutting down the Ho Chi Minh Trail would have been necessary for the South Vietnamese to provide security and a stable government for its people.

Organization of Hanoi's Military Forces—

To understand how decisions made by the Party Central Committee and the Politburo are passed to the operational forces, the next level of military organizations below Hanoi requires consideration. Basically these are Military Regions (MR), geo-political areas controlled by the Region Party Committee and Military Fronts, regular PAVN operational forces, controlled by the Minister of Defense and the Central Military Committee in Hanoi.

Robert Destatte does an excellent job of detailing this organization.

During the French era MR 4 included the three southernmost provinces of what we knew as North Vietnam during our war, plus Quang Tri and Thua Thien Provinces of what we knew as South Vietnam (SVN). [The SVN government in Saigon designated MR1 to include the provinces of Quang Tri, Thua Thien, Quang Nam, Quang Tin and Quang Ngai.]

When the country was divided in 1954, Quang Tri & Thua Thien were detached from MR4 and attached to MR5 (at that time called Inter-Region 5), and designated the Northern sub-region of MR5. These two provinces remained subordinate to MR5 until April-June 1966.

Initially PAVN divided SVN into two military Fronts, B1 and B2 Fronts. B1 Front encompassed the provinces from the DMZ down to approximately the 12th Parallel (down to the southern borders of Khanh Hoa & Dac Lac Provinces).

B1 Front was commonly referred to as MR5. B1 Front and Military Region 5 refer to the military headquarters for Region 5. Region 5 refers to the Region Party Committee (Khu Uy), which was the Party organization that controlled Communist operations in this region. B1 Front was directly subordinate to the Ministry of National Defense for operational matters. [Military operations in the B1 Front consisted primarily of regular North Vietnamese Army units.]

B2 Front was commonly referred to as Nam Bo. COSVN was the Party entity that controlled Communist operations in B2 Front. B2 Front reported to the Ministry of National Defense on operational matters. [In Vietnamese, Nam Bo means south. Military operations here were of a significantly different nature from the B1 Front as close coordination with local and regional forces of the National Liberation Front were vital; the North Vietnamese Army regular units could not go it alone this deep into South Vietnam.]

B2 Front went through several reorganizations and realignments, but in general it was divided into:

-MR 6 (aka Southernmost Central Region/Cuc Nam Trung Bo; roughly Ninh Thuan, Binh Thuan, Tuyen Duc, and part of Lam Dong province),
-MR 7 (Eastern Nam Bo)
-MR 8 (Central Nam Bo)
-MR 9 (Western Nam Bo)
-MR10 (roughly Quang Duc, Phuoc Long, Lam Dong Provinces), and the Saigon-Gia Dinh Special Zone.

In May 1964 PAVN created a third military Front command, called B3 Front (aka Western Highlands Front). B3 Front headquarters was physically located in Cambodia near the tri-border point. It controlled communist regular units in this region—roughly Kontum, Pleiku, and Dac Lac Provinces. The PAVN forces that fought in the first large battle in the Ia Drang were subordinate to B3 Front. B3 Front reported directly to the Ministry of National Defense in Hanoi on operational matters. The Region 5 Party Committee remained the senior Party authority in this region.

In April 1966 PAVN established a fourth military Front Command in the South. It was designated B4 Front (aka Military Region Tri-Thien-Hue). The Politburo also established a separate Region Party Committee (Khu Uy Tri-Thien-Hue) to exercise Party control in this region. B4 Front commanded all PAVN regular units in Thua Thien Province and Southern Quang Tri Province. [*The B4 Front included most of the 3rd Brigade AO.*] Its headquarters was located in the A Shau-A Luoi area. It reported directly to the Ministry of National Defense on operational matters.

Two months later, June 1966, PAVN established the fifth and final military Front in the South, B5 Front (aka Highway 9—Northern Quang Tri Front). B5 Front commanded all PAVN regular units north of Highway 9 in Quang Tri Province and the DMZ area. [*This included the northern part of the 3rd Brigade AO.*] Its headquarters was located in Vinh Linh District Quang Binh Province on the north side of the DMZ. The Party Committee for the Vinh Linh Special Zone might have exercised Party control in this region.

From June 1966 till the end of the war, B1 Front (aka MR5) controlled regular forces in the coastal provinces from Quang Tin Province down to and including Khanh Hoa Province. Its headquarters was located in the area generally west of Kham Duc.[66]

The 3rd Brigade was fighting primarily against the B4 Front around Ripcord, Gladiator, O'Reilly, Barnett, and Rakkasan and on occasion against the B5 Front around Khe Sanh and Shepard.

An explanation is also appropriate for understanding equivalent officer rank. The NVA/PAVN officer ranks are basically the same as US officer ranks up through the grade of colonel. After colonel, progression is as follows:[67]

Vietnamese	U. S. Equivalent
General	General of the Army
Lieutenant General	General
Major General	Lieutenant General
Brigadier General	Major General
Senior Colonel	Brigadier General

Hanoi's military forces in the field followed rather conventional lines, but where and when they were to be committed to battle, particularly for offensive purpose, was very tightly dictated by the political bureaucracy of the communist party in Hanoi.

11

Interviewing North Vietnamese Army Officers

Getting the North Vietnamese Military Story—

In June 2001, we met in Hanoi with our official point of contact, the Foreign Press Center of the Ministry of Foreign Affairs, and they reaffirmed that Senior General Van Tien Dung, still hospitalized, could not meet with us. They also reaffirmed the impracticality of a meeting with Major General Chu Phuong Doi, former commander of the 324B Division who lived way up north in Cao Bang. After months of time for preparation, the Socialistic Republic of Vietnam stated that they had no senior Ripcord veterans in the Hanoi area with whom we could talk. As the reader has learned, I finally had the opportunity to interview with General Doi in May 2004.

We decided to visit the People's Army Publishing House with great expectations for hitting it big there, only to find another major disappointment. Their little ten by twelve meter hole-in-the-wall sales outlet had no available index of published works, nor, apparently, any publications relevant to the battle for Ripcord in their store.

The first piece of the puzzle to fell into place serendipitously, with nothing scheduled for the next day, Wednesday, 6 June, Colonel Pham Van Dinh suggested that we visit the Army Museum there in Hanoi. Shortly after arriving at the museum, it became obvious why Colonel Dinh had suggested this place to visit. When we got there, Dinh contacted a PAVN female captain and we sat down for tea and a chat. Soon she departed to go talk with her boss and we went over to view the 175mm Self-Propelled Artillery piece which they proudly displayed.

(Author)

Lt Col (Ret) Fred Spaulding and Col Pham Van Dinh with the 175 mm
Self-Propelled Gun at the Army Museum in Hanoi

I explained Colonel Pham Van Dinh's presence with us in the Prologue. At Courtney Frobenius' suggestion, I hired Dinh as our interpreter/guide/door-opener because of: his unique relationship with the government of the Socialist Republic of Vietnam as a serving officer in the People's Army of Vietnam; he currently resided in Hue; and, my earlier service with him during Lam Son 719 in 1971. Colonel Dinh surrendered his ARVN infantry regiment and Camp Carroll to the North Vietnamese during the North's Easter Offensive 1972. The departing US Army left two batteries of four 175mm guns each to the Army of the Republic of Vietnam. One battery of 175s had been located at the critical defensive bastion of Camp Carroll. The principal artillery support weapon of the PAVN for the Easter Offensive was the 130mm gun with a range of 27,500 meters. The ARVN 175 mm gun was the only weapon that could provide counter-battery fire against the PAVN 130mm gun. This 175 surrendered to the PAVN at Camp Carroll is a highly prized possession of the Army Museum in Hanoi.

The Museum Director was understandably pleased to see Colonel Dinh.

Colonel Le Ma Luong's Take on PAVN Forces at Ripcord—

Colonel Luong was friendly and cheerful and wanted to talk with us. As we joined him in drinking tea, he sent for his key staff officers and for his Museum photographer. The staff, including an English speaking female Lieutenant Colonel, seemed to very much enjoy the gathering and discussions.

To our surprise and delight, we found that the Director of the Army Museum served as an infantry company commander in Thua Tien Province in 1970 and fought in some of the battle for Ripcord. Out of his company of 90 men, 35 were killed in the few weeks his company participated in the battle. He stated they were ordered to "attack, attack to keep pressure on Ripcord." To maintain constant pressure, Colonel Luong emphasized that the 304B; 324B and 325 Divisions were rotated into the battle. This provided the first indication of the 325 Division's involvement as a participant in the battle and that the NVA practiced a rotation of divisional units.[68] Hearing this from a senior serving officer with an appreciation of military history, the information proved quite impressive.

(Fred Spaulding)

Colonel Le Ma Luong, Director of the Army Museum in Hanoi
Colonel Pham Van Dinh and Captain Trinh Le Phuong

It is not insignificant that five of the six officers we interviewed had been the Deputy Commander and Political Officer of their respective units. Most people knowledgeable of the military organizations in Communist countries agree that the Commander is commander in name only and the final authority rests with the Political Officer. The Vietnamese government authority readily assumes that Political Officers are more reliable to provide "proper" answers.

Mr. Nguyen The Cuong of the Foreign Press Center of the Ministry of Foreign Affairs acted as our official point of contact for our visit. We talked with him at the Ministry office upon our arrival in Hanoi. He apologized for not being able to schedule anyone for us to interview. I reminded him when we were scheduled to leave Hanoi for Hue and also told him that we could adjust that schedule if he located a person knowledgeable of the Ripcord battle. I implored him to keep trying and asked if US Ambassador Peterson might be able to help since he was very much interested in our visit. (Important names are no good unless you can drop one now and then.) I called Mr. Cuong that afternoon and twice the next day. Late that afternoon, Mr. Cuong left a message for me to call his office. When I called, he said he had located a senior officer that we could meet with the next morning before we had to leave to catch the flight to Hue.

Brigadier General Bui Pham Ky, Deputy Commander and Political Officer of the 324B Division in 1970—

The only officer that the Foreign Press Center of the Ministry of Foreign Affairs arranged for us to interview in Hanoi happened to be with Brigadier General Bui Pham Ky, the former Deputy Commander and Political Officer of the 324B Division in 1970. The interview, conducted at the Ministry of Foreign Affairs, with Mr. Nguyen The Cuong of the Foreign Press Center of the Ministry of Foreign Affairs acting as the official interpreter. The government officials turned my personal interpreter, Colonel Pham Van Dinh, away at the door and forbade him to be in the room. A man in civilian clothes, presumed to be from the Ministry of Internal Affairs (their secret police), set to the left of General Ky, while a uniformed military officer, presumed to represent the Ministry of Defense had been seated to the general's right.[69]

General Ky did not look happy to be there. (He smiled only once in the two hours there; I'll tell that story later.) General Ky and Mr. Coung did not seem happy for us to take pictures of them, but that did not stop us. All four of them seemed unhappily surprised when they learned that I had a movie camera running throughout the time of the interview. In appreciation, I presented General Ky with a Polaroid picture of himself taken at the interview and with a Ripcord memento coin. Mr. Coung received a picture, Ripcord coin, and a cash gift for his children, in appreciation of his services.

I asked General Ky where the 324B Division located its headquarters during the battle for Ripcord. He immediately turned to the left and conferred with the man in mufti before he would give an answer and so it went for virtually every question.

Brigadier General Bui Pham Ky responded that the 324B Division located its headquarters just north of FSB Barnett. (This could have been the division base area, but it was not likely to have been the 324B Division Command Post during the Ripcord battle—the command group would have been much closer to Ripcord. General Doi verified this assumption when he informed me that his forward Command Post had been co-located with the 803rd Regt CP, southwest of Hill 902. He explained that the area northwest and south of Barnett contained considerable logistical caches and facilities, hospitals, and bivouac sites.[70] This is the same area where Lt Col Chuck Shay took his 2nd

Battalion, 502nd Infantry "STRIKE FORCE" and did such a superb job of locating and destroying the enemy's base camps.

Chuck carried a large piece of wood known as The Shillelagh. A shillelagh is a large club or cudgel of blackthorn or oak from Shillelagh, County Wicklow, Ireland. St. Patrick reportedly used the shillelagh in defense of his followers. A charismatic and great combat leader, Chuck Shay, had been admired, respected, and liked by most of his subordinates, but I'm sure more than one soldier thought, "That crazy mother just might hit me with that big stick!" John Delveccio used this valley battle as the setting for his superb novel, *The 13th Valley*, where he most poignantly described the 2/502's fierce firefights with the North Vietnamese enemy and the miserable struggle with the jungle and seemingly endless days in the boonies. To the STRIKE FORCE troopers, Chuck Shay was known as Shamrock. To Delveccio, Shay was the Green Man.

(Fred Spaulding)

Brigadier General Bui Pham Ky, Deputy Commander and Political Officer
of the 324B Division in 1970

I asked General Ky if he had any questions for me. After seeming tense and bored for a couple of hours, he gave a wry smile and asked, "What happened to General Zais?" General Melvin Zais, a two-star general, commanded the 101st Airborne Division at the time of the battle for Dong Ap Bia—better known as Hamburger Hill. Our 3rd Brigade fought that battle in 1969, one year earlier than Ripcord. Zais received a lot of adverse press and Congressional criticism as a result of that battle. Notwithstanding, he later received a promotion to three stars and stayed in Vietnam to command the 24th Corps with headquarters in Danang. General Zais received his promotion to a fourth star before a normal retirement. He died a few years ago.

Why did General Ky ask this question and why with a smirk more than a smile? He had been there at Hamburger Hill and he knew he lost a lot of men, but he saw it as a victory. He also knew General Zais got in hot water about the battle. He also knew that Hamburger Hill became somewhat of a turning point in the war as discussed in Chapter 1, Strategic Setting. Ky, happily, stuck me with the needle Ky's KIA loss ratio of over ten to one at Dong Ap Bia apparently did not bother him at all. Ky knew of the major negative political impact that savage and brutal battle had on both American soldiers and the American public.

General Ky remained probably all too aware that not until after Hamburger Hill did President Nixon announce his peace plan and the first withdrawal of combat units. An American disaster at Ripcord could have caused a major acceleration of US ground forces withdrawals. That would be worth a lot of PAVN lives.

I asked Brigadier General Bui Pham Ky which of our weapons systems was more effective—close air support by jet aircraft or helicopter gunships? He did not say helicopter gunships, he quickly said, 'The AH-1 Cobra!' The Cobra, a basic Huey light cargo helicopter built by Bell Helicopter Company and modified to be a streamlined aerial weapons platform. The Cobra came armed with rockets and machine guns and, with two Army aviators flying it, it quickly became the choice of weapons to support US infantry soldiers in close contact, day or night. Ky went on to point out that the jet aircraft had great difficulty hitting their targets in the mountains.

The US troops and NVA both well understood the difficulties experienced by aerial bombardment in hitting the correct target in mountainous terrain. First, the location of the target had to be communicated to the Forward Air Controller (FAC), usually an Air Force pilot in a fixed wing propeller driven aircraft, who normally operated three to five thousand feet above the terrain.

The FAC had to visually verify the target location initially reported via the radio nets and marked by smoke "popped" on the ground by the troops. The FAC would then try to mark the target for the strike aircraft by employing a 2.75 inch rocket smoke round fired from a wing store on his aircraft. More often than not, these rockets proved very inaccurate. The aircraft used by the FAC could not always turn to get a safe firing angle while keeping the target in sight sometimes causing more than one attempt to get off the marking round. The pilots of the high performance jet aircraft, sometimes flying above the clouds, but always high above jungle and mountains that all pretty much looked alike, would experience difficulty in locating the marking rounds which often took time and the marking smoke, often subjected to winds and rain, would drift or fade. After confirming the target with the FAC and getting cleared in "hot," the jet aircraft would then enter a steep dive and launch its ordnance five to seven thousand feet above the surface. In addition to all of the problems in delivering ordnance on the target by fast moving jet aircraft, the enemy frequently would see the FAC and marking round and have sufficient time to move and or take cover for protection.

In line with the difficulty of hitting the target is the misplaced bomb or napalm falling on US troops, euphemistically called "friendly fire." Unfortunately most soldiers can tell of one or more friendly fire incidents. Watching parts of your buddies bodies fly through the air or trying to extinguish flaming napalm on their bodies is the worst kind of battle experience.

General Ky stated that they did not worry about B-52s, which may be a bit of post-war bravado. The NVA frequently learned of planned bombings by listening to US radios. They also observed that when US troops started to back out of an area that a B-52 strike might be forthcoming, so they left the area too. When they observed helicopters flying in the area the NVA assumed that no B-52 or heavy artillery attacks were to be expected. When the B-52s hit enemy in the box (a reference to the pattern of exploding bombs on the ground), it amounted to total devastation. We have gone in and found the few remaining survivors staggering, blinded, and bleeding from all orifices

General Ky spoke of his troops detailed knowledge of FSB Ripcord pointing out that it was first established in 1968. General Ky operated in the area for several years prior to the Ripcord battle and his soldiers had extensive first-hand knowledge of the latticed trails combing the valley floors, the bunkers occupied and, then, reoccupied. They knew the location of the supply caches and medical aid stations throughout the vast tunnel complexes.

When asked what his plan of attack was for Ripcord, General Ky, almost too quickly, stated that they used the tactics learned from higher headquarters. He explained these as:

1. Besiege.

2. Infiltrate the approach.

3. Attack with infantry.

4. Block all enemy reinforcement routes.

5. Quickly withdraw.

Others have explained NVA/VC tactics as Four Fast and One Slow. This means: Fast Advance, Fast Assault, Fast Clearance of the Battlefield and Fast Withdrawal. All actions based on Slow Preparation.[71] These two explanations are not consistent and that is why they are both believable. General Ky described preparation with a long "Besiege" and "Infiltrate the approach" instead of "Fast Assault." A smart enemy uses the tactics that fit the situation.

There wasn't much time between the end of the interview with General Ky and our departure flight from Hanoi to Hue. The ride to the airport was filled with quick glimpses of landmarks of Hanoi. The stark contrast between the bustle of the seven times larger, more modern Saigon and the much smaller, ancient capitol city of Hanoi proved startling. The modern five star hotel that overlooked Hanoi's Westlake had been a nice surprise. As we were about to depart I experienced an upwelling of mixed emotions upon the realization that I had just visited the capital of the government that had tried to kill all of my troopers. Also, thoughts about the interview raced through my mind…What more could he have told us? Why did it take so long to locate a PAVN general living in Hanoi? Surely other senior officers lived in the capitol area. Why did they not allow Col Dinh into the interview? When I asked Dinh, he just shrugged his shoulders.

The flight to Hue, via Vietnam Airline A320 jet transport, approached along the beautiful South China Sea shoreline with its pristine white sandy beaches and multiple coves that invited exploration. How I would love to have visited the old Eagle Beach and had a day or two to snorkel around the beds of coral. We flew into Hue-Phu Bai Airport, the former home of an OV-1 Mohawk Aerial Reconnaissance Company and about one hundred helicopters of the 101st Airborne Division and numerous single and twin engine utility aircraft. A bustling, very busy airfield with bunkers and revetments everywhere the last time I saw it. Now, only one very small building remained on the parking apron. There was not another aircraft anywhere on the airfield. In fact, not even a single car could be seen after the taxis departed.

The Ministry of Foreign Affairs had informed me that the PAVN helicopter that used to be at Phu Bai was no longer there and that I would not be able to visit the Ripcord firebase. Having traveled to many small airports around the world, I grew accustomed to seeing a few Cessna and Piper aircraft at virtually every airport in the universe. In the absence of the helicopter, I had hoped to be able to charter a small aircraft for a fly over Ripcord, but there was <u>nothing</u> at Phu Bai!

Colonel Dinh got us checked into a very nice hotel on the Perfume River and sent us off for a brief visit to the old Eagle Beach, the former rest area for the 101st Airborne Division. Dinh invited us for dinner at his home that night. During our sightseeing, Dinh busily lined up two former PAVN officers, BG Nuoi and Major Thuoc, for us to interview the next day. He did this on his own without working through the Ministry of Foreign Affairs. (We think.)

Brigadier General Duong Ba Nuoi, former Deputy Commander and Political Officer of Military Zone (Corp) 4—

General Nuoi, who agreed to be interviewed, had been located in Hue by Colonel Pham Van Dinh. Although confined to a wheelchair, General Nuoi appeared overjoyed to have us come to his home and talk with him. Bright and smiling, he genuinely interested in trying to help us. During the course of the interview, none of the individuals present represented the Ministry of Foreign Affairs or the Ministry of Internal Affairs.

(Fred Spaulding)

General Nuoi at his home near Hue.

The home of this retired old warrior, equivalent to major general in US ranks, would be considered modest to poor by US standards. His wheel chair had been fabricated from an old metal office chair which looked like something left behind by US forces. His arthritic hands appeared twisted with the fingers curled down and stiff. He dressed in cotton pajamas that hung on his very thin and frail frame. His wife graciously served tea as the children and grandchildren who crowded the house were gently shooed out of the way for our visit.

The enemy order of battle continued to expand as we interviewed Brigadier General Duong Ba Nuoi in Hue on 8 June 2001. General Nuoi was the Deputy Commander of Zone 4 in 1970. This Zone included Thua Tien, Quang Tri, Quang Binh, and Ha Tinh Provinces. The last two listed provinces were north of the Demilitarized Zone in North Vietnam. The Zone headquarters was in Vinh, North Vietnam. The North Vietnamese also knew Zone 4 as MR4.

In response to the question of what PAVN forces were in the Ripcord area, General Nuoi responded the 324B and 304B Divisions. When asked if there were any more major forces in the Ripcord battle, General Nuoi said, "The 304 Div and 324B Division stay, the 325 Division and 308 Division come and go."[72] And so the 308 Division had been added to the possible enemy order of battle.

General Nuoi said they were keeping pressure on Ripcord and building their forces for a major offensive operation against FSB Ripcord. He said this offensive was planned for August 1970. This was a startling revelation even though we should have deduced it at the time. The US occupation of FSB Ripcord not only positioned American forces to fire 155 mm artillery onto the Ho Chi Minh trail and to facilitate air strikes in the area during poor weather, it also served as an obvious potential forward base for launching ground strikes into the A Shau. It also presented a juicy target close to their support bases. The overwhelming concern for the NVA remained the control of the high ground along the Ho Chi Minh Trail.

General Nuoi stated explicitly that the NVA were quite intent on the destruction of Ripcord and the forces defending it; the primary goal of the planned August 1970 offensive operation.

Below is a breakout of the regiments of these four divisions:[73]

304B Division	**308 Division**
9th Inf Regt	36th Inf Regt
24th Inf Regt	88th Inf Regt
66th Inf Regt	102nd Inf Regt
68th Arty Regt	

324B Division	**325 Division**
29th Inf Regt	18th Inf Regt
803rd Inf Regt	95th Inf Regt
812th Inf Regt	101st Inf Regt
6th Inf Regt Regional Force (OPCON)	

The strength of the infantry companies in the PAVN units approximated the field strength of US infantry companies in the bush—an average of about

90 men per company. The US battalion would normally be larger because it consisted of four infantry companies per battalion to the norm of three infantry companies in the PAVN battalion. Both the US and PAVN armies normally had three infantry battalions per regiment. On the other hand, we have seen that Viet Cong/NVA regional force regiments such as the 6th Tri-Thein, might have more than three battalions.

A close look at the artillery in the 304B Division is impressive. The 68th Artillery Regiment was established in 1955 as part of the 304th Infantry Division. The 540th, 640th and 940th Pack Artillery Battalions were assigned to the three infantry regiments of the 304th. The 840th Pack Artillery Battalion was at division level and had the 91st and the 93rd Mountain Artillery Companies and the 111th Mortar Company as organic units. This tube artillery is comparable to that organic artillery assigned to a US division. US divisions normally have 8-inch howitzers and 175mm gun tubes in support from corps level.

During the siege of Khe Sanh in 1968, the 68th obtained and employed 18 DKB (122mm Rocket Launchers), 18 DKZ (82mm Recoilless Rifles) and fifty-four 82mm mortars. Additionally, two D74 (122mmRocket) battalions with 24 launchers provided support to the 304 Division.[74] This is a very substantial amount of artillery support. Each of the four divisions would have a similar capability. US divisions in Vietnam did not have this type of rocket launcher support, but alternately, had substantial air support.

Major Ho Van Thuoc, Operations Officer Thua Tien Province Regional Forces in 1970—

Major Ho Van Thuoc, who in 1970 as the Operations Officer for the Thua Tien Province Regional Forces, was interviewed in Hue on 8 June 1970. Across the Perfume River on the north bank of Hue, surrounding the former Royal Citadel lies a neighborhood seasoned with time. Major Thuoc lived in a section where many PAVN families currently live. He was not comfortable with the idea of Americans, with their military haircuts, coming to his house and being observed by his neighbors. Col Dinh arranged for Major Thuoc to be transported by van to Dinh's Sunflower Hotel for the interview. The Spartan setting in the back of the hotel, with a single light bulb hanging from the ceiling, allowed sufficient space for a table with four chairs and a rotating fan in a room partly used for storage.

Thuoc, not feeling well, walked unsteadily. He looked much older than his 65 years. Still, he seemed pleased to come and talk with us.

Major Thuoc described their mission as "[T]o kill as many as possible and push you out of the mountains."[75]

Major Ho Van Thuoc stated that the 6th Infantry Regiment of Regional Forces consisted of eight battle-hardened infantry battalions of local Viet Cong whose ranks had been filled with regular soldiers from the North. A regiment with eight battalions, although most unusual, but as a regional force spread throughout the highly active Thua Thien Province, remains within the realm of possibilities. Dave Palmer, in his *Summons Of The Trumpet*, reported that the 5th and 6th Regiments near Hue had eight battalions totaling seventy-five hundred men.

Major Thuoc added that in May 1970 the 6th Infantry Regiment was placed under operational control of the 324B Division "to attack Ripcord." Surprisingly, Major Thuoc said that he strongly recommended against attacking Ripcord, but they attacked anyway and, he admitted, that they "lost too many people." He estimated that they lost over 500 killed and wounded from the 6th Infantry Regiment. Major Thuoc further reported on the death of one battalion commander, along with over 100 of the men from his battalion being killed, at Ripcord.

The rationalization of North Vietnamese losses, while perplexing, is always interesting. Ambassador Maxwell Taylor expressed his admiration for the enemy: "The ability of the Vietcong continuously to rebuild their units and to make good their losses is one of the mysteries of this guerrilla war…Not only do the Vietcong units have the recuperative powers of the phoenix, but they have an amazing ability to maintain morale."[76] Stanley Karnow reports that in Hanoi after the war, "A communist veteran of the Khe Sanh battle recalled the carnage inflicted on his comrades, disclosing to me that some North Vietnamese and Viet Cong units suffered as much as 90 percent losses under the relentless downpour of American bombs, napalm and artillery shells. Giap, who was rarely troubled by heavy human tolls, flew to the front in January 1968 to inspect the situation personally—and he nearly became a casualty himself when a flight of thirty-six B-52s dropped a thousand tons of bombs near his field headquarters."[77]

Monitoring US Radio Traffic—

Major Thuoc told us that they listened to our radios all the time. He said their radio intercept squads could understand English, as well as, French and Spanish. Thuoc told us that they knew "when and where you move."[78] Stu Vance of the CIA concluded in 1969 that the enemy had more than 600 listening posts—200 of them manned by people who knew English. They were part of an espionage organization with agents, secret ink, couriers, and microdots as sophisticated as anything the Allies had in World War II.[79] A 101st Airborne Division pilot of the 2nd Squadron, 17th Cavalry was on the receiving end of this North Vietnamese radio intercept effort while on a reconnaissance mission around Ripcord in April 1970. He recounted, "I was the front seat in the AH-1 of a Charlie Troop 2/17 Cav Pink Team. The mission was going smoothly when we hear on the radio, 'Condor 22, Chief Warrant Officer 2 Mike Allan, we are going to kill you.' Boy that was unnerving!"

Major Thuoc grew tired. He said he could talk with us later, but now he needed to be taken home. We did not get a chance for a second interview.

Senior Colonel Nguyen Quoc Khanh former Operations Officer of the 324B Division in 1970—

Senior Colonel Nguyen Quoc Khanh served as the Operations Officer of the 324B Division in 1970. Mr. Nguyen The Cuong of the Foreign Press Center of the Ministry of Foreign Affairs in Hanoi "found" Senior Colonel Khanh for the interview after I had given Mr. Cuong a cash gift for his children.

(Fred Spaulding)

Senior Colonel Nguyen Quoc Khanh and MG (R) Ben Harrison
*(Above the door are pictures of Khanh in the French War, The American War
and the Chinese War)*

Located on Dien Bien Phu Street, Senior Colonel Khanh's home, unusually large and well furnished, looked quite nice in one of Hue's finest neighborhoods. As with virtually all Vietnamese homes, it lacked air-conditioning. Khanh, like Colonel Dinh, owns a hotel in Hue City. He seemed very proud of the photos on the wall above the windowed double-door; they showed him in uniform while serving in the French War, the American War, and the Chinese War as they are known to the Communist Vietnamese.

Senior Colonel Khanh, a gracious host, proffered tea and showed us to a comfortable sitting area, but he could not or did not hide his tenseness.

He defined their mission as "To carry out serious battle and defeat you so we can control the high points along the Ho Chi Minh Trail. To destroy, set by set, one by one, the American bases to force the American Army to leave." They believed that if they destroyed two or three American bases that the American forces would leave.[80]

Khanh was asked if there was a plan to bring in more forces to attack Ripcord. He replied, "We can not talk about specific plans, but we were going to attack and take all high ground." (There was an interpreter allegedly from the Ministry of Foreign Affairs, probably the secret police, present and it is believed that this inhibited and constrained Senior Colonel Khanh in some of his responses.)

The statement about not being able to talk "about specific plans" and "we were going to attack and take all the high ground." is interpreted to mean that the complete destruction of Ripcord had been ordered. The conviction and determination demonstrated by Senior Colonel Khanh as he told of the plan to attack Ripcord and destroy it, conveyed that, as was the case in the Ia Drang Valley five years earlier, and Tet of 1968 two years earlier, major battle-field losses would not deter them from the offensive.

Though smiling sometimes through gritted teeth, Senior Colonel Khanh talked of attacking and controlling all of the high ground along the Ho Chi Minh Trail. He wrung his hands and squeezed alternate fists. His commitment and determination being clearly transmitted without need for language interpretation.

Senior Colonel Khanh possessed several neatly bound maps, which he displayed with obvious pride. There were numerous markings on the maps with unit positions and logistical facilities. His maps were based on old French map data; he identified FSB Ripcord as Hill 935 instead of 927 as shown on US topographic maps.

Khanh indicated the placement of a number of the antiaircraft units around Ripcord which were later transferred to Laos to defend against the upcoming 1971 Operation Lam Son 719 along Highway 9 to Tchepone. He added, "Yes, we mobilized all the air defense we had." The courageous and daring air crewmen of the 101st Aviation Group would have certainly appreciated it if they had started this transfer to the northwest before the evacuation of Ripcord on July 23rd.

Senior Colonel Khanh was asked what we (the US) did best, or he feared most at Ripcord. He said, "You have fire support from helicopter gunships and you occupied the high ground in an area where we could not move and made it difficult to attack you because of the steep hill." With the clearing of fields of fire, and the emplacement of barrier wire, the hill looked even more steep and foreboding. Then in typical Communist dialectic double talk, Khanh said, "The worst thing you did was to stay on a hilltop isolated so that it made it easy for us to eliminate you one by one."

Colonel Nguyen Ba Van—

The reader will recall from the Prologue that Colonel Van was "introduced" to me by a business associate of Lieutenant General Teddy Allen as my first contact for getting the North Vietnamese side of the Ripcord battle.

Colonel Nguyen Ba Van was interviewed in his home in Cu Chi. He was most gracious and seemed to genuinely want to help us. (I believe he much appreciated the $700 I had previously had delivered to him.) Unfortunately Colonel Van was not a lieutenant who was wounded in the Ripcord battle as we had earlier been told. In June and July of 1970, Colonel Van was a sergeant in a unit near Khe Sanh.[81] He had general knowledge of the forces and battles in the area, but little specific information about the Ripcord battle.

What did we learn from our interviews?—

Our NVA interviewees consistently stated that the 304B Division and the 324B Division remained in the Ripcord area while the 308 Division and the 325 Division would "come and go."

Another source of input on enemy strength at Ripcord comes from the 3 September 96 report of the Joint Task Force-Full Accounting for Case 1648 (Howard and Beals) which places the enemy's 6th PAVN Regt as occupying Hill 1000 from April through August 1970. The report also located the 29th Regiment of the 324B Division south of Hill 1000 and the 803rd Regiment, 324B Division southeast of Hill 805.[82] (The bodies of Howard and Beals were not found.) These enemy location reports provided by the JTF-FA are fairly consistent with general Doi's inputs. We do not know how many of the eight battalions in the 6th Regional Force Regiment were under the operational control of the 324B Division. The 1st and 2nd Battalions are specifically mentioned in the official 324B history.

101st Airborne Division intelligence estimated the enemy strength around Ripcord to be as many as six to eight battalions of infantry. From our interviews, one could conclude that there were possibly eleven to fourteen battalions of infantry around Ripcord and we have not yet located the 324B Division's 812th Regiment. Quite likely, the 812th had been withdrawn from battle to be reconstituted after crippling losses, as was the normal practice of the PAVN. On the other hand, some of the battalions of the 812th could have been there working for one of the other three regiments. General Doi's answer to my question about the 812th was short and vague.

The 6th Regional Force Regiment was in such strength in a complex of fighting positions and connecting trenches that they successively and successfully repelled on 6 July, the Reconnaissance Team Bravo, 2/506th Infantry wounding all team members and on 7 July, they inflicted heavy casualties on Delta Company 2/506th forcing their withdrawal. On 8 July, the 2/506th launched a battalion-controlled assault against Hill 1000; once again, the 6th Regt brutally defended the hill top. On 17 July the 6th Regt successfully defended the Hill 1000 on the northern slope with heavy casualties to the battalion-controlled attack by the Reconnaissance Platoon and A and B Companies of Lieutenant Colonel Otis Livingston's 2/501st Infantry. The 6th Regt remained in control of Hill 1000 until August and placed heavy fire on our helicopters during the Ripcord extraction on 23 July.

All of the North Vietnamese officers interviewed consistently expressed the spirit of the offensive at the time of the Ripcord battle. They were determined to take the fight to the Americans and cause great casualties among the Americans no matter the cost in lives to the North Vietnamese military.

My estimate of the price in lives the North Vietnamese Army paid at Ripcord, from possibly eleven (certainly eight) infantry battalions, four artillery battalions, one anti-aircraft battalion, one sapper battalion (reinforced), three machine gun companies, and hundreds of porters and support troops from the 304B Division, amounted to a minimum of 2400 soldiers killed in action and several thousand more wounded.[83]

12

Hanoi's Strategy Changes

Early in the American War, the North Vietnamese and NLF adopted the same classic strategy used by the Viet Minh to defeat the French to defeat the Americans and their allies in South Vietnam. This strategy followed the three-phase methodology of Mao Tse—Tung. Phase One called for insurgents to gain control of the population and conduct limited guerrilla and terrorist operations. Phase Two required the formation of regular military units to attack small or isolated government forces. In Phase Three, the insurgent forces become large and powerful and together with the Vietnamese *"khoi nghi"* (the general uprising of the people), the government is overthrown.[84] As noted earlier, the North Vietnamese modified this strategy in 1963 when they sent NVA cadres to the NLF in the South and, again, in 1964 when they sent regular NVA units to the South and, most notably, in 1965, when they launched a major offensive operation against the US Army's 1st Cavalry Division in the Ia Drang Valley. The forces of North Vietnam suffered heavy losses in terms of both men and equipment, on the order of 10 to 1, at the hands of the 1st Cavalry Division. The loss of 305 men killed in action, as suffered by the 1st Cavalry Division, are also considered very heavy by American standards.

The American high command concluded that at this 10 to 1 ratio, we, the Americans, could beat them. The North Vietnamese high commands concluded that even though they will lose many soldiers, they, the North Vietnamese, could cause great losses to the Americans and in the end, win the long struggle.

As we examined the battle for Ripcord from the viewpoint of Hanoi, we concluded that there had been a shift in strategy with the North Vietnamese moving more deliberately to the offensive. More recent research has revealed an American naiveté; indeed, it clearly illuminates the American government's blindness and stupidity. Lieutenant General Nguyen Van Vinh (a South-erner), Deputy Chief of Staff of the People's Army of Vietnam, also served as the Director of the Reunification Department of the *Lao Dong* Party in Hanoi. Vinh wrote in the February 1966 *Hoc Tap*, the official journal of the *Lao Dong* Party, an article entitled, "The Vietnamese People On The Road to Victory." Donald S. Zagoria, in his book, *Vietnam Triangle*, published in 1967, has summarized General Vinh's sanguine outlook on the situation in South Vietnam as follows:[85]

1. An alien army is incapable of pacifying South Vietnam.

2. The NLF armed forces can bring about the disintegration of the Saigon army and thus leave military action wholly in the hands of the United States forces, exposing once and for all the foreign "imperial-ist" nature of the war and strengthening the NLF appeal for a popu-larly-backed united front.

3. The widespread United States bombing of North Vietnam is ineffec-tual against a war effort based on a primarily agricultural economy.

4. The NLF can inflict an increasingly heavy toll of casualties on the American forces, thereby strengthening American domestic pressure for a settlement.

5. The number of American troops actively fighting in South Vietnam will never be sufficiently large to reach the ten-to-one (or greater) ratio required to defeat a guerilla force.

It is terribly disappointing and disturbing that information such as the above quote, and much more, being readily available to the American public and to the government in 1966 and 1967 and that our national civilian and military leadership failed in their duties to develop a rational and effective win or end strategy. This failure cost 30,000 American and over a million Viet-namese lives in Vietnam during 1968–1972.

The shift in strategy to the offensive that we saw in our operational area in 1970 had its roots well into the past. It was not strategic outlook that determined the PAVN operations on the battlefield, but the hard cold reality of resources.

After the Ia Drang Valley battle of late 1965, it took two years for the Central Military Committee and the Politburo to order another major offensive—Tet in January 1968. This time the losses were even more horrendous; especially to the Viet Cong/National Liberation Front forces. Whether this was a deliberate, expected, and welcome outcome for the Central Military Committee and Politburo in Hanoi continues to be debated today.

Then in 1970, slightly more than two years after Tet 1968, the Central Military Committee and the Politburo again decided to take the offensive. In addition to the two years for NVA recovery, the offensive in the Ripcord area occurred after the Marines had disengaged and withdrawn from the area, the major withdrawal of US forces from Vietnam was well underway with the first US Army division, the 9th Infantry, starting withdrawal one year before the Ripcord battle. Also significant to the overall strategic situation with the withdrawal of US forces, were major redeployment shifts of South Vietnamese forces. The 101st Airborne Division was the last full strength American division in Vietnam.

The Paris Peace talks had been ongoing for over a year and a half. The Politburo in Hanoi well remembered the disruption of the Ho Chi Minh Trail, just one year earlier, when the 101st Airborne Division established fire support bases on the high ground along both sides of the A Shau significantly interdicting that portion of the Ho Chi Minh Trail. The PAVN illustrated their determination to defend that area no matter the cost in lives at Dong Ap Bia—Hamburger Hill.

The Politburo also gained some confidence for planning their next offensive as a result of Pham Van Dong's visit to Beijing in March 1970. Zhou Enlai assured Dong that Lon Nol would not send his Cambodian forces against the North Vietnamese sanctuaries.[86]

We asked each of our interviewees why the offensive pressure continued in the Ripcord area when in the past when the PAVN forces would strike and then when US/ARVN forces made a strong counterstrike, the PAVN would fade back into the jungle for a substantial period to recover. But most notably, starting 1 July 1970, the PAVN applied continuous offensive pressure. What happened to the old guerrilla tactic of, "You come, we go. You go, we come?" The interviewees all answered the same. They replied that they were ordered to conduct continuous offensive actions to control the high ground that protected the Ho Chi Minh Trail. The purpose was to kill the Americans so they would more quickly withdraw from Vietnam. When asked the question who ordered this offensive in the Zone 4 area, they responded unequivocally, the "Central Military Committee in Ha Noi—Gen VO NGUYEN GIAP." This strategy of Hanoi applied equally to the Ripcord battlefield, as well as, to the American public opinion. Ironically, due to the denial of the area to the news media, the PAVN paid dearly at Ripcord for virtually no public opinion gain. American public opinion was not concerned about what they did not know.

The writing of General Giap in January 1970 helped us to understand the shift in strategy of the North Vietnamese. Giap believed that the war would become, ultimately, a conventional conflict, with big divisions clashing in showdown battles. Giap wrote: "Great strides would be made only through *regular war* in which the main forces fight in a concentrated manner" (his italics).[87] This helps to explain the clarity with which the North Vietnamese officers that we interviewed seemed to understand their mission. After all, with General Giap personally in command, they remembered Dien Bien Phu where 50,000 Viet Minh concentrated to face 16,000 French troops. And they thought of losing 23,000 in that one fight was as a reasonable price to pay for victory.

We have learned that a much broader battle area than Ripcord changed at this time. From "The Southern Laos—Route 9 Counter-Offensive Campaign—1971,"

Robert Destatte has translated the following summary:

> In June 1970, the PAVN high command began to reinforce the 968th Infantry Division (responsible for ground operations to secure the Ho Chi Minh Trail through Laos). In July 1970, the Central Party Military Affairs Committee directed the integration of HQs of Group 559 and the 968th Division to simplify command and control in Central and South Laos. By September 1970, the main force units of the high command and MR5 had confirmed their tactical plans and began conducting practice maneuvers.[88]
>
> In October 1970, the high command directed the establishment of Binh Doan 70 [B.70, which was equivalent to a combat corps command]. Binh Doan 70 included the 304th, 308th, and 320th Infantry Divisions and units from the various branches. These units were the core of the mobile combat force and the core of the campaign operations. By mid-October 1970, basic preparations were complete. The PAVN high command, however, was concerned about a possible major US/RVNAF strike across the DMZ into southern MR4, and had some reservations about the readiness status of units responsible for defending that area [i.e., units of B.5 Front

(the DMZ and northern Quang Tri Province area) and MR 4 units located in southern MR4].[89]

Hanoi was making big plans and FSB Ripcord was in their way. So—they took the offensive and brought the fight to us and stayed with us. That is until we most wisely, thanks to Brigadier General Sid Berry, withdrew from Ripcord on 23 July.

Keith Nolan's book, **RIPCORD**, describes the 23 July 1970 extraction and withdrawal in riveting detail.

At the 24 October 1987 Ripcord Association Reunion, Chuck Hawkins asked General Berry, "Did we know, did we understand what the enemy really intended? Did we have a sense that they were trying to get to the lowlands, or did they simply want to embarrass some American or Vietnamese units?"

General Berry responded, "I think, yes, their long-range aim was to get to the lowlands and the population. But I think they absolutely intended to eliminate the Americans on and around Ripcord. It seems to me that the whole focus of their gathering at Ripcord is the hole in the doughnut. And if they had been able to eliminate an American unit and seize that firebase, I think—and this is my guess too—I think they thought that would have speeded the disillusionment of the American people and American members of Congress with our being in Vietnam, and would have led to a stronger demand that we come out more quickly. But again, we both are recognizing that as a long-range aim, as always, they looked at the control of the country and its people. But I think elimination of Ripcord and the people on and around it was one of their intermediate steps."[90]

Our interviews of June 2001 in Vietnam with PAVN officers who were in the Ripcord area in 1970, confirm General Berry's belief at the time, but most of the PAVN officers clearly indicated that controlling the high ground along the A Shau Valley/Ho Chi Minh Trail was their first priority.

A North Vietnamese Strategic Pattern?

Looking back at the long war in Vietnam, the NVA did not launch a major offensive (Tet 1968) for two years after their very large losses in the Ia Drang Valley in November 1965. The NVA did not launch a major offensive (Ripcord 1970) for two years after their very large losses in Tet 1968. The NVA did not launch a major offensive (Easter Offensive 1972) for two years after their very large losses at Ripcord in June-July 1970. That is what I call a tactical and strategic victory for the 3rd Brigade, for the 101st Airborne Division and for the US Army! Mission accomplished!

*   *   *

Irrespective of how history is recorded, happy young children seem to glow as illustrated by these three who just caught a goldfish in Westlake in Hanoi in front of our hotel on 6 June 2001.

Happy Kids in Hanoi!

13

Hanoi's Allies

The News Media—

It should not be surprising that North Vietnamese strategy was influenced to a considerable degree by foreign news media including the media agencies and personnel of the United States.

In 1962, the number of US advisors in Vietnam increased from 700 to 12,000. (1963 witnessed the addition of another 3000 advisors.) Along with this extraordinary increase in American military activity in Vietnam, came representatives of the news media. Many observers and veterans of the Vietnam War blame the news media for being *a*, if not *the*, major reason for our failures in Vietnam. Most of these observers have a point of reference around the time of the 1968 Tet offensive when the Viet Cong suffered massive losses, but the news media seemed to interpret the situation as America losing the war. However, critical reporting by U.S. and international news media began long before 1968. Present in Vietnam in 1962 were: Homer Bigart of the *New York Times* followed by David Halberstam, Neil Sheehan of UPI, Nick Turner of Reuters, Peter Arnett of AP, et al.

One of the first major operations with U.S. participation occurred on Thanksgiving Day 1962, when forty-five American helicopters with over two hundred American air crewmen and advisors on board, launched an attack on a suspected VC base near Saigon. The South Vietnamese military did not want news media coverage and U.S. Ambassador Nolting and MACV Commander, General Harkins, honored this. David Halberstam became so outraged that he reported in the *Times,*

The reason given is security. This is, of course, stupid, naïve and indeed insulting to the patriotism and intelligence of every American newspaperman and every American newspaper represented here. You can bet the V.C. knew what was happening. You can bet Hanoi knew what was happening.[91]

Halberstam, while at the American Embassy Fourth of July picnic in 1963 refused to shake hands with MACV Commander General Paul D. Harkins. On one occasion at a restaurant, he slammed his fist on the table and shouted, "Paul D. Harkins should be court-martialed and shot."[92]

Mieczyslaw Maneli, a Polish member of the International Control Commission, was very impressed with the outspoken hostility towards the American embassy displayed by Halberstam and Sheehan. A. J. Langguth reported that while visiting in Hanoi, "Maneli urged Pham Van Dong to grant Halberstam and Sheehan visas and let them enter North Vietnam. Dong refused saying. "We are not interested in building up the prestige of American journalists." Maneli suspected that Hanoi leadership worried that accurate reports from the North would help the Pentagon to improve its strategy. He knew that Giap had once described the American Joint Chiefs as even less expert in fighting Vietnam's kind of war than the French had been, and slower to learn from their mistakes. Dong said, "The United States could be defeated sooner if it did not get tips from its journalists."[93]

The strategy of North Vietnam seemed keenly and continuously focused on American public opinion. When Stephen Young visited in Paris in 1995, he asked Colonel Bui Tin (the North Vietnamese officer who officially received the surrender of South Vietnam in 1975) how they intended to defeat American forces, to which Bui replied: "By fighting a long war which would break their will to help South Vietnam." Bui Tin quoted Ho Chi Minh as saying:

We don't need to win military victories, we only need to hit them until they give up and get out." In explaining the importance of the anti-war movement in the United States, Colonel Bui Tin said: "It was essential to our strategy. Support for the war from our rear was completely secure while the American rear was vulnerable. Every day our leadership would listen to world news over the radio at 9 a.m. to follow the growth of the American antiwar movement. Visits to Hanoi by people like Jane Fonda and former Attorney General Ramsey Clark and church ministers gave us confidence that we should hold on in the face of battlefield reverses. We were elated when Jane Fonda, wearing a red Vietnamese dress, said at a press conference that she was ashamed of American actions in the war and that she would struggle along with us.

He further stated that the Politburo paid attention to these visits by Americans to Hanoi because: "Those people represented the conscience of America. The conscience of America was part of its war-making capability, and we were turning that power in our favor. America lost because of its democracy; through dissent and protest it lost the ability to mobilize a will to win."[94]

Lieutenant Colonel Frank Miller, the US Defense Attaché in Hanoi in 2001–2002, proved especially helpful in my research for this book. In response to my question about Russian and other influence on North Vietnamese strategy, Colonel Miller responded in January 2002:

> While the Vietnamese have been adamant in the past that they received no help, recent events involving the discovery of a North Korean pilots' cemetery and other pressure from China have forced them to back down.
>
> The key for the Russians is the timing, since advisors and observers from many different countries were here [North Vietnam] at different times. The Cuban presence is well known. Less known, though, is the presence of Indian advisors in the DMZ area.

The Soviet Union and China—

It is difficult to get an accurate picture of Russian and Chinese influence on North Vietnamese strategy simply because it changed frequently. The Chinese were an early and major supporter/supplier of North Vietnam, e.g., in 1962 alone, the *Viet Cong* guerrillas were supplied with over ninety thousand rifles and machine guns.[95] Some of these were delivered directly to the South by Chinese ships. Even well before this, the arrival of the Chinese at the border of Vietnam in November and December 1949 provided the decisive change that altered the balance of logistics in favor of the *Viet Minh* against the French. Notwithstanding this timely and critical help, centuries of mistrust and hostility between China and Vietnam were again made fresh when China supported the French at the Geneva Conference in 1954. China's Chairman Mao Tse-tung, urged Vietnam to fight the traditional struggle of protracted conflict. This suggestion seemed to serve Mao's own purpose by tying down the Vietnamese in a protracted conflict, conserving his own forces, and placing an increased military and political burden on the United States.

China brought its engineers into the area north of Hanoi beginning in July 1965. Numerous Chinese soldiers manned and equipped antiaircraft positions, which they previously established. The mutual distrust of the Chinese and North Vietnamese manifested itself in the Chinese fortifying these positions against their neighbors on the ground as well as against the attacking American aircraft. For their part, the Vietnamese stole equipment and supplies from the Chinese at every opportunity. The Chinese troop strength in North Vietnam probably peaked at about 70,000. A periodic rotation of these troops would see about 300,000 Chinese participating in the war.[96] Ilya V. Gaiduk placed the number of Chinese in North Vietnam in 1967 as between 60,000 to 100,000. Kent Sears has refined this number:[97] "China has opened its records on the number of uniformed Chinese troops sent to aid their Communist friends in Hanoi. In all, China sent 327,000 uniformed troops to North Vietnam. Chinese historian Chen Jian wrote "Although Beijing's support may have fallen short of Hanoi's expectations, without this support, the history, even the outcome, of the Vietnam War might have been different."

In addition to the very substantial military equipment and large numbers of troops China provided North Vietnam, the North Vietnamese aircraft were allowed to safely land at Chinese bases when being pursued by Americans.

The Vietnamese openly welcomed and praised the help from China, yet never trusted them. Prime Minister Pham Van Dong expressed the true feeling about China when he said Mao "was always ready to fight to the last Vietnamese."[98] Of course the world knew China was not genuine in their support of North Vietnam when China in February 1972 embraced President Nixon and later, when China actually invaded Vietnam's northern border in February 1979. Some observers have theorized that the attack of Vietnam by China may also have been in retaliation for Vietnam's 1978 attack of Pol Pot, China's ally.

Former senior PAVN staff officer Colonel Bui Tin said: "The Chinese believed in fighting only with guerillas, but we had a different approach. The Chinese were reluctant to help us. Soviet aid made the war possible. Le Duan (Secretary General of the Vietnamese Communist party) once told Mao Tsetung that if you help us, we are sure to win; if you don't, we will still win, but we will have to sacrifice one or two million more soldiers to do so."[99]

The Chinese repeatedly stated their support of the Communist Party of North Vietnam, but consistently in terms of people's revolutions and wars of liberation over time. An article by Marshal Lin Piao appearing in the September 3, 1965 issue of the Peking Review is probably reflects the best-known statement of Chinese policy in support of North Vietnam. Donald S. Zagoria stated that the article may have been intended "to serve notice on the West of China's expansionist ambitions and can therefore be reasonably compared with Hitler's *Mein Kampf*."[100]

Several North Vietnamese leaders made speeches and issued statements rejecting the Chinese approach to people's liberation. The consistent theme from the North Vietnamese stated that only by taking the offensive could the North Vietnamese defeat the Americans and their Saigon puppets.

The North Vietnamese began to look more and more towards the Soviet Union for support of their struggle to unite the two Vietnams.

The Russians supplied large quantities of sophisticated and expensive military equipment and training for the North Vietnamese Army, Air Force and Navy. The first shipments from the Soviets began in January 1965. The support grew rapidly and steadily and by 1968 accounted for fifty percent of all socialist aid. According to classified reports from the Soviet Embassy in Hanoi, their aid amounted to over $582 million US dollars by 1968.[101]

It is fascinating to note that this great influx of Soviet aid (1965 to 1967) occurred at the same time that the North Vietnamese replaced the Soviet advisors in their intelligence offices with Chinese and recalled Vietnamese then training in the Soviet Union. In 1967, the North Vietnamese again flipped, ordering out the Chinese advisors, and replacing them once again with Soviets.

An example of the political acumen of the North Vietnamese in dealing with both the Soviets and the Chinese can best be illustrated when the Chinese refused to allow the transit of Soviet supplies to North Vietnam across the Chinese roads and railways in 1967. The North Vietnamese Communists gained an agreement whereby they would receive the Soviet shipments at the Soviet-Chinese border and escort the shipments across China to the North Vietnamese border.

Kent Sears concluded:

> At the height of the War, the Soviet Union had some 55,000 'Advisors' in North Vietnam. They were installing air defense systems, building, operating and maintaining SAM (Surface to Air Missiles) sites, plus they provided training and logistical support for the North Vietnamese military.[102] Sears also reported that General Van Tien Dung's 1975 final campaign 'was supported by a total of 700 (maneuverable) Soviet tanks', i.e. Soviet armor, burning Soviet gas and firing Soviet ammunition.[103]

The Soviet Union received some pretty good payback from the North Vietnamese in the form of US military equipment and weaponry that they turned over to the Soviets for exploitation. Between May 1965 and early 1967, more than seven hundred pieces of US military equipment, including parts of aircraft, missiles, radar, and photoreconnaissance equipment were delivered to the Soviet Union from North Vietnam.[104] Notwithstanding this impressive amount of US military equipment turned over to the Soviets, the North Vietnamese repeatedly violated the agreement to turn over equipment. A specific case involved a downed F-111, an item that remained a point of high-level negotiation between Marshal Grechko and General Pham Van Dong.[105]

A North Vietnamese journalist and a Soviet journalist concluded in January 1968 that the Soviet Union supplied about seventy-five to eighty percent of all assistance received, yet wielded only about four or five percent of influence on Hanoi policies.[106]

Also of major significance, the Soviet Union provided extensive construction equipment necessary to vastly improve the throughput of the Ho Chi Minh Trail. As always, it remained the position of the Soviet Union to encourage and support wars of liberation, but privately, the Russians urged the Vietnamese to refrain from trying to "liberate" South Vietnam. The Kremlin preferred to preach Soviet peaceful coexistence with the United States, the hated enemy of the Vietnamese.

Robert Destatte prepared a "talking points" paper about foreign involvement with American prisoners of war for the Chairman of the Joint Chiefs of Staff in August 1990. Bob updated and removed classified information 16 September 1996. This paper details some of the frequently changing relationships between the Communist Triangle—Moscow/Peking/Hanoi.

Its instructive and illuminating points are provided below:[107]

> GENERAL: Until the early 1990s the Socialist Republic of Vietnam (SRV) intelligence and security services relied on the Soviet, East German, Cuban, Czech, Hungarian, Polish, and Bulgarian state security services for various types of operational, training, and technical support. The relationships were limited primarily to technical assistance and exchanges of information.
>
> Prior to 1979, as a general rule, the Vietnamese did not permit Soviet KGB and GRU advisers to enter Vietnamese Ministry of Interior and military intelligence facilities and working areas. The Vietnamese limited Soviet intelligence advisors to meetings with department heads and office chiefs in designated visitor reception areas.

After the 1979 border war with China, the relationship experienced some changes, and KGB/GRU contacts with Socialist Republic of Vietnam services increased across the board. For example, by mid-1980, Soviet GRU personnel were working closely with, and reportedly supervising some People's Army of Vietnam Signal Intelligence components. These changes, however, are not relevant to the wartime relationships that effected Soviet access to American POWs.

HISTORY OF THE SOCIALIST REPUBLIC OF VIETNAM'S RELATIONSHIP WITH THE SOVIETS AND CHINESE:

During the first Indochina War (1945–1954), the People's Republic of China (PRC) was the primary foreign advisor to the Vietnamese intelligence and security services.

In 1951, the first Soviet advisers appeared in Vietnam.

In 1954, Soviet KGB advisors replaced Chinese advisers.

In 1958, a Soviet KGB advisory group arrived in Hanoi to assist the Vietnamese Ministry of Public Security [renamed the Ministry of Interior in June 1975]. Soviet KGB advisers were assigned to each staff-line department of the Vietnamese Ministry of Public Security as well as the People's Army of Vietnam's (PAVN's) Military Security Department. Soviet GRU advisers were assigned to the General Research Department [i.e., Military Intelligence Department], of the PAVN General Staff.

In 1959, the Vietnamese Ministry of Public Security and the KGB concluded an agreement for Vietnamese personnel to receive training in the Soviet Union.

By late 1963, Vietnamese Communist Party officials had become alarmed by KGB recruitment operations against Vietnamese party officials and trainees in the Soviet Union. In 1964, Vietnamese authorities recalled all Ministry of Public Security and Military Intelligence Department trainees from the Soviet Union; initiated an investigation of all officials who had received training in the Soviet Union or who had close contacts with Soviet intelligence; and began a general tightening up of security. The investigation and subsequent actions became known in Vietnamese circles as the "H Affair"

Between 1965 and 1967, the PRC Ministry of Public Security replaced the Soviet Union as the primary foreign adviser to the Vietnamese intelligence and security services. Ultimately caught in the middle of the Sino-Soviet conflict and the turmoil caused by the Chinese Cultural Revolution, Hanoi decided to limit PRC influence and ordered PRC advisers withdrawn. KGB advisers replaced the PRC advisers in 1967.

The "H Affair" reached a denouement of sorts when Vietnamese authorities began arresting people in August 1967. By March 1968 they had arrested more than 300 senior party and military officers, including two Central Committee members and several colonels. As of 1974, at least 15 of these persons remained in prison or under house arrest.

SOVIET BLOC AND CHINESE ACCESS TO AMERICAN POWs:

The KGB provided Vietnamese services military and political information about the U.S. and helped them draw up questionnaires for interrogating U.S. POWs. Although Hanoi accepted requirements from the Soviets and the Chinese and provided sanitized interrogation reports to them, Hanoi never allowed either the Soviet KGB and GRU, or the Chinese Ministry of Public Security to interrogate U.S. POWs.

The Vietnamese permitted a Russian KGB officer named Nichiporenko to speak with a CIA officer for 2–3 hours shortly before the officer was released from the Hanoi POW camps in 1973. The CIA officer characterized the incident as a rambling conversation, rather than an interrogation.

Another CIA officer, named Lewis, who was captured by PAVN forces during the final offensive in April 1975, reported that although he was never questioned by any Soviets, the detailed nature of the questions the Vietnamese asked led him to suspect that the Soviets were involved in preparing the questions.

There also was an incident in which a newly captured American pilot was questioned in the presence of a Caucasian at an air defense site near the point of capture in North Vietnam.

There were a few instances in which Chinese air defense troops operating north of Hanoi conducted superficial tactical interrogations of a POW immediately after capture; however, we are not aware of any other instances in which Chinese were permitted to interrogate an American POW.

Two Caucasian interrogators who appear to have been Cubans were introduced into one prison (the Zoo) in Hanoi in August 1967. The introduction of the apparent Cubans coincided with the expulsion of Chinese intelligence advisers and appears to be a manifestation of Vietnam's reorientation toward the Soviet Bloc for advice and assistance in August 1967. The POWs nicknamed the activities of the apparent Cuban interrogators the "Cuban Program." One of these interrogators subjected most of the 19 American POWs in the "Cuban program" to brutal mistreatment, which led to the death of one of the 19 POWs. The program ended in about July 1968.

CONCLUSIONS:

American POWs encountered foreign news representatives, a small number of alleged Soviet and East European personnel, and a few superficial tactical interrogations by Chinese who captured American air crewmen north of Hanoi (Chinese gun crews were active in that area); however, the "Cuban Program" marked the first and only time that non-Vietnamese were overtly involved in the direct exploitation of American POWs.

Hanoi apparently accepted requirements from the Soviets and the Chinese and provided sanitized interrogation reports to them. Soviet, Chinese, and other communist bloc personnel did assist the North Vietnamese in many military related functions, but had only rare and casual contact with American POWs. To the best of our knowledge, with the exceptions just noted, Hanoi never allowed the KGB, GRU, or Chinese Ministry of Public Security to have direct access to U.S. POWs.

While the Soviets undoubtedly were interested, the Vietnamese apparently were not willing to permit Soviet personnel to interrogate U.S. POWs. In view of the history of their relationship, illustrated by the "H Affair," it is not surprising that the Vietnamese did not permit the Soviets to have direct access to our POWs.

Cuban Support—

Cuba really wanted to help the enemy of the United States at that time—North Vietnam. Cuba's help certainly could not match of the magnitude of the Soviet Union or China, but, nonetheless, proved substantial and came at a critical time. When Robert Walz, owner and operator of Last Frontiers Expeditions and Safaris, based in Boulder, Colorado, learned of my interest in the Cuban connection with North Vietnam, he said he would arrange for me to meet in March 2002 with a Cuban in Havana who had spent considerable time in North Vietnam during the war.

Roberto Salas is a world-renowned photographer. Roberto is a friend, personal photographer and biographer of Fidel Castro. He co-authored the book, *Fidel's Cuba*, published in the United States in 1998.

Salas was in North Vietnam 1966–67 and went into Laos in 1968 via Dien Bien Phu. He returned to North Vietnam in 1972. Roberto speaks fluent English and seems exceptionally well qualified in American cuss words. I went to his studio at 9 AM the morning after our big party with Fidel Castro on Friday night, 1 March 2002. When I arrived he informed me that he did not get in from the Fidel party until 5:30 that morning. He regretted that we did not meet on Friday as planned as he personally wanted to introduce me to Castro.

Salas said he did not specialize in "spot news photography," but tended to go for the lasting and artistic opportunities. All of the work I saw in his studio was done using black and white photography. He did not have any pictures of fighting in Vietnam. The closest thing he had was the picture below with NVA soldiers raising their AK-47s skyward. He said the picture showed the spirit and dedication of the soldiers willing to die for what they believed in. It became obvious that he had never been in combat with a small unit himself to learn what soldiers really fight for.

Roberto Salas in Quang Binh, North Vietnam took the above picture in 1972. Quang Binh is the southernmost province of what was North Vietnam.

The Fahey/Klein Studio in Los Angeles had offered this print signed by Roberto Salas, for sale for $1200. (All of Salas's prints were priced for at least $1200. Communism pays for some people.)

Salas said his travels were somewhat restricted as his North Vietnamese hosts were concerned about his safety. A guide/escort, a driver and a bodyguard always accompanied him. Salas traveled down to the DMZ and looked south across the bridge over the Ben Hai River.

Castro continued his intense interest in supporting the North Vietnamese and his determination to visit the "war front" in South Vietnam finally materialized in September 1973. Vivo writes according to Destatte's translation, that Prime Minister Pham Van Dong and General Vo Nguyen Giap accompanied Castro's delegation to Quang Tri Province in the South. The delegation departed Hanoi's Gia Lam airport aboard an AN-24, and after a 1 hour and 15 minute flight landed in Dong Hoi, the capital city of Quang Binh Province. From Dong Hoi, the delegation traveled 40 kilometers by "jeep" to Vinh Linh, and from there continued down to Dong Ha town, Quang Tri Province—the destination "of Castro's dreams." As an aside, Vivo writes that Castro slept less than two hours a day during this final week of his visit to Vietnam. While in Quang Tri, Castro traveled out Highway 9 to "high point 241, which the Vietnamese call "Tam Lam" [sic] Base." [Note: this was the old US/SVN Camp Carroll Combat Base] Here Castro and his delegation met with PAVN troops. After his visit with PAVN troops at the old Camp Carroll Combat Base, Castro and his delegation returned on Highway 9 to a former US/SVN base at Cam Lo Town.

Thăm các chiến sỹ QĐND Việt Nam trên đường Hồ Chi Minh (1973)

The Vietnamese caption is translated to "…Visiting combatants of the People's Army of Vietnam on the Ho Chi Minh Trail (1973)."

Robert Destatte notes that Vivo claims in Chapter VII that Cuban Ambassadors in various countries and the innumerable agents that Cuba dispatched to foreign countries initiated all of the international movements in support of Vietnam. The number of scholarships in Cuba for students from Vietnam increased. The fates of the two countries became bound together in thousands of ways, including technological fields and in particular cinematography.

Fascinating, in that of all of the senior leaders of the Socialist Republic of Vietnam, in their many speeches and writings, no one gives credit for the Liberation of all of Vietnam to anyone except the people of Vietnam. On the other hand, Cuban writer and former Ambassador Raul Valdes Vivo says Cuba arranged for support of the Liberation of Vietnam from countries all over the world. (See, Appendix E.)

Douglas Pike reported that apparently, Hanoi and Havana enjoyed a uniquely close relationship. In its external relations, the National Liberation Front placed Cuba second only to the NLF's relations with Hanoi. And since the NLF seems an extension of, rather than separate from, the government in Hanoi, one could argue that Hanoi considered Cuba its closest fraternal socialist ally. Cuba sent its first aid to the NLF in February 1965.[108]

The Soviet Union with 55,000 advisors/workers, thousands of heavy weapons, vehicles, ammunition and other vital equipment, supplies and spare parts clearly must be North Vietnam's greatest supporter and bill payer. China also provided massive aid and material and alternated as one of North Vietnam's most influential advisors and supporters. The ebb and flow of Soviet versus Chinese support and influence will long continue to be a rich and complex area of study for historians for many decades. Cuba earned its place as a major contributor to the success of the North Vietnamese by its consistent support in embassies throughout the world and its major construction effort on the Ho Chi Minh Trail in 1973–1974 which accelerated Hanoi's march to victory.

This massive and sustained foreign support to the communist government of North Vietnam and the paramount importance that Hanoi placed on the Ho Chi Minh Trail, manifested itself in the 3rd Brigade 101st Airborne Division Area of Operations in 1970 by the determination of PAVN forces to spend whatever lives needed to deny us the mountain ridges controlling the A Shau Valley and the high ground around FSB Ripcord.

14

Hanoi's Distortions

Vietnamese Xenophobia—

Half a century after the Vietnamese overthrew the French hold on their country, we see Vietnamese xenophobia combining with Communist dogma to produce a grossly distorted history of the Vietnam War. General Van Tien Dung's book, *Our Great Spring Victory*, presents an interesting example of this phenomenon. Dung praises the great strategy of the Party Central Committee and the brilliant and timely decisions of both the Politburo and the Central Military Committee. He repeatedly brags about the large forces of the People's Army with their modern equipment and technological weapons. He never, never mentions or gives credit any place in the book to the Soviet Union or any foreign power for the billions of dollars worth of equipment, the large training cadres operating in Vietnam and the many schools and training courses hosted in the Soviet Union and Cuba. The Russians provided virtually all of the jet aircraft and sophisticated air defense weapons and, yet, the words "Soviet" or "Russian" are not found anywhere in the book. The preferred Vietnamese Communist view exemplifies a great victory for the Central Party Committee as Dung reports that on April 29, 1970, "In this final day of the period determined by the Political Bureau for the liberation of Saigon, the fighters wrote on their helmets, on their sleeves, on their gun slings the immortal proclamation of President Ho Chi Minh: *Forward! Total victory is ours!*"[109]

The subject of Russian/Soviet influence came up during our discussions with Ambassador Douglas B. (Pete) Peterson at the US Embassy in Hanoi.

Peterson, a former POW, became the first US ambassador to the Socialist Republic of Vietnam. Ambassador Peterson explained that not giving credit to any other country represented their normal behavior. He emphasized that the Russians now hate the Vietnamese and added that the Russians are very bitter.

Dung proved equally careful to never use the words "South Vietnam or SVN." For him, the Republic of Vietnam (RVN) never existed; nor did the former Army of the Republic of Vietnam (ARVN). The government officials of SVN are referred to asd the American lackeys or American puppets. The ARVN are often called Saigon troops, or Saigon's generals, or Saigon's 23rd Division, etc. He never once recognizes that South Vietnam existed although he talks of things in the south.[110]

Stanley Karnow observed, on a visit to Vietnam in 1981, "a land not only ravaged by a generation of almost uninterrupted conflict. But governed by an inept and repressive regime incompetent to cope with the challenge of recovery."[111] Twenty years later, on our visit to the American Embassy in Hanoi, Ambassador Peterson told us that the government of Vietnam proved grossly inept, still.

The real shocker came when Ambassador Peterson candidly informed us that there no one was really in charge of the government. He said there was no one to whom he could go to really get anything done. How could this be in a totalitarian state? Peterson further stated that in addition to the lethargic bureaucracy, the National Assembly consistently blocked most all attempts to modernize and effectively govern the country. There are clear signs that the individual politicians are guarding their power and control to enrich themselves and their families. The National Assembly, composed primarily of local party bosses, many of whom make their fortune by graft and extortion. Maybe they learned something from the United States politicians after all?

Distortion and Propaganda—

The National Military Museum in Ho Chi Minh City (formerly Saigon) has a large, very nicely done addition built in 1996. It is a Requiem for photographers and artists killed in the Vietnam War. The exhibits are quite impressive—awesome, spectacular, dramatic, horrifying, and sickening. Unfortunately, exceptionally talented Communist propagandists provided the captions for the exhibits. The new building represents a world class exhibit for Communist hagiography and propaganda. To most Americans who read the captions for the first time, they are quick to recognize the ridiculous or patently unbelievable. Even though few Americans actually see the exhibits, thousands of Vietnamese school children and tourists from other countries read these captions daily and probably believe most of what they say.

It is very interesting to note that severe cleavages exist within Vietnam today. Membership in the *Lao Dong* (Communist) Party is 5:1 in favor of the Northerners. Country-wide, only three percent of the eighty million people of Vietnam belong to the Communist Party. The Northerners remain staunchly Communist while the South maintains clear differences. Only legitimate members of the Communist Party are eligible to vote in elections thus maintaining total control now as they did in the Vietnam War with the United States.

One exhibit at the museum, although not in the Requiem building, presented a mannequin dressed in US Army fatigues, a US helmet, sergeant's stripes, a M-16 rifle in his hand and, on his chest, the wings of a Master Aviator, clearly a misrepresentation of facts.

A large number of books and articles about the Vietnam War have been published by agencies of the Socialist Republic of Vietnam or licensed publishing organizations. It was disappointing to learn from experts, like Robert Destatte and Courtney Frobenius, who have read many of these books, that just because it is an "official" history or government publication, it may not be true and/or accurate. In most cases it clearly will be inaccurate if that is what is needed to make the Party and the Socialist Republic look good. This has certainly been the case concerning the battle for Ripcord.

It was not until 1997 that the government acknowledged that the North Vietnamese military suffered 1.6 million killed.[112]

Former CIA analyst Merle L. Pribbenow points out in his enlightening article, "The Fog of War: The Vietnamese View of the Ia Drang Battle," the wild extent some Vietnamese "historians" have gone to in reporting misleading and inaccurate battle results. He uses "The Plei Me Victory: Looking Back after 30 Years." Military History Institute and 3rd Corps 1995, and "The 304 Division, Vol. II 1990;" both published by the People's Army Publishing House in Hanoi, to illustrate several distortions and unfounded conclusions.[113]

The propensity to see things as one chooses to is not limited to the Communists. Stanley Karnow reported that, "When McNamara made the first of his many trips to Vietnam in May 1962, he looked at the figures and concluded optimistically after only forty-eight hours in the country that "every quantitative measurement…shows that we are winning the war."[114]

Interpreter Nguyen Ba Bang informed us that Colonel Nguyen Ba Van thought that the War Records Center in Quang Tri had a great deal of information, i.e., maps, journals, etc., pertaining to the battles in the Ripcord area. Colonel Van visited Quang Tri on my behalf, but said he could not gain any information without the permission of the Minister of Defense. We thought we had this well in hand with a request through the American ambassador and the Minister of Foreign Affairs. My interest in the Quang Tri War Records Center was mentioned several times in email correspondence with the Foreign Press Center of the Ministry of Foreign Affairs. There was never any specific response with reference to the Quang Tri War Records Center. The records are probably still "Top Secret."

In early discussions with Colonel Dinh in Ho Chi Minh City, I said that I hoped he would be of assistance in getting information when we visited the War Records Center in his neighboring city of Quang Tri. He gave a blank stare (which is not unusual in communicating with someone not quickly fluent in your language) and then said that yes, he had many friends in Quang Tri. Finally on our third day in Hue, Colonel Dinh said that we could visit Quang Tri and try and find the War Records Center, but they probably would have records pertaining only to some of their local forces. The big hope for a bonanza at the Quang Tri War Records Center ended in yet another frustrating disappointment. I was learning what Courtney Frobenius had told me, "Any difficult subject is approached in the same manner: Without comment!" Colonel Van had told me that my mission was too difficult because it involved national secrets.

The bureaucratic barriers encountered in our search for the view from Hanoi alerted us to the fact that it would be difficult to find and talk with the right people and these "right" people might not tell us the truth or the whole truth. The Socialist Republic of Vietnam is a totalitarian government operated in accordance with the dogma of the Communist Party. Everyone is suspect. Nothing is more important than sustaining the Central Party in power.

The soldiers of the PAVN learned that from day one, big brother was watching. Every soldier became a member of a three-person cell. Everyday he is subjected to the practice of *Kiem Thao*. Each member of the three-person cell evaluates the words and actions of him and the other two cell members and delivers daily critiques of all. In addition to self-confession and self-criticism, the soldier learns respect for others and confidence in his leaders. The cell members are told to give to each other the same loyalty and support expected of brothers.[115]

There is a Department of Internal Affairs that watches all other government Departments, the entire population and all foreign visitors. My request for a visit and my requests for interviews had to be cleared through this Ministry of Internal Affairs. Military officers "retired" for many years still come under the authority of the Minister of Defense and are directly controlled by the appropriate military branches and agencies.

Internal security remains tight, as it must in a Communist state. There still is unrest in the Central Highlands, especially among the native Montagnards. Concern for internal security probably also comes from the fact that it has been only five years since the uprising in Thai Binh Province, just south of Hanoi. The uprising was general and widespread and the People's Army was called out to restore order. The area remained "off limits" to foreign visitors for six months.[116] Like any police state, Vietnam maintains internal security by fear and constant surveillance.

Local police stations keep "family books" on who lives in each house. No one can stay in that house except the occupants listed in the book. If a friend comes to town, you must go to the police station and register him as a guest, if the police approve, then he can sleep there.

Thanks to a tip from Bob Destatte, in his DoD capacity of expert in POW and MIA affairs, I made a request for North Vietnamese News Agency (VNA) photographs, allegedly made at Ripcord in 1970. The request, presented to the Joint Task Force-Full Accounting, Commander in Chief, Pacific, Headquarters, Camp H. M. Smith, Hawaii, had been filled when the JTF-FA Headquarters had received seven photos in February 2001 in response to their request to the government of Vietnam in connection with the case of the missing bodies of Spc Howard and PFC Beals, D Co, 2/506th Inf.

Five of the seven photographs showed bodies alleged to be Americans killed on Hill 935. This was the designation used by the PAVN for Fire Support Base Ripcord. The number "935" is the elevation in meters of this high point as shown on the old French maps used by the PAVN.

The PAVN never penetrated FSB Ripcord while US forces occupied it. In the fast-paced withdrawal from Ripcord, with incoming shells exploding and dust everywhere, there was one American body in a body bag mistakenly left on Ripcord, which had been later recovered intact. There is no way that the Vietnamese News Agency could have taken photographs of American soldiers killed on Hill 935, they just weren't there.

In the photograph (MN 7466) shown below, the Vietnamese News Agency caption read, *"During the campaign to surround and pressure high point 935, Liberation Troops shot down 97 American aircraft. The UH-1D Combat helicopter wreckage was set afire."* Note the North Vietnamese soldier (upper left in the photo) scrounging around in the wreckage.

(JTF-FA)

Photo by Vietnamese News Agency alleged to have been taken on FSB Ripcord.

The claim that 97 American aircraft were destroyed at Hill 935 (Ripcord) is patently preposterous and propaganda in the extreme!

We had three aircraft destroyed at Ripcord: a CH-47 shot down on 8 July; another CH-47 shot down on 17 July; and the third CH-47, lost during the extraction on 23 July—a very, very long way from 97 aircraft being destroyed at Ripcord.

The losses and damages to Army helicopters during the siege of Ripcord, while significant, never approached the numbers claimed by the PAVN. Only the Chinooks listed above were actually shot down on the firebase. For the four-month plus period, a total of six helicopters were destroyed by combat actions. In a letter from Headquarters, 101st Airborne Division to the Commanding General, XXIV corps, dated 23 July 1970, the following losses and damages were sustained in the Ripcord area from 13 March through 23 July:

UH1H (Huey)

    Destroyed: 3   Major Damage: 10   Minor damage: 13

OH6A (Scout)

    Destroyed: 1   Major Damage: 4   Minor damage: 1

CH47 (Chinook)

    Destroyed: 2   Major Damage: 3   Minor damage: 5

60 aircraft received combat damage requiring minor repair.

In preceding chapters, there were numerous claims made by the North Vietnamese of US casualties and equipment destroyed. One document ridiculously claimed that 2000 US soldiers had been killed and 170 aircraft destroyed by the end of June. In addition to these numbers, it was stated that during the 1–23 July siege, 1700 US soldiers were killed and 97 aircraft destroyed for total claims of 4100 US KIA and 267 aircraft destroyed.

The facts are that we suffered 175 US KIA by the end of June and lost another 75 soldiers during the siege for total number of 250 US KIA. By the end of June, we reported 3 aircraft destroyed and 7 with major damage. During the siege we lost an additional 3 aircraft and had 10 more with major damage for totals of 6 destroyed and 17 with major damage for the entire four-month battle in the Ripcord area.

The next photograph from the Vietnamese News Agency (MN 7451) shows two PAVN soldiers walking or running in the jungle passing a body lying face-up on the ground. There is a helmet beside the body and an M-16 rifle without a magazine resting on what appears to be a log or tree root. The JTF-FA experts judged that "both the helmet and the rifle appear to have been placed in their positions rather than randomly falling where they lay." The Vietnamese News Agency caption read: "Bodies of American Soldiers Annihilated on High Point 935." This is, of course, ludicrous as no vegetation whatsoever grew on Hill 935 (Ripcord)

(JTF-FA)

Photo by Vietnamese News Agency alleged to be on
Hill 935 (FSB Ripcord)

Interviews with North Vietnamese Army Officers—

It was reported earlier that five of the six officers we interviewed in 2001 had
been the Deputy Commander and Political Officer of their unit at one time
during their army service. The Vietnamese government authority assumed
that Political Officers would know the "correct" answers.

I asked Brigadier General Bui Pham Ky, Deputy Commander and Political
Officer of the 324B Division in 1970, if they gained much intelligence from
our Kit Carson Scouts. He hesitated and I repeated Kit Carson Scouts—further stating that they were former North Vietnamese soldiers or Viet Cong
National Liberation Front soldiers who had either *Chu Hoi'd* under the surrender program or had been captured and put through special training and
then assigned to American frontline fighting units. Ky responded that he was
in our area for five years and commanded two divisions and he never heard of
Kit Carson Scouts. And that, dear reader, represents what might be called the
Party Line.[117]

General Ky knew about General Zais at Hamburger Hill. It remains illogi-
cal and simply impossible for General Ky not to have heard of Kit Carson
Scouts. General Ky did not want to admit that: a North Vietnamese soldier

would ever betray the North and work for the "American puppets"; that they, the NVA, had been unable to gain intelligence from these former soldiers of the North; and that they were profoundly embarrassed by the large numbers of them. In 1969 alone, more than 47,000 former enemy soldiers rallied to the side of the South Vietnam government.

There were three interviews where the Ministry of Foreign Affairs provided the interpreter and three interviews where Colonel Dinh acted as our interpreter. The interviews with the Ministry of Foreign Affairs interpreters were noticeably more constrained and reserved. The interviewees remained guarded and answered slowly and deliberately. With only Colonel Dinh present, the interviewees appeared warm, receptive, and anxious to try and answer our questions.

The Enigma of Colonel Pham Van Dinh—

Colonel Pham Van Dinh is a bit of an enigma and should be discussed in this chapter dealing with possible obfuscation and distortion. Dinh is significantly taller than the average Vietnamese soldier. On our 2001 visit, he still stood ramrod straight with shoulders back and chin in. Dinh first came to the attention of American officers in the 101st Airborne Division as the leader, trainer and first commander of the *Hoc Bao*. The *Hoc Bao* or Black Panthers were a 200-man strong company assigned to Headquarters, 1st Infantry Division in Hue City. They wore Black Berets and were equal to the best of our elite Ranger and Special Forces troops: Airborne and super gung ho!

Then a major, the spotlight seemed to find Dinh (or he found it). In the fight for Dong Ap Bia-Hamburger Hill, Major Dinh led an ARVN attack and he was the first soldier to reach the mountain's peak. During Tet 1968, the 2nd Brigade 101st Airborne Division and the 1st Infantry Division, ARVN, recaptured Hue. Major Dinh was photographed climbing to the top of the big flagpole at the Citadel in Hue City as he hauled down the North Vietnamese Red Star and raised the flag of the Republic of Vietnam.

After turning over command of the 3rd Brigade, 101st Airborne Division in December 1970 (and getting my much cherished Army Commendation Medal), I became the Senior Advisor to Brigadier General Pham Van Phu, Commanding General, 1st Infantry Division, ARVN, with Headquarters in Hue City. Major Pham Van Dinh was then the Executive Officer of the 54th Infantry Regiment, of the 1st Infantry Division, ARVN. Because of his great reputation, extra height, and always-present Black Beret, I remembered him.

At one point in my advisor tour with them, the entire division had a searing experience during Operation Lam Son 719 into Laos in 1971. The 1st Infantry Division, ARVN, took many, many casualties (KIA,MIA, and POW); losing one regimental commander and five battalion commanders KIA.

After Lam Son 719 two of the five regiments in the 1st Infantry Division were moved to the newly created 3rd Infantry Division along the Demilitarized Zone (DMZ). Dinh, promoted to lieutenant colonel, received command of the 56th Infantry Regiment, a newly formed unit. In mid-March 1972, the 56th Regt replaced the 2nd Regt at Camp Carroll. As the 56th Regimental Commander, LTC Dinh also assumed command of Camp Carroll, the bastion for the defense of South Vietnam from any invasion by the North Vietnamese across the DMZ.

On 30 March 1972, two years after the last major offensive of the North Vietnamese (centered on the FSB Ripcord area), the North Vietnamese again went on the offensive. The NVA launched multiple attacks across the DMZ in what is known as the Easter Offensive of 1972. The precise timing could have been keyed on the exchange of regiments at Camp Carroll.

Camp Carroll was well designed and heavily fortified (recall this was also the alternate CP for our 3rd Brigade, 101st Airborne Division). There were 21 pieces of artillery at Carroll, including four 175mm guns. (These were transferred to the ARVN upon the withdrawal of the US Army artillery unit from Vietnam). The battle, or non-battle, of Camp Carroll has been well documented and interestingly covered by Colonel G. H. Turley, USMC, Retired, in his extraordinary book, *The Easter Offensive*,[118] and by Dale Andrade in his fine book, *Trial By Fire: The 1972 Easter Offensive*.[119]

The NVA attacked all across the DMZ. The American advisory net became very busy as Dinh's advisor, Lt Col Bill Camper, US Army, reported that he had been unable to consult with then Lt Col Dinh. Camper tried to enter a conference room where he understood Dinh had met with his officers, but the Vietnamese regimental executive officer blocked Camper from entering.[120]

By noon on Easter Sunday, Camp Carroll and the 1500 South Vietnamese soldiers in and around Carroll, had withstood several artillery bombardments and three ground attacks. Suddenly, the shelling stopped. Lt Col Dinh went to the underground bunker of the American advisors and informed them of his plan to surrender and asked the Americans to join him. The American officers refused and suggested a plan to breakout of the encirclement using the two M-41 tanks and three other tracked vehicles. Dinh quickly stopped them saying that it would not work. Dinh suggested that the Americans walk out with them for the surrender and try to slip away in the tall grass. Lt Col Camper said they would not surrender and would find a way out.[121]

Lt Col Camper, his assistant, Major Joe Brown, US Army, and their ARVN radio operators left the fortress and were immediately pinned down by PAVN rifle fire. They received a radio call from the American advisory team at the 3rd ARVN Division headquarters saying that a US Army CH-47 Chinook, then delivering artillery re-supply to Mai Loc (just two kilometers south of them), would come over to pick them up. Camper advised the Chinook pilot to land at the "chopper pad inside Camp Carroll as it would be impossible for him to make a pick-up at their pinned down location. The advisory team slipped back into Carroll and they and about 100 ARVN soldiers escaped on the Chinook. Camper personally beat off any ARVN soldier that tried to board without his individual weapon.[122]

Not all of the South Vietnamese military surrendered at Camp Carroll. The South Vietnamese Marine artillery battery at Camp Carroll radioed their commander that they would not surrender. This brave Marine battery lowered its guns and fired point blank into the North Vietnamese soldiers walking in through the front gates of Camp Carroll! They fought to the last Marine. *Semper Fi*!!

As we visited the Army Museum in Hanoi and Colonel Dinh showed us the 175 from Camp Carroll, I indicated that I was aware of the surrender. Colonel Dinh immediately began to tell me how he personally called in a Chinook helicopter to take out his advisors so they would not be taken by the NVA, certainly not the way Lt Col Camper remembers the surrender.

I am still uncertain of Colonel Dinh's status. He owns a small hotel near his home in Hue City where he renovated the hotel restaurant. I sent Dinh some questions by email. A few days later, in his return email, he apologized for his slow response because the PAVN had him working in Quang Tri. He added, "I just come from Quang Tri two days ago. As you know, I 'm still working in Army, not retired."

(Author)

Old French Hoa Lo Prison—Later the Hanoi Hilton for POWs

We thought it a bit strange that on three occasions, one in Ho Chi Minh City and twice in Hanoi, Dinh came to our hotel and called from the lobby. I asked him to come up to the room each time. He would not leave the lobby. Dinh apparently believed he was being observed.

On 2–3 June 2002 I visited with Colonel Dinh in Hattiesburg, Mississippi. Professor Andrew Wiest, University of Southern Mississippi is the Director of the nationally recognized and honored Studies Abroad Program for Vietnam et al. Professor Wiest and USM arranged for Colonel Dinh to spend one month at the University for the purpose of conducting interviews and lectures. Professor Wiest, author of military history books, is writing a book about Colonel Dinh and I expect the enigma will soon be solved. Shortly after Colonel Dinh returned to Vietnam, we received word that he had a stroke and could not communicate in any way. Late in 2003 we learned that Colonel Dinh had begun a slow recovery from the stroke. We had a good visit in Colonel Dinh's nice new home in Hue in June 2004. He looks good and understands what you are saying, but cannot talk. His right arm and right leg are limp. His recovery continues.

15

Operations of the 308 and 325 Divisions

During the June 2001 interview, Brigadier General Duong Ba Nuoi, Deputy Commander of Zone 4 in 1970, made strong statements that, in the Ripcord area, the 324B and the 304B Divisions would "stay", and that the 308 and 325 Divisions would "come and go." Zone 4 included; Thua Tien, Quang Tri, Quang Binh, and Ha Tinh Provinces with the headquarters located in Vinh, North Vietnam. The North Vietnamese also knew Zone 4 as Military Region 4.

The very limited intelligence that we received in the 3rd Brigade spoke only of the 29th and 803rd Regiments of the 324B Division and the 6th Regiment (Regional Force) independent force committed to the Ripcord battle. Chapters 2 through 8 described the operations of the 324B Division in the Ripcord area.

To complete "The View From Hanoi," we needed the records of not only the 324B Division and the 6th Regiment; we needed to also obtain the records of the 304B Division, 308 Division, and the 325 Division. Lieutenant Colonel Frank Miller, US Defense Attaché, American Embassy, Hanoi, put me in touch with Ken Conboy in Jakarta, Indonesia.

Ken Conboy does security assessments in Indonesia and is a published military historian of battles in Southeast Asia. Ken was kind and gracious enough (with relay help from his wife, Janet, in Cincinnati, Ohio) to provide me with the pertinent parts of the histories of the 304 Division and the 325 Division.

207

The 308 Division—

Notwithstanding the repeated insistence by Brigadier General Duong Ba Nuoi that the 308 division came and went during the Ripcord battle, we obtained no evidence which proved 308 Division units direct involvement during the Ripcord battle in 1970.

Lieutenant Colonel Frank Miller located the "official" history of the 308 Division. He bought it in a used bookstore and sent it to me for our use. Trang Frobenius, wife of Courtney Frobenius, interpreted the history of the 308 Division and concluded that:

> In October 1970, the 308th was in training in North Vietnam (Chuong My, Thach That, Quoc Oai and Ba Vi [due west of Hanoi] and at the Da River at Hoa Binh; also in Xuan Mai and Nui Muc. All of these places are in North Vietnam, west and to the southwest of Hanoi.
>
> During Tet 1970, the 308th was working on flood protection (dikes) at Tu Hy Hung and the Tich River at Thach Dat and Ha Tay (all in the North).
>
> In May 1970, Army Corps B-70 was formed, on paper, which included the 308th, 304th and 320th Divisions along with supporting units. All of these divisions were veteran divisions of the PAVN, having fought in the French campaigns. On 7 September 1970, inspecting cadres began the trip for reconnaissance of the zones south along Road 9.
>
> Half-month later [approximately 22 September 1970]: Regiment 88, leading the 308th, moved from Ha Tay to Hung Nguyen Nghe An and then to Thach Ban Quang Binh; the division followed." Preparations began for the PAVN Counter Offensive to Lam Son 719. Yet again, another sign of increased aggressiveness on the part of the PAVN to take the fight to the US forces in our operational area.

(*The fact that this information appears in the official history is truly interesting because Operation Lam Son 719, which was supposed to be Top Secret, was not launched until 8 February 1971.*)

The 325 Division—

Bob Destatte translated the entire 325 Division published history some time ago. The following paragraphs summarize the 325th Division's activities during 1970. "The division apparently sent one or more replacement battalions to Region Tri-Thien-Hue (B4 Front) sometime between October 1969 and March 1970. There was no indication that any replacement battalion trained

by the 325th Division took part in the battle for Ripcord. Destatte does conclude that some of these fourteen infantry battalions were in a reinforcing
position for the nine to twelve 324B infantry battalions in the Ripcord area.
This would allow the commander of the 324B Division to be more daring in
the commitment of his resources against Ripcord. (The 101st Airborne Division had only eight infantry battalions.)

Bob reported:

> There were several generations of the 325th Division. For example, the
> 325A (18A, 95A, 101A Regiments) arrived in the Western Highlands
> Front (B3 Front) in March 1965. Meanwhile the 325B was formed and
> began training for movement to the South. The 101B Regt arrived in the
> Western Highlands Front as an independent regiment in September 1965.
> The 325B (18B, 95B, 101C Regiments) arrived in B3 Front in May 1966.
> With the arrival of the 325B, the 325A was disbanded and its cadre and
> component units reassigned to new duties and missions. Among the seven
> regiments of the first two 325 Divisions (A and B), only the 18A (aka
> E.12) and 95B remained in the Western Highlands and Region 5 (B1
> Front) until April 1975. The 101A Regiment (aka E.16) moved down to
> Eastern Nam Bo (MR7 in B2 Front) immediately after the 1966 Spring-
> Summer phase of operations in the Western Highlands. The 33rd Regi-
> ment (i.e., the 101B and 101C Regiments) moved down to operate in
> Eastern Nam Bo at the end of 1968. The 95A Regiment (aka E.10) and
> the 18B (aka E.20) moved down to Eastern Nam Bo at the end of 1968,
> and then down to the Mekong Delta at the end of 1969.
>
> By 1968 the 325th was in its fourth generation, the 325D Division.
> After the spring 1969 phase of operations in Quang Tri Province, the 95D
> Regiment withdrew to Quang Binh Province, NVN. After completing its
> mission to help expand the Truong Son Road (HCM Trail), the 18D Reg-
> iment returned to Quang Binh Province. The division was preparing to
> move the 101E Regiment down to Quang Tri to open the next phase of
> operations in the summer of 1969, when it received orders converting the
> division to a training unit—its new mission would be to form and train
> replacement units for the Southern theaters.
>
> The division's new mission notwithstanding, the Central Party Military
> Affairs Committee and the General Political Directorate of PAVN gave
> clear guidance that the division would remain a mobile main force unit and
> must be ready to carry out combat missions in the various theaters. In the
> summer of 1969, the division made changes in its table of organization and
> equipment appropriate to its new training mission. However, the division
> and regimental staff elements retained their old tables of organization and
> equipment so they could be ready at all times to revert to a mobile main
> force division.

The division disbanded its supporting arms units and converted them into infantry units, and reorganized its combat battalions into 16 replacement battalions. On 18 July 1969 these battalions began the training program that would prepare them to march off to become replacement units in the South. During the autumn and winter of 1969, the division sent these 16 battalions to reinforce the various fronts in the South.

The 3rd and 15th Battalions of the 101E Regiment departed their home base on 16 October 1969, en route to the Nam Bo (the Southern Region, aka B2 Front). Between the end of October and the beginning of March 1970, the division sent the remaining 14 battalions, one by one, south to reinforce Nam Bo (B2 Front), the Western Highlands Front (B3 Front), Region 5 (B1 Front), and Region Tri-Thien (B4 Front). [Although there is no specific mention of the battalions of the 325 Division participating in the Ripcord battles, some of these remaining 14 battalions were in a reinforcing position in the Ripcord area. These battalions in a "reinforcing position" meant to the 3rd Brigade, 101st Airborne Division, that the 324B Division and the 6th Regiment would be in a much stronger position to attack and keep offensive pressure on FSB Ripcord and the 3rd Brigade units operating in the field around Ripcord.]

The Southern Fronts" requirements continued to increase. At the beginning of 1970, the Ministry of Defense assigned to the division cadre for 15 battalions, moved the division up to Thanh Hoa Province, and instructed it to build a new division. The 15 groups of battalion cadre included three groups from Military Region 3, three groups from the Left Bank Military Region, three groups from Military Region 4, two groups from the Viet Bac Military Region, two groups from the Navy Headquarters, one group from Headquarters Artillery Command, and one group from Headquarters Sapper Command.

During May 1970, the division's cadre spread out to recruit troops from nine provinces and 25 ministries and general directorates that included 310 national and regional agencies. The division took in 5,672 new recruits during the first recruiting drive. The new recruits included 377 Party members, 4,758 Party Youth Group members, 688 soldiers with college educations, and 1,892 who were high school graduates. This force was organized into nine training battalions. During the second recruiting phase the division selected men from Hanoi and the universities. The division received nearly 2,000 new soldiers during the second recruiting phase. The division organized these new recruits were into three training battalions.

In mid-September 1970, the 1st and 8th Battalions departed to reinforce units serving in Central and Southern Laos. During November and December 1970, the division sent an additional eight battalions into battle. The 3rd Battalion traveled the greatest distance. After an exceptionally arduous foot march that covered a distance of nearly 1,600 kilometers, with the men carrying all their equipment on their shoulders, the unit arrived at the Highway 4—Kampong Saom Front where they became replacements for the 101D and 95A Regiments performing "international duty" helping Hanoi's friends in Southern Cambodia.

At the end of 1970, two battalions remained in the division. At the direction of the General Staff, the division modified the 18th Battalion's training and table of organization and equipment so that it could operate as an independent battalion. At the end of February 1971, the 18th Battalion moved down to the Mekong Delta where it took part in continuous fighting. In March 1971, the division dispatched its last replacement battalion and received orders to move its regiments up to Ha Bac Province and continue its training missions.

(*This look at the 325 Division does not provide any detailed information on the operations of the Division in the Tri-Thien Theater; just the possibility of support of the replacement battalions sent to the area. It does give us an interesting view of the process of reconstitution of a PAVN division by recruitment and the creation of replacement battalions. And it has addressed Brigadier General Duong Ba Nuoi's assertion that the 325 and 308 Divisions always "come and go" in our operational area.*)

Epilogue

Much has been learned about the North Vietnamese Army with respect to the battle for Ripcord. Regrettably, there is still much we do not know. We will, probably, never know the truth, and certainly not the whole truth. This is the reality of life in the Socialistic Republic of Vietnam with its totalitarian rule; ever present fear of individuals of their own government and no mandate for the preservation of an accurate account of history. Instead, there is a mandate to alter, obfuscate, change and distort both history and reality to serve the needs of the *Lao Dong* Party (the Communist Vietnam Worker's Party).

The "official" histories of PAVN units against whom we fought fail miserably as true historical documents. But even in their distorted, manipulated reporting, they do contribute to our understanding of our battles. For that, we are grateful. The strategic importance of FSB Ripcord is clearly stated in the 324B Division history: "Hill 935 (FSB Ripcord) was located in the mountain jungles of Phong Dien district. The top of the hill was approximately 350 meters wide by 550 meters long, and it was the key to opening our route back down to the lowlands."

Courtney Frobenius reports that the only battles lionized by the Vietnamese are those in which they won, or claim to have won, a great victory: Ap Bac, Hamburger Hill, Cu Chi, the beginning of the 1972 Nguyen Hue (Easter) Offensive, the final Ho Chi Minh 1975 Offensive, etc. The simple fact that the Ripcord battle has remained unreported or at least under reported by the Vietnamese press says nothing less than it proved a vast and embarrassing failure from the perspective of the North Vietnamese.

Robert Destatte comments that:

> In 1997 I interviewed a retired Russian air defense officer in Latvia, who had been an advisor to a Vietnamese Surface-to-Air-Missile Regiment in the southern region of NVN (Nghe An, Ha Tinh, Quang Binh Provinces)

in 1970–71. The regiment he advised took part in PAVN's campaign to counter our Operation Lam Son 719 in the Highway 9 corridor in Laos in early 1971. The North Vietnamese would not even permit him and the other advisors to the regiment to carry maps with them. The advisors had to rely largely on road signs and conversations with their counterparts and local residents to learn where they were. The actions that the Russian officer described illustrated the Vietnamese's obsessive secrecy and security consciousness.

The North Vietnamese officers interviewed, including General Doi, repeatedly denied that they ever had any foreign officers advising or accompanying any of their units.

As distorted and convoluted as the North Vietnamese histories may be, we have learned some important things about their Communist Party and the People's Army of Vietnam:

- The 324B Division and the 6th Thua Thein Regiment operated in strength in the Ripcord, Coc Muen, Hills 805, 902 and 1000 area long before the first air assaults by the 3rd Brigade in March 1970.

- The PAVN in the general Ripcord AO had already established underground bunker complexes, gun and mortar emplacements, supply caches and medical facilities.

- The 324B Division was given a division mission (their first-ever division mission) to "up root" and destroy FSB Ripcord with all division assets reinforced by the 6th Thua Thein Regiment and the 7th Sapper Battalion with the 304B Division in support.

- Hanoi's leaders never wavered from their conviction that the United States would fold and eventually leave South Vietnam.

- Hanoi believed it imperative to take the offensive against the Americans to accelerate their withdrawal no matter the cost to themselves in human lives.

- The North Vietnamese forces operating in the South in 1970 literally had been starving in their base areas in the mountain jungles. They had lost a great deal of support from local Viet Cong infrastructure primarily due to the exhaustion of VC resources, men and material during the 1968 Tet Offensive and, as a direct result of the subsequent effectiveness of the

Phuong Hoang (Phoenix) Program, which began in 1968, got underway in 1969, and was in full swing by1970. These two factors combined, cleaved the rice producing coastal littoral areas from the supply chain, which led to the Highland redoubts of the NVA.

- They greatly feared our helicopter gunships and respected our airmobile tactics.

- Their primary strategic concern focused on maintaining the flow of men and materials down the Ho Chi Minh Trail and keeping open the supply chain from the coastal lowlands to the highlands to feed their troops.

- The North Vietnamese could not have won in the next several decades without the support of the Soviet Union and/or China.

- The PAVN with its great concentration of men and supporting firepower and its singular mission, never once penetrated the defensive perimeter of FSB Ripcord.

- The mission to destroy FSB O'Reilly, a less formidable firebase than Ripcord, was also a failure of the significantly weakened 324B Division. O'Reilly was closed at the beginning of the monsoon season as earlier planned by the ARVN.

- Even though positioned in the nearby area, the crippled 324B Division played no significant role in the critical and strategically important PAVN 1971 Counter Offensive to Lam Son 719.

Having read a draft version of this Epilogue, Courtney Frobenius stated:

> I am certain that both the brass and a great many of the men would have wanted to fight the final battle of Ripcord—and win it, certainly—but the overall political environment of withdrawal, Vietnamization and holding down US casualties foreclosed on that command decision. Why I think the battle was so victorious for the US, was that you denied them what they sought most, a political victory at a very critical juncture of the war, for had they been able to achieve getting to the top of the hill, the withdrawal process most certainly would have been vastly accelerated and the Vietnamization program all but aborted, which is exactly what they wanted. They wanted us out of there in the worst way and as fast as possible; that, I believe, is why they expended so much treasure on you. They just didn't

expend that much treasure unless there was a strategic objective in view. In the end, they were in no shape to secure the plains of Hue as they had hoped, and were so bloodied they were withdrawn from active offense, thus gaining critical time for the RVN (which they didn't take adequate advantage of).

There were very few significant engagements fought from the decision to begin withdrawal, starting in May 1969, until withdrawal was actually finally affected, by December 1972; Ripcord stands as a monument of success during that entire period of the time. It was a very major contributor to their second offensive of the war (the *Nguyen Hue* or Easter Offensive) being delayed until March 1972, nearly two-full years after the battle of Ripcord had been fought. Without the success of Ripcord that offensive would have been advanced a full year.

We most tragically lost too many of our comrades during the battle for Ripcord and the final siege. As I stated in Chapter 10, my estimate of the price the North Vietnamese paid during the siege of Ripcord from at least eight infantry battalions, four artillery battalions, four 120mm mortar companies, one anti-aircraft battalion, one sapper battalion (reinforced), three machine gun companies, and thousands of porters and support troops from the 304B Division was a minimum of 2400 killed and several thousand more wounded. This estimate is based on their order of battle, our many fire fights, the horrendous pounding by our gunships, artillery, mortars, quad-fifties, tac air and B-52 bombers for twenty days and nights plus the saturation fires after our withdrawal, and my interviews with Colonel Le Ma Luong and Major Ho Van Thuoc when no representatives of the Ministry of the Interior (secret police), Ministry of Defense nor Ministry of Foreign Affairs were present.

We still don't know the precise details of how the PAVN leaders and soldiers fought at Ripcord or their actual losses (no Vietnamese histories or documents ever mention any of their losses in any of their battles), but that does not alter the great pride we feel for the way our own American soldiers fought for their buddies, their unit and their country. God Bless each and every one of them!

We had many, many heroes on the 3rd Brigade team during the March-August battle for Ripcord. Special recognition is due the following Medal of Honor and Distinguished Service Cross recipients:

Medal of Honor:

Private First Class David Coleman Kays, D Co, 1/506th Inf	7 May 1970
Lt Col Andre Cavaro Lucas, Hq, 2/506th Inf (Posthumous Award)	23 Jul 1970
Cpl Frank Rocco Fratellenico, B Co, 2/502nd Inf (Posthumous Award)	20 Aug 1970

Distinguished Service Cross:

Platoon Sergeant William Lawrence, Jr., C Co, 2/501st	9 Apr 1970
Sergeant First Class Jesse A. Isaac, B Co, 1/506th Inf	25 Apr 1970
Private First Class Kenneth J. David, D co, 1/506th Inf	7 May 1970
Captain David F. Rich, B Btry, 2/319th Arty	5–17 Jul 1970
Sergeant John W. Kreckel, A Co, 2/506th (Posthumous Award)	22 Jul 1970

As I look at the names of our KIA listed below, I don't compare the numbers of enemy KIA or their loss ratio of more than thirty to one during the siege, but believe that our price paid was far too high.

Note: "Date KIA 19700312" is year, 1970, month 03 Mar and date 12 for Mar 12, 1970.

Last Name	First & Middle	Rank	Date KIA	Company	Battalion	Regiment
DAVIS	DUDLEY	1LT	19700312	A Co	2nd Bn	506th Inf
HEATER	DANIEL NEIL	SP4	19700312	A Co	2nd Bn	506th Inf
SHANOR	GERALD DELMAR	CPL	19700312	A Co	2nd Bn	506th Inf
GOOSEN	ROBERT HENRY	SP4	19700313	A Co	2nd Bn	501st Inf
JACKSON	BENJAMIN FRANKLIN	SP4	19700313	E Co	2nd Bn	501st Inf
DOBSON	CECIL LEE	SP4	19700314	A Co	1st Bn	506th Inf
HAUSWIRTH	GERALD RICHARD	1LT	19700314	A Co	1st Bn	506th Inf
CARSON	PAUL DAVID	SGT	19700315	A Co	2nd Bn	501st Inf
STANLEY	JAMES STEVEN	SP4	19700316	C Co	2nd Bn	506th Inf
GILBERTSON	CARL LOUIS	SP4	19700317	D Co	1st Bn	506th Inf
BLAKE	DALE ADAMS	PFC	19700320	C Co	1st Bn	506th Inf
DAVIS	JAMES LEONARD	SGT	19700320	C Co	1st Bn	506th Inf
HARRIS	HAROLD RAY	SP4	19700320	C Co	1st Bn	506th Inf
KNIEPER	PHILIP GEORGE JR	CPL	19700320	C Co	1st Bn	506th Inf
KURTH	JAMES PETER	SP4	19700320	C Co	1st Bn	506th Inf
LEONARD	RONALD FRED	SP4	19700320	C Co	1st Bn	506th Inf
LOVATO	RUDOLPH DANIEL	SP4	19700320	C Co	1st Bn	506th Inf
MC GUIRE	MICHAEL JOSEPH	PFC	19700320	C Co	1st Bn	506th Inf
STACEY	GARY ROSS	SP4	19700320	C Co	1st Bn	506th Inf
WALKER	WILLIE TERRY JR	SP4	19700320	C Co	1st Bn	506th Inf
WELLS	TINSLEY JACK JR	SP4	19700320	C Co	1st Bn	506th Inf
MORRILL	DENNIS LEROY	PFC	19700320	B Co	326th Engr Bn	
THOMPSON	ROBERT NOEL	PFC	19700320	B Co	326th Eng Bn	
WANTO	JOHN PAUL	SSG	19700321	A Co	1st Bn	506th Inf
SAMS	JOHN WILBUR JR	PFC	19700322	C Co	1st Bn	506th Inf
MC KEE	DONALD WAYNE	PFC	19700324	C Co	1st Bn	506th Inf
SHELL	MARVIN	SGT	19700326	B Co	2nd Bn	506th Inf
HAYES	HARRY ELLIS	1LT	19700331	B Co	2nd Bn	506th Inf
SHRINER	THOMAS JOHN	SSG	19700331	B Co	2nd Bn	506th Inf
TAPP	NEWTON LEE	PFC	19700331	B Co	2nd Bn	506th Inf
BARNETT	CARL EUGENE	CPL	19700401	C Co	2nd Bn	506th Inf
HEIMARK	DON RAY	SGT	19700401	C Co	2nd Bn	506th Inf
RAGSDALE	DONALD RAY O	CPL	19700401	C Co	2nd Bn	506th Inf
RATCLIFF	TERRY WARD	SSG	19700401	C Co	2nd Bn	506th Inf
UNDERDOWN	GEORGE MICHAEL	SGT	19700401	C Co	2nd Bn	506th Inf
WALL	WILLIAM PENN III	2LT	19700401	C Co	2nd Bn	506th Inf
SWAIN	MILTON TRUMAN	SP4	19700401	B Co	326th Engr Bn	
WILSON	JOHN WILLIAM	1LT	19700403	B Co	2nd Bn	506th Inf
CHRISTMAN	LAWRENCE PAUL	CPL	19700406	C Co	2nd Bn	506th Inf
GOODSON	CARL BRADFORD	SP4	19700406	C Co	2nd Bn	506th Inf
STEWARD	STEVE LEE	SGT	19700406	C Co	2nd Bn	506th Inf
FRINK	PAUL JOSEPH	SGT	19700407	D Co	1st Bn	506th Inf
OSBORN	LYNN ARTHUR	SP4	19700408	D Co	2nd Bn	506th Inf
CLAY	HERMAN ALLEN JR	CPL	19700409	B Co	2nd Bn	501st Inf
MACE	JAMES DOYLE	SSG	19700409	B Co	2nd Bn	501st Inf

NELSON	LEROY	CPL	19700409 B Co	2nd Bn	501st Inf
SELMAN	CHARLES GEORGE	CPL	19700409 E Co	2nd Bn	501st Inf
SISTRUNK	DONALD WAYNE	SSG	19700410 B Co	2nd Bn	501st Inf
KAYS	DAVID COLEMAN	PFC	19700410 A Co	1st Bn	506th Inf
BARTLEY	WALTER CARL JR	SGT	19700415 A Co	2nd Bn	506th Inf
DAFLER	DEAN BLAIN	SGT	19700415 A Co	2nd Bn	506th Inf
STEFFLER	CHARLES ERVIN	SGT	19700415 A Co	2nd Bn	506th Inf
YOUNG	BOBBY ARTHUR	SGT	19700415 A Co	2nd Bn	506th Inf
HEINZ	DENNIS RALPH	CPL	19700416 D Co	2nd Bn	501st Inf
PEERY	NORMAN DOUGLAS	CPL	19700417 B Co	2nd Bn	501st Inf
HAAKINSON	WILLIAM H III	SGT	19700418 A Co	1st Bn	506th Inf
FREY	DEAN LEE	SSG	19700419 A Co	2nd Bn	501st Inf
JARRETT	JAMES DALE	SSG	19700419 B Co	2nd Bn	501st Inf
JOSEPH	JEFFREY JOEL	SSG	19700419 B Co	2nd Bn	501st Inf
LOCKETT	JAMES EDWARD	SSG	19700420 C Co	1st Bn	506th Inf
LONGMIRE	KENT WILLIAM	SGT	19700420 C Co	1st Bn	506th Inf
NICKS	BENJAMIN ARNOLD III	SGT	19700423 E Co	2nd Bn	501st Inf
WORLEY	GARRY LEE	CPL	19700423 A Co	2nd Bn	501st Inf
CLINE	RONALD GREER	PFC	19700425 B Co	1st Bn	506th Inf
MAGEE	BOYD	SGT	19700425 C Co	1st Bn	506th Inf
SEBASTIAN	BILLY JOE	CPL	19700425 B Co	1st Bn	506th Inf
KOTROUS	EUDELL LEO	CPL	19700426 B Co	1st Bn	506th Inf
BERNER	EDGAR DAVIDSON	CWO	19700429 HHC		3rd Bde
KLAVES	JEFFREY JOHN	SP4	19700429 HHC		3rd Bde
BOGGS	ROBERT SIDNEY	CPL	19700429 A Co	2nd Bn	501st Inf
HUNTER	DENNIS WAYNE	CPL	19700429 A Co	2nd Bn	501st Inf
PATTEN	CARL EUGENE	CPL	19700429 A Co	2nd Bn	501st Inf
SNYDER	ROY HARRISON	SGT	19700429 A Co	2nd Bn	501st Inf
STIEVE	WILLIAM JOHN	SGT	19700429 A Co	2nd Bn	501st Inf
WALKER	LINWOOD ALFERONIA	CPL	19700429 E Co	2nd Bn	501st Inf
WORTMANN	FREDERICK EDWARD	SGT	19700429 A Co	2nd Bn	501st Inf
JONES	LARRY NEAL	SGT	19700430 E Co	2nd Bn	501st Inf
SHANNON	ROBERT JOSEPH	SGT	19700430 A Co	2nd Bn	501st Inf
HORTON	DONNIE EDWARD	SGT	19700430 A Co	2nd Bn	502nd Inf
TETKOSKI	LEON ANTHONY	SFC	19700430 A Co	1st Bn	506th Inf
BARRETT	JOHN HAROLD	SP4	19700501 B Co	1st Bn	506th Inf
COLLETT	ROBERT LEE JR	SSG	19700501 B Co	1st Bn	506th Inf
HENSHAW	LARRY ROY	SGT	19700501 B Co	1st Bn	506th Inf
HILL	JIMMY ARNOLD	SGT	19700501 B Co	1st Bn	506th Inf
KAUFMAN	THOMAS JAY	PFC	19700501 B Co	1st Bn	506th Inf
LANCE	SAMUEL STEPHEN	PFC	19700501 B Co	1st Bn	506th Inf
NOLT	CALVIN EUGENE	SP4	19700501 B Co	1st Bn	506th Inf
ANTLE	MICHAEL LOUIS	SGT	19700506 C Co	2nd Bn	501st Inf
BENNETT	GEORGE WILLY JR	CPL	19700506 A Co	2nd Bn	501st Inf
BOWMAN	MELVIN	SGT	19700506 C Co	2nd Bn	501st Inf
CHAVEZ	GREGORY ANTON	SGT	19700506 A Co	2nd Bn	501st Inf

DAY	DOUGLAS WAYNE	CPL	19700506	A Co	2nd Bn	501st Inf
DENTON	ROBERT ANTHONY	SSG	19700506	A Co	2nd Bn	501st Inf
DILLER	JAY THOMAS	SGT	19700506	C Co	2nd Bn	501st Inf
DOOLITTLE	JON HILIARE	SSG	19700506	C Co	2nd Bn	501st Inf
FOUTZ	KENNETH LEE	SSG	19700506	C Co	2nd Bn	501st Inf
GORDON	LAWRENCE LEE	CPL	19700506	A Co	2nd Bn	501st Inf
HAWLEY	RICHARD A JR	CPT	19700506	E Co	2nd Bn	501st Inf
HINDMAN	TOMMY IVAN	CPL	19700506	C Co	2nd Bn	501st Inf
JENNINGS	JAMES DALE	SGT	19700506	HHC	2nd Bn	501st Inf
LEWIS	FRANK FREDERICK	SGT	19700506	A Co	2nd Bn	501st Inf
LONG	RAYMOND LEON JR	CSM	19700506	HHC		3rd Bde
OGDEN	DAVID ELLIS	SSG	19700506	E Co	2nd Bn	501st Inf
REAGAN	DICKIE WALTER	SGT	19700506	E Co	2nd Bn	501st Inf
SNYDER	GARY FOSTER	SFC	19700506	A Co	2nd Bn	501st Inf
VAN BEUKERING	RONALD DALE	SP4	19700506	A Co	2nd Bn	501st Inf
VESER	EDWARD	SGT	19700506	E Co	2nd Bn	501st Inf
WARFIELD	PHILLIP RAY	CPL	19700506	C Co	2nd Bn	501st Inf
WIDEN	JOHN GEORGE	SGT	19700506	A Co	2nd Bn	501st Inf
WILLEY	JOHN JAMES	SSG	19700506	A Co	2nd Bn	501st Inf
ZIEGENFELDER	FREDERICK P	SSG	19700506	A Co	2nd Bn	501st Inf
BERGER	ROBERT FRANCIS	CPL	19700507	D Co	1st Bn	506th Inf
COOK	PETER ALLAN	PFC	19700507	D Co	1st Bn	506th Inf
FLETCHER	LAWRENCE EUGENE	1LT	19700507	D Co	1st Bn	506th Inf
GONZALEZ	JOSE ALBERTO	CPL	19700507	D Co	1st Bn	506th Inf
JACKSON	LLOYD WILNER	SGT	19700507	A Co	2nd Bn	506th Inf
LOHENRY	ROBERT RAYMOND	CPL	19700507	D Co	1st Bn	506th Inf
MC CRANIE	DAVID CARROLL	SGT	19700507	A Co	1st Bn	506th Inf
REDMOND	JOSEPH VERN	SSG	19700507	D Co	1st Bn	506th Inf
SMILEY	RONALD OWEN	1LT	19700510	D Co	1st Bn	506th Inf
MILBURN	ALBERT	SSG	19700511	D Co	2nd Bn	506th Inf
LOWE	ROBERT ERNEST	SGT	19700514	A Co	2nd Bn	506th Inf
CHRISTOPHERSON	DAVID LYN	CPL	19700516	A Co	2nd Bn	506th Inf
JONES	DAVID LAWRENCE	SSG	19700516	A Co	2nd Bn	506th Inf
MARIANI	JOHN ROY	CPL	19700516	A Co	2nd Bn	506th Inf
MAUNEY	GERALD CLINTON	SGT	19700516	A Co	2nd Bn	506th Inf
MC CULLOUGH	BILLY RAY	SGT	19700516	A Co	2nd Bn	506th Inf
DARLING	JOHN EDWARD JR	1LT	19700518	HHC	2nd Bn	506th Inf
STONE	HARRY JAMES	SGT	19700518	HHC	2nd Bn	506th Inf
JOHNSON	THOMAS WAYNE	CPL	19700519	D Co	1st Bn	506th Inf
GROSS	ALAN HARRY	CPL	19700523	A Co	1st Bn	506th Inf
SCHOFIELD	CECIL CLAYTON	SFC	19700523	A Co	1st Bn	506th Inf
VERLIHAY	FRANK T JR	1LT	19700523	A Co	1st Bn	506th Inf
SMITH	JERRY LYNN	1LT	19700525	D Co	1st Bn	506th Inf
NORRIS	WIELAND CLYDE	PFC	19700603	A Co	2nd Bn	506th Inf
SMITH	WINFRED LEE	SGT	19700608	A Co	2nd Bn	506th Inf
MADDOX	MARCUS WAYNE	CPL	19700616	D Co	2nd Bn	501st Inf

BUSH	MARK JOEL	SGT	19700622	HHC	1st Bn	506th Inf
BALDINI	MICHAEL LOUIS	CPL	19700623	D Co	1st Bn	506th Inf
ROWLEY	DONALD ALBERT	CPL	19700623	D Co	1st Bn	506th Inf
CAPUANO	GEORGE ANTHONY	SGT	19700624	A Co	1st Bn	506th Inf
HICKS	JAMES BEN	SGT	19700624	A Co	1st Bn	506th Inf
RINGHOLM	JOHN AZEL	CPL	19700624	A Co	1st Bn	506th Inf
BARNES	RICHARD LOUIS	CPL	19700625	A Co	1st Bn	506th Inf
MEEHAN	DALE PATRICK	CPL	19700625	A Co	1st Bn	506th Inf
RITTER	DENNIS LEE	CPL	19700625	A Co	1st Bn	506th Inf
SNIDER	MARVIN DALE	CPL	19700625	A Co	1st Bn	506th Inf
CAMBAS	VICTOR BYRON	SSG	19700626	B Co	1st Bn	506th Inf
CLIBURN	HALQUA DALE	SSG	19700626	B Co	1st Bn	506th Inf
GARZA	JOHN ANGEL	CPL	19700626	B Co	1st Bn	506th Inf
KOERNER	RODNEY LEE	CPL	19700626	B Co	1st Bn	506th Inf
MC DOWELL	GERALD LEE	SGT	19700627	B Co	1st Bn	506th Inf
CONRARDY	RICHARD JOHN	PFC	19700702	C Co	2nd Bn	506th Inf
HERNDON	THOMAS HAYDEN	SGT	19700702	C Co	2nd Bn	506th Inf
HEWITT	THOMAS THEODORE	CPT	19700702	C Co	2nd Bn	506th Inf
LENZ	LEE NEWLUN	SGT	19700702	E Co	2nd Bn	506th Inf
RADCLIFF	ROBERT PAUL JR	SP4	19700702	C Co	2nd Bn	506th Inf
SUMRALL	ROGER DALE	SGT	19700702	E Co	2nd Bn	506th Inf
ZOLLER	ROBERT WILLIAM II	SP4	19700702	C Co	2nd Bn	506th Inf
UTECHT	ROBERT STEPHEN	CPL	19700703	B Co	2nd Bn	506th Inf
MICKENS	CARL LAWRENCE	CPL	19700704	C Co	2nd Bn	501st Inf
ROBINSON	JIMMIE LEE	SGT	19700704	C Co	2nd Bn	501st Inf
SULLIVAN	WILLIAM LEE	1LT	19700704	C Co	2nd Bn	501st Inf
THADEN	GARY DENNIS	SGT	19700704	C Co	2nd Bn	501st Inf
LYONS	WILLIAM PERRY	SP4	19700704	A Co	2nd Bn	502nd Inf
RAY	WILLIAM CLAYTON	SGT	19700704	58th Inf Plt Scout Dog		
STONE	FOREST MICHAEL	SP4	19700705	D Trp	2nd Sqdn	17th Cav
WAYMIRE	MICHAEL KARL	SGT	19700705	C Co	2nd Bn	501st Inf
PORTER	SANDY HILLY	SSG	19700706	D Co	2nd Bn	506th Inf
GRIMM	MICHAEL JOSEPH	CPL	19700707	D Co	2nd Bn	506th Inf
RISINGER	GERALD LEE	SGT	19700707	D Co	2nd Bn	506th Inf
CRUSE	STANLEY JOE	SGT	19700708	Trp D	2nd Sqd	17th Cav
FRANK	HAROLD LEROY	SGT	19700708	Trp D	2nd Sqd	17th Cav
MC DERMOTT	JOSEPH F III	SP4	19700708	Trp D	2nd Sqd	17th Cav
MC EWING	HARRY	PFC	19700708	Trp D	2nd Sqd	17th Cav
STROUD	ALLEN RALPH	SSG	19700708	Trp D	2nd Sqd	17th Cav
WALKER	WALTER LEWIS	SFC	19700708	Trp D	2nd Sqd	17th Cav
HUPP	JAMES EARL	SP4	19700708	D Co	2nd Bn	506th Inf
SCOTT	RICKEY LEROY	CPL	19700708	D Co	2nd Bn	506th Inf
DODGE	GREGORY ALEXIS	SGT	19700709	E Co	2nd Bn	506th Inf
BOHAN	PATRICK JOHN	PFC	19700710	Trp D	2nd Sqd	17th Cav
DE FOOR	VICTOR LEE	CPL	19700710	Trp D	2nd Sqd	17th Cav
RAYMOND	FREDRICK CAROL JR	SP4	19700710	Trp D	2nd Sqd	17th Cav

HIVELY	DANIEL RICHARD	SGT	19700710 B Co	2nd Bn	506th Inf
GUIMOND	PAUL GERALD	SSG	19700714 D Co	2nd Bn	501st Inf
HEMBREE	JAMES THOMAS JR	SSG	19700714 D Co	2nd Bn	501st Inf
HUFFINE	DENNIS WILLARD	SGT	19700714 D Co	2nd Bn	501st Inf
JONES	WILLIAM EDWARD	SSG	19700714 D Co	2nd Bn	501st Inf
KEISTER	JOHN LOY	SGT	19700714 D Co	2nd Bn	501st Inf
PALM	TERRY ALAN	1LT	19700714 D Co	2nd Bn	501st Inf
SCHNEIDER	GARY LEE	SSG	19700714 D Co	2nd Bn	501st Inf
UTTER	KEITH EDWARD	CPL	19700714 D Co	2nd Bn	501st Inf
MILLER	BURKE HOLBROOK	CPL	19700718 A Btry	2nd Bn	11th Arty
BEYL	DAVID ROBERT	SGT	19700718 D Co	2nd Bn	501st Inf
ROLLASON	WILLIAM DAVID	SGT	19700718 E Co	2nd Bn	501st Inf
WALKER	MICHAEL ALLEN	SGT	19700718 A Co	159th Avn Bn	
PLETT	LARRY JOE	PFC	19700720 B Btry	2nd Bn	319th Arty
BROWNING	BILL GWINN	CPL	19700720 D Co	1st Bn	506th Inf
CARROLL	SAMUEL T JR	SGT	19700720 D Co	1st Bn	506th Inf
DE WULF	PATRICK THOMAS	CPL	19700720 D Co	1st Bn	506th Inf
KNOTT	JOHN CHARLES	CPL	19700720 D Co	1st Bn	506th Inf
VALLE	ELOY RUBEN	SP4	19700720 D Co	1st Bn	506th Inf
CALHOUN	DURL GENE	SGT	19700720 B Co	326th Eng Bn	
FISHER	DENNIS FAY	SGT	19700720 B Co	326th Eng Bn	
JOHNSON	DAVID EARL	SGT	19700721 A Btry	2nd Bn	11th Arty
KALSU	JAMES ROBERT	1LT	19700721 A Btry	2nd Bn	11th Arty
ASHER	FRANK LOUIS	CPL	19700721 D Co	1st Bn	506th Inf
FLORES	ROBERTO C	SGT	19700721 B Co	2nd Bn	506th Inf
HAYS	ROBERT BRADFORD	CPL	19700721 D Co	1st Bn	506th Inf
HUK	PETER PAUL	CPL	19700721 D Co	1st Bn	506th Inf
MAUNE	FRANCIS EDWARD	CPL	19700721 B Co	2nd Bn	506th Inf
WORKMAN	DONALD RENAY	CPT	19700721 D Co	1st Bn	506th Inf
LAW	BRENT ROBIN	SGT	19700721 326th	Med Bn	
BABICH	JOHN MICHAEL	CPL	19700722 A Co	2nd Bn	506th Inf
BIXBY	VIRGIL MARTIN	CPL	19700722 A Co	2nd Bn	506th Inf
BROWN	ROBERT JOSEPH JR	CPL	19700722 A Co	2nd Bn	506th Inf
DIEHL	STANLEY GENE	SSG	19700722 D Co	2nd Bn	506th Inf
DRAPER	MARK GREGORY	SGT	19700722 A Co	2nd Bn	506th Inf
FRIES	DANNY JOE	CPL	19700722 A Co	2nd Bn	506th Inf
JOURNELL	ROBERT MASON III	SP4	19700722 A Co	2nd Bn	506th Inf
KRECKEL	JOHN WILLIAM	SSG	19700722 A Co	2nd Bn	506th Inf
OLSON	STEVEN ALLAN	2LT	19700722 A Co	2nd Bn	506th Inf
PAHISSA	WILLIAM ANTHONY	1LT	19700722 A Co	2nd Bn	506th Inf
SCHULTZ	THOMAS RUSSELL	SGT	19700722 A Co	2nd Bn	506th Inf
SEVERSON	DONALD JON	SP4	19700722 A Co	2nd Bn	506th Inf
SINGLETON	GERALD BLAINE	SSG	19700722 A Co	2nd Bn	506th Inf
WARNER	WILFRED WESLEY JR	SGT	19700723 D Co	2nd Bn	501st Inf
ALLEN	GUS	CPL	19700723 A Co	2nd Bn	506th Inf
LUCAS	ANDRE CAVARO	LTC	19700723 HHC	2nd Bn	506th Inf

TANNER	KENNETH PAUL	MAJ	19700723 HHC	2nd Bn	506th Inf
MC DOWELL	LARRY JAMES	CPL	19700727 B Co	2nd Bn	506th Inf
NEAL	HARVEY RAY	SGT	19700727 A Co	2nd Bn	506th Inf
NORRIS	GRADY LEE	SFC	19700727 B CO	1ST BN	506TH INF
BROWN	LAURENCE GORDON	SGT	19700728 D Co	1st Bn	506th Inf
BAIZ	LEE THOMAS	SP4	19700729 B Co	1st Bn	502nd Inf
RAYMER	CARROLL EDWARD JR	CPL	19700808 D Co	3rd Bn	187th Inf
SORENSEN	KENNETH JAY	SGT	19700810 HHC	3rd Bn	187th Inf
BAHRKE	RUSSELL LEROY JR	CPL	19700813 E Co	2nd Bn	502nd Inf
HUTTIE	FREDERICK E III	SSG	19700815 D Co	2nd Bn	502nd Inf
WASHENIK	GARY LEE	SSG	19700816 A Co	1st Bn	506th Inf
FRATELLENICO	FRANK ROCCO	CPL	19700819 B Co	2nd Bn	502nd Inf
JONES	MARSHALL KEENE	SGT	19700820 C Co	2nd Bn	502nd Inf
MILLER	PAUL	SGT	19700820 C Co	2nd Bn	502nd Inf
JOHNSON	BEN ODELL	SGT	19700821 HHC	2nd Bn	502nd Inf
SILVERMAN	SHELDON	SSG	19700824 A Co	2nd Bn	502nd Inf
STILL	JERRY MELTON	CPL	19700825 HHC	2nd Bn	501st Inf
MUNCEY	JAY ALLAN	SP4	19700828 D Co	2nd Bn	501st Inf

In addition to the 247 soldiers listed in the table above, PFC STEPHEN J. HARBER, C Co, 2nd Bn, 506th Infantry was killed on 2 July 1970 and his body was not recovered. SSGT LEWIS HOWARD, JR. and SP4 CHARLES E. BEALS of D Co, 2nd Bn, 506th Infantry were killed on 7 July 1970 and their bodies not recovered.

Acknowledgements

Twenty-one years ago, in 1983, a few soldiers who had fought in the battle for Fire Support Base Ripcord got together and formed the Ripcord Association. Rodney B. "Chip" Collins (now deceased), Ray "Blackie" Blackburn and John "Custer" Mihalko started the *Ripcord Report* Newsletter 1 July 1985, "For Friends and Survivors of FSB RIPCORD, RVN." Chuck Hawkins, Frank Marshall and John Sherbo joined this small group and they organized the first reunion of the Ripcord Association held in John Mihalko's hometown of Whippany, New Jersey in October 1986. For several years Chuck Hawkins supplied the sustaining effort for the Association by maintaining addresses and by writing and getting out the quarterly newsletter. For the last six years, Fred Spaulding has been the driving force and has arranged outstanding reunions. Fred handles the bookkeeping and checking account. Chuck Hawkins continued to write the *Ripcord Report*, maintain the association's Archives, and he also designed and maintained the Ripcord web site until the fall of 2003. Gary and Patty Radford arrange for and pay for the reproduction and mailing of the Ripcord Report as a gift to the Association. Frank Marshall has taken over as editor of the newsletter and keeper of the web site and is doing a super job. Dennis Bloomingdale has contributed his vital professional expertise in final design for publication of the newsletter.

From the very start, the Ripcord Association has helped the veterans of Ripcord and their families and friends understand the service, sacrifices and suffering of the Ripcord veterans. The Association is unique in several ways. It includes men and their families and friends from all twenty-six units and various branches and services of our Army and the Department of Defense. There are no Association officers, no rules, no bylaws and no dues. The Association helped to provide significant closure for many of its members. Further closure was very greatly facilitated by the July 2000 publication of Keith Nolan's superb book, *Ripcord Screaming Eagles Under Siege Vietnam, 1970*. The magnificent October 2000 reunion organized and conducted primarily by Jim Campbell, with vital help from Fred Spaulding, put a sparkling cap on this closure effort with a formal welcome home celebration and memorial ceremony in Shreveport, Louisiana.

Although some thought had been given for some our Association members going to Vietnam early in Keith Nolan's research, the task and travel simply seemed too daunting and too difficult. Actual publication of Nolan's book made knowledge of the North Vietnamese side even more intriguing and more compelling, hence, the publication of this book. Nolan told how we fought the battle, but he could not tell us how the NVA fought it. Many, many questions remained unanswered.

Every author who writes Acknowledgements must have the terrible fear as do I, that enough good things will not be said, or worse, some most deserving person will be left out.

I certainly would have never attempted the trip to Vietnam or made the extensive preparations necessary without the encouragement, advice and specific contacts provided by my old friend and airborne-aviator comrade, Lieutenant General (Retired) Teddy Allen, former commander of the 101st Airborne Division. Thanks to a referral and recommendation by my old boss, Lieutenant General (Retired) John H. Cushman, also airborne-aviator comrade and former commander of the 101st Airborne Division, Courtney Frobenius came up on my need net. Courtney is an exceptional Vietnam expert serving two one-year wartime tours. He was a combat infantry platoon and company commander. Courtney also served as a Regional Force and Popular Force Advisor and the People's Self Defense Force Advisor for all of Phu Yen Province. He provided an incredible amount of valuable advice, assistance and wise counsel for both my research and my writing. Courtney's wife, Trang, provided much needed contacts in Vietnam and a summary translation of pertinent parts of the North Vietnamese 308 Division's official unit history. Courtney's help extended into the composition of this book.

US Ambassador Douglas B. "Pete" Peterson asked the Vietnamese Minister of Foreign Affairs to support our visit and research effort in Vietnam. He provided interesting background on the workings (or non-workings) of the Socialist Republic of Vietnam. Lieutenant Colonel Frank L. Miller, Jr., US Defense Attaché in Hanoi, personally sought and procured documents for me in military bookstores in Vietnam. Frank introduced me via email to Ken Conboy, author of *The NVA and Viet Cong* and *Elite forces of India and Pakistan* and other military histories. Conboy does security assessments in Indonesia and, from Jakarta, sent me the pertinent parts of the Vietnamese language histories of the 304 Division and the 325 Division.

As the Vietnamese Ministry of Foreign Affairs faltered on locating North Vietnamese veterans of the Ripcord battle to meet with me, Courtney Frobenius put me in touch with Colonel Pham Van Dinh. Colonel Dinh was the lieutenant colonel in the Army of the Republic of Vietnam who surrendered his regiment and Camp Carroll to the invading North Vietnamese Army during the Easter Offensive of 1972. Colonel Dinh proved indispensable in facilitating my interviewing six North Vietnamese Army officers who participated in the battle for Ripcord.

Robert J. Destatte played a most vital role in helping to identify, locate, and translate North Vietnamese writings. Destatte served nine years in Vietnam with the US Army and Defense Intelligence Agency and from 1993 until his retirement 1 August 2001, served as the principal staff officer in the Prisoner of War and Missing Personnel Affairs Office of the Secretary of Defense.

Bob Destatte provided an enormous amount of not just translations, but learned interpretations of Vietnamese books, documents, and publications that greatly broadened and enhanced our understanding the North Vietnamese side of the FSB Ripcord battle. Bob's insights on the influence and support of North Vietnam by the Soviet Union, China, and Cuba prove both fascinating and illuminating.

Merle Pribbenow, a colleague of Destatte and a former CIA officer with extensive experience in Vietnam, provided the key resource for this book, a translation of the "official" history of our primary adversary in the Ripcord area, the North Vietnamese 324B Division.

Randy White assisted in obtaining information on aviation cavalry and rangers in the 101st. Randy spent a lot of time and personal resources gathering about 19,000 pages of official records. He also posted and facilitated my many requests for data at his web site for L Company, 75th Ranger Regiment and its many links to 101st Aviation units. Randy served as a Sergeant in L Company when it was OPCON to the 2nd Squadron, 17th Cavalry of the 101st in 1970.

Kent Sears, Ph.D., spent a total of 19 years in Vietnam starting in 1965. He provided a strategic perspective on the 101st Airborne Division and the fighting and costly casualties within the northern provinces of South Vietnam.

Jim Campbell, a treasured friend and great asset to the Ripcord Association, provided significant and much appreciated encouragement.

Keith Nolan did a fine job identifying the soldiers killed during the 1–23 July siege of Ripcord. Since the battle for Ripcord actually started in March, continued through the operations of the 2nd Battalion, 502nd Infantry of the following August, and the siege of FSB O'Reilly in August, I sought the names of soldiers, both in and supporting the 3rd Brigade, who were reported killed in the total fight for Ripcord. Indeed, three soldiers died on 12 March, the first day that troops assaulted onto Hill 927-to-become-FSB Ripcord, just as there were three soldiers killed on 23 July, the day Ripcord closed. John Shepard introduced me to www.VirtualWall.org. Having trouble extracting pertinent data, I contacted the Virtual Wall webmaster, Ken Davis. Ken was eager to try and help and then put me in email touch with the real creator of the Virtual Wall database, Richard Coffelt, an Army veteran of the Korean War. Coffelt and Vietnam War veterans, David Argabright and Richard Arnold, developed an extensive database of 58,202 names from the Wall in three digital formats. With their coaching, I worked through the names of those 526 KIAs in 1970 combat in the northern provinces, to identify 250 soldiers from ten different battalions, plus the 58th Infantry Scout Dog Platoon, who paid the ultimate price in our Ripcord battle.

Responding to a posting on an Army Aviation web site, Malcolm W. Jones, Jr., offered to help and provided me with a copy of his book, *Four Condors*. This book captured the raw perspective of air cavalrymen of the 101st Airborne Division during the Ripcord battle. The web site for C Troop, 2nd Squadron, 17th Cavalry can be found at www.cav-condors.org/.

Don Moore provided not only top-quality illustrations, but also professional advice. Don knows infantry fighting; he served as a Marine Corps Gunnery Sergeant and Combat Artist in our northern South Vietnam AO during 1968–69.

My June 2001 trip to Vietnam was made much more productive and less grinding by the warm companionship, note taking, video taking, photo taking, voice recordings and suggestions of my very special and dear friend, Fred Spaulding.

Professor Andrew Wiest, Ph D, University of Southern Mississippi, Director of the internationally acclaimed and honored Vietnam Studies Abroad Program, author of several military histories, spent considerable time providing wise counsel and vital assistance in my writing effort and preparation for publication. Andy's Studies Abroad Program Co-Director, Professor Brian O'Neil asked me to accompany the university group on their 2004 visit to

Vietnam. This led to the critical interview with Major General Chu Phuong Doi and facilitated the completion of this book.

Jerry Tiarsmith, a veteran and an adjunct faculty member with the Department of History, the University of Alabama-Birmingham, where he teaches courses on War in the Modern World and America in Vietnam, did a superb job editing the entire manuscript, however, any mistakes, errors, or shortcomings are mine and mine alone.

All profit from the sale of my book will go to the Ripcord Association for the benefit of the great soldiers who fought the battle of Ripcord.

Thanks to all and especially to my wife, Carolyn.

Appendix A

The Ripcord Association Reunion in October 2000

The 2000 Ripcord reunion included:

- A memorial ceremony dedicating a plaque to Ripcord veterans.

- A luncheon at the Barksdale Air Force Officers Club with B. G. Burkett, author of *Stolen Valor*, as the speaker.

- Tours, fishing, golf and an afternoon at the Louisiana Downs Race Track where Ripcord veterans had a race named in their honor.

- Dinner at the Shreveport Yacht Club with evening cruises on the lake and a dinner at Shreveport's finest Cajun restaurant with NFL great Rocky Bleier, wounded Vietnam veteran and holder of four Super Bowl champion rings, as speaker. The son and daughter of Lieutenant Bob Kalsu, the only NFL player killed in Vietnam, were honored at this dinner. (Bob was actually the only professional athlete to give his life for his country in Vietnam.)

- A banquet followed by dancing to live music after a speech by Lieutenant General Randy House, Deputy Commander in Chief, US Pacific Command, known to the troops as Captain Randy House, Phoenix 16, Air Mission Commander for the evacuation of Ripcord on 23 July 1970. (He actually was flying Lead and assumed control of the helicopter lift elements as incoming fire began to seriously disrupt the operation.) Randy earlier had flown Lead for the insertion of troops on Ripcord 1 April 1970.

• The memorial dedication was preceded by a B-52 fly-by. The Red River Pipe and Drum Group and the 156th Louisiana National Guard Band provided ceremonial music. The 101st Airborne Division Color Guard, the Barksdale Air Force Base Saber Cordon Honor Guard and the C. E. Byrd High School ROTC Honor Guard performed during the placing of ten wreaths at the Ripcord Memorial. Mrs. Wilma Knight, mother of Wieland Norris who was killed at Ripcord, placed one of the wreaths. Wieland"s brother, a very emotional Chuck Norris, also paid his respects.

I delivered the following Ripcord Memorial Dedication speech:

> Thank you, Fred. Colonel Spaulding has recognized our distinguished guests and organizations participating in this memorial dedication today. Let me add my most sincere personal appreciation for your presence today and your great contributions in service to our nation.
>
> It is fitting and appropriate that permanent recognition of the veterans of the battles for Fire Support Base Ripcord be placed here in this Memorial Plaza that already recognizes the veterans of America's wars; World War I, "the war to end all wars," the Second World War, as a friend of mine said, everyone knew about it, is was in all the papers, and the Korean War, "the Forgotten War." Today we add the Vietnam War. You might call it "the Misunderstood War." Some call World War II the Good war as opposed to Korea and Vietnam. The Second World War was indeed, in scope and significance, the most important event of the entire 20th Century. But there are no "Good" wars, as all wars rob us of our young men and women. They are simply, America's wars.
>
> The World War II Generation, the Greatest Generation, deserves all the praise we can heap upon it—they defeated the totalitarian and evil governments of Germany and Japan; restored Europe and Japan and developed a mighty and economically healthy America. But it may be time to recognize the Vietnam War Generation. The Vietnam War Generation contained Communism, restored democracy in Panama, stopped the Iraqis in the Middle East, won the Cold War, and caused the collapse of the Soviet Union. It has been the Vietnam War Generation that has made the United States the most technologically advanced and wealthiest nation in the world!! It is the Vietnam War Generation that has brought about more racial harmony and reduced gender bias in our society.
>
> It is our purpose today to honor all men and women who have fought for our country in all wars, but we pay special tribute to the Vietnam War

Generation as we recognize two groups of America's Best—those who made it back and those who did not! This group of survivors seated with you today represent the Army, Navy, Marine Corps and Air Force veterans that participated in the five months of costly battles for Fire Support Base Ripcord, March through July, 1970. We certainly take no joy in the numbers, but the losses of Hamburger Hill fade to a small fraction of those who fought their last battle at Ripcord.

And their names indeed are, "Graven not so much in stone as in the hearts of men."

And they served in the spirit of the words on the Confederate Memorial in Arlington National Cemetery, "not for fame or reward, not for place or for rank, but in simple obedience to duty, as they understood it."

I believe these men would be honored to have written on their memorial the same words as found in Washington on the Tomb of the Unknown Soldier—"I am the unknown soldier, and I may have died in vain...,but if I were alive...and my country called, I'd do it over again."

It is hard to believe that it has taken thirty years to have the story of Ripcord told. It's also hard to believe that some of us occasionally, still have terrifying nightmares of Vietnam. But the story finally has been told and all of us are deeply appreciative of the exacting and scholarly research that Keith Nolan has done for his tenth book on the Vietnam War. Keith has written moving, shocking, and sad; sometimes emotionally draining, but more often, inspiring stories about our comrades.

Ripcord, Screaming Eagles Under Siege, is not just a tribute to the 356 soldiers that Keith has written about in his book, it is a tribute to the hundreds of thousands, yes, <u>hundreds of thousands</u> of Army and Marine infantrymen who fought on the ground in Vietnam and the Army and Air Force and Navy and Marine brave aircrews who time and again provided crucial fire support and medical evacuation. Thank you, Keith Nolan!!

Will Rogers once said, "It's not the things we don't know that get us into trouble. It's the things we know that just ain't so." This applies in spades to Vietnam veterans.

Our Misunderstood War is sometimes called, "the dirty little war." To help put the Vietnam War in perspective, James Webb reminds us that Vietnam was no way a "little" war, it was the most costly war the United States Marine Corps has ever fought! Five times as many dead Marines as World War I, three times as many dead Marines as in Korea, <u>and more total killed and wounded Marines in the five years the Marines were in Vietnam than in the entire three and one half years of World War II!</u>

As grateful as I am to Keith Nolan and Presidio Press for bringing us this magnificent book that is sure to become one of the true classics of the Vietnam War, I feel compelled to take issue with one of their key editorial assertions. In the Introduction, it is stated that, at Ripcord, "The enemy victory was total." Simply not so!

The mission of the 101st Airborne Division was to ONE, destroy as much of the North Vietnamese Army and their equipment and supplies as possible, TWO, to deny safe havens for the enemy to use to strike the populated coastal areas and THREE, gain time for the South Vietnamese military to improve their combat effectiveness. Our soldiers accomplished their mission. It was not until three years after the 101st withdrew from Vietnam, that the North Vietnamese were able to invade with a 22 division conventional force, leaving only one division in all of North Vietnam. The forward assembly of these forces was made easy by the Kissinger drafted Paris Peace Accords. The United States reneged on its promise of air support and military supplies to South Vietnam. President Ford pleaded with Congress to support the South Vietnamese but was rebuffed and denied. As our higher command in the 101st chose not to continue the fight at Ripcord, our country chose not to support the South Vietnamese any longer. It could be analogous to a football team never putting the offensive squad on the field, or probably more accurately, the entire team walking off the field at the start of the fourth quarter.

Nonetheless, it was a noble cause and a just war against an evil and cruelly oppressive North Vietnamese government that was trying to destroy its neighbor—a government that proclaimed that is better to kill ten innocent people than miss one potential enemy.

Our military forces followed the orders of the National Military Authority with courage and honor.

To the two groups of Vietnam Veterans that we honor today—

To the group that did not return, you have our most sincere respect and appreciation for your dedication and sacrifice—you shall forever remain young!

To the group of Vietnam Veterans that made it back. Welcome Home!

To all Veterans and your Families, we salute you!

APPENDIX B

Proposed Itinerary

Draft 15–25 April 2001 Itinerary for Maj Gen Ben L. Harrison (Ret.) *

* Names(s) in parentheses () indicates individual(s) responsible for making arrangements.

15 April	Arrive HCMC on JAL Flight 759 at 9:20 pm. Clear customs and immigration, meet guide and driver, transfer to hotel (Request Hotel Delta Caravelle at $70). (Mr. Luong Thanh Nghi/Col Nguyen Ba Van)
16 April	9:00 am departure for the Cu Chi Tunnels accompanied by Col Nguyen Ba Van (Ret). Tour the tunnels and return to HCMC for a brief city tour: Dong Khoi St, Notre Dame Cathedral, the Colonial Post Office, the Rex and Continental Hotels and the Re-unification Palace. Return to hotel. Dinner with Col Nguyen Ba Van at 6:30 pm. Return to hotel. (Mr. Luong Thanh Nghi/Col Nguyen Ba Van)

17 April   Early check out and transfer to the airport for Vietnam Airline's Flight VN-918 departing for Hanoi at 7:00 am. (Mr. Luong Thanh Nghi/Col Nguyen Ba Van)

Arrive Hanoi at 9:00 am. Meet guide and driver, transfer to hotel. (Request Metropol Hotel $100) (Mr. Luong Thanh Nghi/Col Nguyen Ba Van)

Afternoon courtesy calls:

1:00 pm   Luong Thanh Nghi, Dep Dir, VN Foreign Press Center (Mr Nghi)

2:00 pm   Amb Peterson, US Ambassador to SRV (Harrison)
Lt Col Rennie M. Cory Jr (LTC Cory is the Cdr of the JTF for MIAs—the son of an old comrade of mine)(Harrison) [Rennie and all aboard a Russian MI-17 Helicopter were killed in a fiery crash just before we arrived.]

3:00 pm   SG Nguyen Van Giap (Mr. Luong Thanh Nghi/Col Nguyen Ba Van)

5:00 pm   Meet SG Tien Van Dung at his house, present gift to Mrs Dung; proceed to dinner given by MG Harrison (Ask General Dung his restaurant preference and book it.) (Mr. Luong Thanh Nghi/Col Nguyen Ba Van)

18 April   All day meetings:
SG Tien Van Dung (Mr. Luong Thanh Nghi/Col Nguyen Ba Van)
PAVN Division, regimental, battalion and company commander participants in the Ripcord battles (Mr. Luong Thanh Nghi/Col Nguyen Ba Van)

| | 6:30 pm   Dinner for discussion participants given by MG Harrison (Mr. Luong Thanh Nghi/Col Nguyen Ba Van) |

19 April   All day meetings:
Participants as determined during discussions 18 April.

20 April   Visits to the Ba Muoi Sau (Old Quarter), Hoan Keim Lake, the Ho Chi Minh House on Stilts, the HCM Mausoleum and the One-Pillar Pagoda. (Mr. Luong Thanh Nghi/Col Nguyen Ba Van)

21 April   9:30 am check out of hotel and transfer to Hanoi's Noi Bai Airport to connect with VN-247 departing for Hue at 12:10 pm and arriving at 1:10 pm. Meet guide and driver and proceed to Hotel Huong Giang ($45) and a brief visit to the former US Camp Evans and former FSB Ripcord. Return to hotel. Free evening. (Mr. Luong Thanh Nghi/ Col Nguyen Ba Van)

22 April   8:30 am departure for Quang Tri War Information Records Center. (Mr. Luong Thanh Nghi/Col Nguyen Ba Van) At the conclusion of business at the Records Center, travel to Danang. (Mr. Luong Thanh Nghi/Col Nguyen Van Ba) Col Ng Van Ba to transfer to Hue airport to fly to HCMC. Check into Hotel Furama($125) at China Beach. (Mr. Luong Thanh Nghi)

23 April   Check out of hotel and transfer to the airport at 8:45 am to connect with VN-335 departing for Nha Trang at 10:30 am and arriving Nha Trang at 11:40 am. Check into Hotel Ana Madara ($125). Afternoon tour of the Po Nagar Cham Towers, Nha Trang Harbor, Bao Dai Villas, and the Nha Trang Beach. (Mr. Luong Thanh Nghi)

24 April   Free day for snorkeling for sea shells in Nha Trang and or
                  Cam Ranh Bay. (Mr. Luong Thanh Nghi)

25 April   Check out of hotel and depart for the airport at 0830 to
                  connect with VN-453 departing at 9:30 am and arriving
                  HCMC airport at 10:45. Meet guide and transfer to Hotel
                  Delta Caravelle ($70). Free day until 9:30 pm transfer to
                  the airport to connect with returning JAl Flight 750
                  departing HCMC11:20 pm . (Mr. Luong Thanh Nghi)

APPENDIX C

Vietnam Visit 1–11 June 2001

The visit to Vietnam in search of the North Vietnamese side of the battle for Ripcord in 1970, has been completed. We returned late yesterday. Encouraged and assisted by Lt Gen (Ret) Teddy Allen and advised and coached by Courtney Frobenius, owner and operator of Vietnam-Indochina Tours, it was first scheduled for 29 Nov 2000. Postponed because of Carolyn's TIA, I rescheduled it for March 2001. The Ministry of Foreign Affairs asked me to reschedule for late April, Ten days before my planned 11 Apr departure, the Ministry of Foreign Affairs said, please reschedule for a later time, so 1 Jun became the new date.

Fortunately for me, at that timing of the trip, Fred Spaulding was able to go with me. We are home, healthy and grateful. (Fred lost 14 pounds and I lost 5.)

The Initial Report:

GOOD NEWS:

The trip clearly was a success as we learned significant information about the North Vietnamese forces and their strategy and tactics in the battle for Ripcord in 1970.

The first of our six interviews with North Vietnamese officers was with Colonel (Ret) Nguyen Ba Van, now living in Cu Chi. Teddy Allen located Col Ba for us. Col Ba was a sergeant serving near Khe Sanh at the time of Ripcord, later Deputy Commander and Political Officer of the 9th Division of the People's Army of Vietnam (PAVN) and retired from the position of Political Officer of the Cu Chi District.

Ambassador Peterson was gracious and generous with his time. He made some interesting observations. The Defense Attaché, LTC Frank Miller, offered to assist us.

Mr. Nguyen The Cuong of the Foreign Press Center of the Ministry of Foreign Affairs, arranged for us to interview BG Bui Pham Ky, People's Army of Vietnam, Retired. Ky had been the Deputy Commander and Political Officer of the 324B Division in Thua Tien Province.

With Courtney Frobenius's help and his wife's timely trip to Vietnam, we were able employ the assistance of Colonel (Ret) Pham Van Dinh, living in Hue, whom I had known in the 1st Infantry Division, Army of Vietnam. (Colonel Dinh had been the Commander of the 56th Regiment, 2nd Infantry Division of the Army of Vietnam and Camp Carroll on the DMZ, when he surrendered his forces to the North Vietnamese during the Easter Offensive of the North Vietnamese in 1972. He was flown to Hanoi and made a colonel in the People's Army of Vietnam). Col Dinh took us to the Army Museum in Hanoi where we interviewed the Director, Col Le Ma Luong. He had been an infantry company commander in Thua Tien Province in 1970.

Col Dinh located and arranged for us to interview the following People's Army of Vietnam officers in Hue:

Major (Ret) Ho Van Thuoc, who, in 1970, was the Operations Officer of the Regional forces in Quang Tri Province.

Brig Gen (Ret) Duong Ba Nuoi, who, in 1970 was the Deputy Commander and Political Officer Of Zone 4, which included Thua Tien, Quang Tri, Quang Binh, and Ha Tinh Provinces.

Senior Colonel Nguyen Quoc Khanh, who, in 1970 was the Operations Officer of the 324B Division.

With the help of LTC Miller and Col (Ret) Dinh, we will follow up our search with the People's Army Publishing House for books/reports relating to the battle for Ripcord in 1970.

Our next step is to use our notes, recordings, references and memories to develop a narrative of the North Vietnamese side of the battle for Ripcord. We will offer this to Presidio Press (should they choose to make a second edition of the Ripcord book) to try and recoup the expense of trip to Vietnam. Should they not buy it, we will publish a report (with pictures) and offer it for sale through our Ripcord Association with any money beyond our expenses going to the Association.

General Observations:

In spite of the official propaganda, virtually all of the people are friendly, courteous and quick with a smile; happy to learn that you are an American. Many will tell you that they have a relative(s) in the United States. The children laugh, giggle, romp and play like children all over the world.

Many people speak English. Most signs and menus are also in English. The adventurous person can travel without a guide or interpreter. I, however, would recommend Courtney Frobenius Vietnam-Indochina Tours.

Many people refer to Ho Chi Minh City as Saigon and Saigon is seen on many signs and in print.

The food is good and quite cheap. The taxis are also very cheap.

The three, four and five star hotels we used were excellent and averaged about $70 per night.

Vietnam Airlines fly Airbus 320"s and employ some western pilots.

The landscape is absolutely beautiful!

BAD NEWS:

Japan Airlines does not stock rum!

Senior General Tien Vien Dung, age 81, the overall commander of the PAVN who replaced Giap, was still in the hospital and I could not see him. Lt Gen Din Vang Quang, former commander of the 304 Division, was traveling away from Hanoi and I could not interview him. Ambassador Peterson said that was unfortunate because Quang is the head of the war veteran's organization and loves to talk. I will try and communicate with him by letter.

The People's Army Publishing House sales office in Hanoi was a 10-foot by 20-foot hole in the wall with no list or index of published books/papers available.

The Quang Tri War Records Center had limited information on Quang Tri Regional Forces and apparently nothing on the Ripcord battle. (A visit there was deemed a waste of our limited time.)

Past and present military and government bureaucrats are quite careful to talk the communist party line and extremely parsimonious with information.

Most of the history of the Ripcord battle apparently has not been written or published even though communist military units are known to be careful record keepers.

We could not visit Ripcord because there still is no road through that area. There used to be a government helicopter available in the Hue-Phu Bai area, but there is none now. Our Vietnam Airline A320 jet transport landed there and not another single aircraft of any kind was in sight.

General Observations:

Poverty and a very, very low standard of living is all too readily apparent; especially in the countryside. Rice is still planted and harvested by hand. You sometimes will see a water buffalo used for plowing in the muddy rice paddies.

There are hundreds of thousands of motorbikes in Ho Chi Minh City and Hanoi. The traffic is terrible in the cities and Highway 1 is frequently rough. The motorbike riders and bicycle riders never look as they pull into the traffic and they ignore the incessant horn blowing.

Vietnam Airlines still use several Soviet built AN-24 turbo-prop transports.

It is still a very, very, very long trip! We had a 24-hour layover in Tokyo enroute to Saigon. The return trip was 36 hours from baggage turn-in to pickup including a six-hour wait in Tokyo. It was 57 hours from bed in Saigon to bed at home!!

APPENDIX D

Vietnam Visit 17 May-6 June 2004

Jack Cushman introduced me to Courtney Frobenius, owner/operator of Vietnam-IndoChina Tours. Courtney and his lovely and most gracious wife Trang, arranged the visit to Vietnam for Fred Spaulding and myself in June 2001. Courtney later introduced me to Professor Andrew Wiest, University of Southern Mississippi. Andy started the award winning Vietnam Studies Abroad Program in 2000. For the last three years, the Program's Co-Director, Dr. Brian O'Neil, has conducted the studies tour. From the beginning, the program was most fortunate in having John W. Young, raised in Minnesota, but now living in Picayune, MS participate in the classroom course on the Vietnam War and accompany each group of students to Vietnam for the past four years. John takes the students to the battle site in the Mekong Delta where his under-strength, boat-transported 4th Bn, 47th Infantry was mauled by three VC battalions waiting in ambush. With three VC veterans of the battle looking on, John gives a most moving account of his actions as a Rifle Squad Leader in Charlie Company. For the 2004 Program, Brian me asked to accompany the group and contribute observations about the Vietnam War and from my two tours in Vietnam, 1966–67 and 1970–71.

I left Belton at 5 AM on Monday 17 May. At the Los Angeles airport, I met Prof O'Neil, veteran John Young, Trang Frobenius, Prof John Van Sant from Univ of Alabama Birmingham (John helped lead the first trip as a member of the USM faculty at that time) and Dylan Q. Muoi a New Orleans born Vietnamese young lady who had been on the study two years ago prior, now doing a story for the Washington Post. The fourteen USM students are listed here:

Amelia Steadman, MS International Studies/Spanish, Hattiesburg, MS
Tiffany Beckham, MA European History, Pearl, MS
Kristie Atkinson, Senior in International Studies, Oxford, MS
Chassity Smith, BA History, Magee, MS
William Quinn, BA History, Hattiesburg, MS
Lauren McKee, MA English Literature, Waynesboro, MS
Jessica Shows, BA English Education, Lucedale, MS
Michelle Heard, BS Medical Technology, Richland, MS
Carrie Walker, BS Physics and Mathematics, Oxford, MS
Geoffrey Philabaum, BA Music, Brookhaven, MS
Jason Sokiera, MA History, Allison Park, PA
Jason Stewart (also a student on the 2003 study), MA History, Mobile. AL
Scott Houston, Senior, International Studies, Vicksburg, MS
Justin Sowder, BA History and Political Science
Joining the USM group was:
Joanna Ain, Senior in History, Cornell University, Winchester, MA and
Amber Miller, Junior in Psychology, University of Wisconsin-Eau Claire, Rice Lake, WI

With a two-hour stop in Seoul, we arrived in Saigon after 36 hours at 1 AM on Wednesday, 19 May.

We booked into the very fine old (1925) French Hotel Majestic on the Saigon River. Most folks got to bed about 2 AM and we met for orientation at 10 o'clock. After lunch, we toured Saigon with a long visit to the former South Vietnamese Presidential Palace, now used for tourism and propaganda. We enjoyed a lavish Vietnamese dinner with young and middle age adult friends of Trang's.

On 20 May, we went to the Vinh Nghiem Pagoda and a very interesting visit with the Chief Monk who had gone to school at Yale and Columbia. He had been a member of the protest group that resulted in the emulation of six monks against Pres Diem in the early '60s. The Chief Monk was delightfully entertaining, speaking excellent American with lots of "you know's", but not quite up to date with multiple "like's" That evening, John Young gave a detailed and emotional lecture on his experience as a squad leader in C Co, 4th Bn, 47th Inf, 9th Inf Div with the Mobile Riverine Force on the Rach Gia River in the Delta.

Friday, 21 May, we went by bus to John Young's battle site of Can Giouc. We took a boat on the same canal used by the US Navy for the Riverine Force. We walked the rice paddy dikes as John told of the battle.

On 22 May, we went to My Tho down in the Delta by bus on a nice new highway. The group took a small boat to Thoi San Island, former VC stronghold and now an enterprising tourist attraction. We toured in sampans and had lunch on two small barges.

Sunday, 23 May, we took a two-hour bus ride to visit the highly commercialized tourist attraction of the Cu Chi Tunnels. Many students went into the tunnels while I took their pictures going in and out. Some of them fired SKS and AK-47 rifles. There is a very large temple and a memorial wall to fallen soldiers of both sides.

We passed near the old free-fire zone of the Iron Triangle and many battle sites that had been repeatedly bombed and sprayed with Agent Orange. Everywhere we looked in all directions, the countryside was beautiful with lush greenery and healthy crops. Any damage by Agent Orange has long passed.

24 May in Saigon, we visited the Phuc Yen Garment factory. Lang Xuan Binh and his charming wife started the factory with twenty sewing machines and twenty employees seventeen years ago. They now have several buildings with over 800 employees. Xuan was an English student of Courtney's in Saigon in the mid-nineties and they have been good friends ever since. Their two sons, Phuc and Yen, are going to college in the US. They gave each of us a very nice coat produced by the factory. We also visited a lacquer factory where 16 steps, taking three months, produced beautiful works in a wide variety of art. Several students bought very nice pieces at good prices.

Tues, 25 May, another 4 AM get-up for me for an 6:20 flight for Hanoi, but the students left on a 10:30 flight. Arrived in Hanoi at 8:30 AM, where I was met by Hau, my translator/guide and driver, Teo, in a stick shift Toyota. Courtney and Trang had engaged the HaiVan Tour company on my behalf to locate Maj Gen Doi for me and then take me to visit him. We left from the airport on the north side of Hanoi for Cao Bang—one of the most remote provinces in VN. No airport, only a 300 kilometers of a, washed out, very narrow rough road through beautiful mountains with narrow valleys of lush crops of rice, corn and sugar cane. Got to Cao Bang at 5 PM, good time, so they said. Hau called Gen Doi and he said come on out. He lives ten kilometers west of Cao Bang near the Bang River.

I remained apprehensive since he turned down my invitation to host his family for dinner in Cao Bang. I was certain that he was going to check me out and then decide if he would meet with me Wed morning. To my most pleasant surprise, our critical meeting proved quite warm and cordial from the very start. His wife, 77, and brother, 75, daughter and granddaughter all gathered there. It is customary in Vietnam to ask one's age when first introduced.

Following a customary sharing of tea, I presented him with Hennessey Cognac, Johnny Walker Black Label Scotch, Nolan's book, RIPCORD, my Ripcord coin, my picture autographed to him, a nicely wrapped gift for his wife and one for his daughter. After drinking the customary tea, he said he could no longer drink Cognac and offered beer instead. (He might just sell that bottle of Cognac—$60 in the duty-free store.)

He said he was most appreciative of my coming to Cao Bang. A very, very modest home, it was and is, the home of his family. His son, still in the People's Army, has a nicer, newer house next door.

For some time, we generally discussed both the French War and the American War. I gave him a translation of my questions and the two maps Courtney had prepared for me relative to the French War in his area in 1950 and '52. He put on different glasses stating he had lost the sight in his left eye and that he had gone to Moscow for surgery on his right eye. He smiled saying it was a very nice gift from the Russians. (This is the only time I have ever heard any Vietnamese give credit to the Russians for anything. Notwithstanding the 55,000 Soviets actually in North Vietnam facilitating the war, and billons of dollars provided in supplies and equipment, no papers or books published in the Socialist Republic of Vietnam have ever given any credit to the Russians for their absolutely vital support.)

Doi's wife was smiling and happy to join in the conversation. Several times Gen Doi told me how pleased he was to have me come visit him in his home. He emphasized this with a story of an American veterans group that a few years ago, wanted him to come to Hanoi for talks. He said with a bit of arrogance, "I told them if they wanted to talk to me, they must come to Cao Bang!" I told him that it was I who made that request in 2001. He sat back and smiled broadly and proclaiming he was most happy that I had come to his home this time. He announced he would come to my hotel in the morning. I asked what time and he requested the driver to come at 6 AM. We left in good cheer.

After freshening up at the hotel, Hau, Teo, and I walked around town to find a place for Internet connections, but could not locate one. We had an okay dinner and then went to bed early. The Bang Giang Hotel, considered as the best in town, had air-conditioned rooms only after you closed the windows and turned on the air. However, the lobby and dining areas lacked air-conditioning. I noted several mosquitoes in my room, but did not elect to deploy the mosquito net stored in a cabinet over the head of the bed. The best hotel in town did not take credit cards, did not convert dollars to Dong (Vietnamese currency), or take payment in dollars. Fortunately, the HaiVan travel company paid for all room charges on my behalf.

Waking up early presented no problem as my second-story room overlooked the street market right under my window where vendors sold live ducks and geese beginning at about 5 AM.

Gen Doi promptly arrived at the hotel at 7 AM and immediately announced he could work for only two hours. He enthusiastically talked about his joining Ho Chi Minh 19 Dec 1946 at the age of 24. Ho Chi Minh had returned to Vietnam in 1940 and lived in the Pac Bo caves near Cao Bang. By the time of the battle of Dong Khe, led personally by Ho Chi Minh, Doi rose to the rank of battalion commander in the *Viet Minh*. (In all of our discussions, Gen Doi always referred to his army as the *Viet Minh*, not PAVN or People's Army. He was, and is, hard core, dedicated to the *Viet Minh* purpose of freeing his country from foreign powers. (The *Viet Minh* owed its birth and growth to support given Ho Chi Minh by the Chinese Communist Party.)

Gen Doi provided details of the very significant defeat of LePaige in 1950. Doi was next a battalion commander with the *Pathet Lao* between 1952 and 1954. He said that Ho Chi Minh personally placed him in command of the 209th Regiment at the battle of Dien Bien Phu in 1954. He presented me with a picture made of himself in uniform at the just observed 50th Anniversary of their great victory of Dien Bien Phu. (The cropped picture is on the back of the dust cover.)

Doi remained in the Dien Bien Phu area as a regimental commander until given command of the 324B Division in 1965. He said his mission in 1967 and 1968 was to draw the American Marines into battle along Route 9, in the highlands, to relieve the pressure on the *Viet Cong* forces operating in the highly populated coastal areas. This Hanoi directed strategy evolved into the famous hill fights of 1967 and eventually into the prolonged siege of Khe Sanh in 1968.

He then went on to my questions that he had studied the night before. He cleared up some of the confusion of the official PAVN history of the 324B Division. When I asked a question about what the 1992 published history book said in obvious error, he would reply, "I was not there when they wrote this."

Probably the only really new thing I learned was that he had four companies of 120mm mortars, each with six tubes in our Ripcord area. No wonder we could never silence them!! That was massive firepower potential, but we took out a significant number of them. The most important piece of information that he gave me was that when we evacuated Ripcord on 23 July, he still had one battalion in his division of nine infantry battalions that he had not committed to Ripcord.

Instead of two hours, Gen Doi talked for three hours. More details of the Gen Doi interview will be in my book.

We left Cao Bang about 1100 for the long drive back to Hanoi. We chose a different route taking us through the mountains to Lang Son. We came within a mile of the border with China. Lang Son is a bustling city where trade with China flourishes. Fortunately for us, we had a very good highway for the remaining 110 miles to Hanoi. The Cao Bang-Lang Son area had been occupied by China during the 1979 war.

Earlier on the 26th, the group had met with Ambassador Raymond F. Burghardt at the US Embassy. They received a most interesting briefing from the Defense Attaché, Col Stephen Ball and the chief of the Joint POW/MIA Accounting Command, Lt Col Thomas Smith. The group was invited to attend a rare Recaption ceremony scheduled for the next day when the remains of two recovered, formerly MIAs would be sent via US Air Force C-17 to Hawaii for positive identification before the remains are delivered to the families.

I arrived at the Sunway Hotel for check-in after the group had departed for dinner. Fortunately, Brian called my guide, Hau, on the cell phones telling me that he had left me a note with the location of the restaurant. I took a taxi and enjoyed a fine, fun meal at the Australian owned Al Frescos restaurant.

The next day, Thursday, 27 May, we went out to the Noi Bai Airport for the RECAP Ceremony, and arriving late, we watched it from the terminal. Afterwards, we visited the Hoa Lo Prison "The Hanoi Hilton" which features propaganda about the dastardly crimes of the French against the Vietnamese and the nice, humane treatment of the American prisoners before their release in March 1973. Most of the old French prison has been torn down and replaced by a modern office building by Singapore investors.

Friday, 28 May, we visited the massive Ho Chi Minh Mausoleum and the Soviet Union built Ho Chi Minh Museum. There were over a hundred tour busses there and thousands of people lined up around two blocks for the visit. John Young said this is their Mount Vernon. I said, no, it is their Disney World. All Vietnamese come here, but few Americans visit Mount Vernon.

Ho Chi Minh's body lies in state surrounded by a very stiff military honor guard. Each year his body is flown to Moscow where it is "touched up."

We then toured the Ba Dinh Square, One-Pillar Pagoda, Dien Huu Pagoda, Ho Chi Minh House on Stilts and the old quarter.

We scheduled an early get-up Saturday for the four-hour bus ride to Ha Long Bay. We had a short, four-hour cruise and lunch visiting a large cave and a very few of the three thousand islands in the Bay. Our cruise was cut short so we could return to the hotel for a very rare opportunity to meet with Bao Ninh, author of the world acclaimed *The Sorrow Of War*. Trang and Thom had visited Bao Ninh the evening before to arrange the meeting. He technically is under house arrest, but can venture out on occasion.

Bao Ninh did make it for a meeting with our eager and enthusiastic group as just about everyone had a copy of his book to autograph (many of us hastily buying another copy).

We flew into Phu Bai on Sunday. They have a new terminal since my 2001 visit, but still no aircraft parked there. It seems so strange after having over a hundred helicopters plus a company of Mohawks and a company of L-19 Bird Dogs there in the war. We bussed into the ancient imperial capital, Hue, to check into the newly upgraded Hotel Huong Giang where Fred Spaulding and I had stayed in 2001. The group took a walking tour of Hue and the Citadel while I prepared for my briefing scheduled for 7 to 9 PM.

I thought the briefing and question period went well and I met Trang, Brian and John Young to go to Col Pham Van Dinh's new home. Very nice place next to his small hotel and a new building that he rents to an Internet business.

Dinh had a stroke two years ago and Brian said he is much better this year. Looks more fleshed out and bright. His right side is paralyzed, but he can shuffle along with a cane. Can make a little noise, but can't talk. Good news is he looks healthy and seems to immediately understand anything you say. I asked him if he was ready to put back on his old *Hoc Bao* Black Beret and again climb the flagpole over the Citadel ala Tet '68. He responded with a very big smile and a nod of the head. We stayed a little over an hour and then went to an Italian restaurant. Had Piccata Milanese, pretty good.

Another early departure scheduled for Monday 31 May for Khe Sanh and Camp Carroll. We visited the old Marine base used for the famous four-month siege of the Marines Jan-Apr 68 and the base we used for Lam Son 719 in 1971. A nice Visitors building with displays and dioramas plus a Chinook, a Huey, a T-41 tank and a 105 howitzer have been added since Brian's visit there in 2003. They disassembled the aircraft in Binh Hoa (near Saigon) and transported them by truck for reassembly here at Khe Sanh. They understand the tourist business pretty well.

Immediately to the rear of the visitor's building is the old airstrip, now reduced to red clay after 30 plus years of monsoons and disuse. The round top hill south of the strip is where I stayed in a CONEX 6 foot by 6 foot metal container for the 8 Feb-9 Apr Lam Son 719 Operation into Laos. The hilltop was home to the Command Posts of the 1st Infantry Division and I Corps, Army of Vietnam (ARVN).

Between the strip and my hilltop is Highway 9 and just five miles to the west is the Laotian border.

On the way back we stopped at where Camp Carroll once was. This was a key base for the South Vietnamese for defense of the DMZ. It was also the alternate command post for my 3rd Brigade, 101st Abn Div. At the time of the Easter Offensive April 1972, the North Vietnamese launched a full-scale multi-divisional attack with Soviet T-54 and PT-76 tanks and armored artillery and surrounded the base of 1500 defenders and four batteries of artillery. With the agreement of his officers, then Lt Col Dinh surrendered his 56th Regt and Camp Carroll. The South Vietnamese Marine 105 Artillery Battery refused to surrender and manned their guns killing many of the North Vietnamese as they entered Camp Carroll. Every Marine fought until mortally wounded. *Semper Fidelis!!*

Camp Carroll remained in North Vietnamese hands until the final North Vietnamese victory in April 1975. Fidel Castro visited there in 1973.

On the way back, our guide took a new road that would intersect the old 561 road that led towards Con Tien, and the Bien Hai River—the DMZ. This was at the special request of Amber Miller whose father, Lance Corporal Larry Miller, had fought with a Naval Gunfire Liaison Team in this area. Amber walked and took photos of the old fighting positions for her father.

Had a nice late assembly at 8:30 AM on 1 June and took the bus to Danang and to Hoi An. Hai Van Pass was in the clouds, so did not have a good view of Danang and Monkey Mountain. We stopped at Red Beach in Danang where the first American Marines came ashore 25 Mar 1965 to a large, friendly and enthusiastic welcoming committee of Vietnamese soldiers and American Advisors.

Continuing towards Hoi Ain, we visited a marble factory and a lacquer factory. The folks continued to buy many things, to include, heavy marble chess sets.

We did a walking tour of Hoi An at 3:30 PM and then everyone did power shopping that afternoon and the next day. Not sure how many of them remembered that it was Hoi Ain where Marco Polo passed through on his way to China in the 13th century, but they all remembered that Hoi Ain is where you can get great bargains on tailored clothing. Michelle had a wedding dress and other things made, Geoffery had a tux plus suits tailored and Justin had a suit and six pairs of bell-bottom black jeans made. Many folks had clothes made and wisely had multiple fittings.

Thursday, 3 June, we had an early start for a long ride, first to the ancient, 11th century Cham ruins near My Son and then on to the site of the 1968 My Lai massacre. The local guide here added such horrible fabrications that I turned and walked away. Recommend you skip this place if you visit Vietnam. They don't deserve our tourist trade. A memorial is appropriate, but not the lies and gross distortions.

The professor had a meeting that evening with us all for limited observations

Friday, 4 June, we boarded the bus for a 6:00 AM departure for the Danang Airport to fly back to Saigon. The group checked back into the Majestic Hotel. Much more appreciated this time. The afternoon was free.

Saturday we split into separate tours and individual shopping. We put the baggage in the lobby at 8 PM and had dinner at the Western friendly, noisy Underground Café and departed for the airport at 10:30 PM. Our Asiana Airline flight for Inchon, Korea departed at 0110 Sunday morning.

We arrived in Inchon about 8:00 AM the next day. About half the group bussed into Seoul and the other half hung out at the very new, quite large terminal. We departed on schedule about eight hours later arriving in Los Angeles early at 11 AM the same day, enjoying a 100-mile per hour tailwind.

Amber headed to Milwaukee, Joanna to New York, me to Dallas and Killeen and the group had a two and a half hour delay and got to New Orleans at midnight. The return was about 55 to 60 hours and I was still recovering two days later.

Personal Observations:

Vietnam continues to improve economically since the government renounced the collective-communist business model and adapted the capitalistic approach in 1986. Just since my visit three years ago, there has been significant building of new modern office structures and hotels with more new factories in the suburbs. Saigon and Hanoi have downtown multi-story malls, each with a nice grocery-super market. Not really large compared to the US, but a great improvement for shopping. A few hundred thousand more motorbikes have been added to the over two million in Saigon and a substantial number of new automobiles. The city can't handle much of an increase in autos. The traffic and parking would be impossible.

The factories like the garment factory we visited, are not in a truly free market competition. The very corrupt politicians at the local and national levels tightly control them as they are assigned export quotas et cetera.

The Socialist Republic of Vietnam elects their officials, but only members of the Communist Party can vote. Only 3% of the Vietnamese belong to the Party. About 80% of the members of the Communist Party live in the North. Their crooked politicians may have learned something from Americans after all.

Saigon has more than eight million people and Hanoi close to two million. Hai Phong is the next largest with over a million. These large cities are trying to improve the infrastructure, but that is an almost impossible task. Saigon's eight million are trying to live with the French-built sewer system for two hundred thousand. They probably never will be able to have drinking water piped into the homes and offices.

The other 65 million Vietnamese in the countryside and smaller cities are not much better off than they were 35 years ago. Farming is still done mostly by hand and foot. The good news is, thanks to the International Rice Research Institute and dedicated people like Tom Hargrove, Texas A&M '66, Vietnam is now a major rice exporter.

Highway 1 has been improved, but the entire transportation system is poor. Very, very little has been done for the vast majority of the people living outside of the big cities.

We traveled a great deal through the countryside, but never saw a military unit. In the cities, there are numerous uniformed police and a great number of hired security guards, but I saw only one person with a weapon in the whole country. All young men have compulsory military or social service. The cops don't need guns since fear is solidly implanted. Big Brother watches everybody and everything. Jason's fiancé could not stay in our hotel because she is not a tourist. Trang is staying over for a few days with her sister in Saigon, but she and her sister had to go to the police station to register that she was going to be in the house. The police keep constant check on where every single person is supposed to be.

You get very tired of the incessant hustling by cyclo and motorbike drivers and young kids trying to sell you postcards and books and pretty young ladies wanting to give you a foot massage.

The really good news is the sea of happily smiling faces on the school kids. We visited four schools and saw many young folk. They are quite joyful and love to sing. Most folks in the city seem to be happy. They are excited when my payment or tip includes a US Two Dollar Bill. In the countryside they are working so hard they don't have time to look up to show their serious face.

Good food and drink are readily available at bargain prices, many catering to Western tastes.

The beautiful countryside of tall mountains and lush valleys and beaches with very white sand and interesting coves beckon to the tourist. Go for it!!

Bottom line—Great trip! Glad I had the privilege and pleasure of being with such a fine group of folks. Thank you, University of Southern Mississippi and Trang and Courtney Frobenius!!

APPENDIX E

CUBANS IN VIETNAM DURING THE VIETNAM WAR

Cuban Roberto Salas said in an interview with me in Havana in March 2002, that the North Vietnamese did not at all trust the Chinese that came there to help. They restricted the Chinese to a relatively small area north of Hanoi. On the other hand he said that the Russians played a key role in the air defense of North Vietnam. He said the Russian technology allowed the North Vietnamese to "burst the protective bubble around the B-52s" in December 1972 causing the United States to halt the use of B-52s in the North. Salas claimed that in December 1972, the PAVN shot down 17 B-52s the first day after learning how to penetrate the "protective bubble." The next day they shot down 24 B-52s, the third day they shot down 22 B-52s for a total of 63 downed B-52s and the Americans halted the bombing.

This is gross exaggeration by Salas. In all of LINEBACKER II, the US name for this 1972 campaign, a total of 15 B-52s were lost.

Another interview arranged for me by Bob Walz was with Ismail Sene. Sene was in the Cuban foreign intelligence business and spent 23 years in Eastern Europe. Most of his time was in Czechoslovakia. Sene mentioned that he spoke seven different languages. I said, "Like Vernon Walters." He said, "Oh yes, I met Walters with Kissinger at the Paris Peace Talks." Sene had some interesting stories, but about all he admitted that he knew of the Vietnam War was a visit by Castro to East Berlin in 1977. Castro came to East Berlin to attend the Nonaligned Nation Conference Chaired by Momar

Khadafi. Castro met with General VO Nguyen Giap, The meeting did not go well as Giap had overslept and Castro was furious.

Roberto started out telling me how much the Cuban participation in North Vietnam had been exaggerated. He said that there were no more than twelve Cubans in North Vietnam and they were there just to observe and receive training. As we talked more, sprinkled with his expletives, he said there were no more than 100 Cubans in North Vietnam. More discussion, then Salas said that there was a Cuban engineer brigade there with bulldozers and heavy construction equipment. It is believed that this engineer brigade did extensive work on the Ho Chi Minh Trail. Bob Destatte has advised that this engineer brigade was comprised of 23 men. It had three designations. The official Cuban designation was U.M. 4539. The official Vietnamese designation was Unit A-74. The Cubans in the group called themselves "The Baseball Players." Apparently, the Cubans use the word "brigada" to describe relatively small teams; e.g., "brigada medica" = a medical team or medical group.

Notes

1. Nolan, Keith. *RIPCORD Screaming Eagles Under Siege, Vietnam 1970.* Novato, CA: Presidio Press, 2000. Page 432

2. "Vietnam: Looking Back—At The Facts," Kent G. Sears, Ph. D., reflecting on his nineteen years in Vietnam in his 2001 paper: "Casualties tell the tale."

3. Karnow, Stanley. *Vietnam. A History.* New York: The Viking Press, 1983 Page 248

4. McMaster, H. R. *Dereliction of Duty.* New York: HarperCollins Publishers, Inc., 1997

5. Nolan, Keith. *INTO LAOS The Story of Dewey Canyon II/Lam Son 719 Vietnam 1971.* NovNato, CA: Presidio Press, 1986. Page. 10–11.

6. "The Southern Laos—Route 9 Counter-Offensive Campaign—1971." The Institute for Military Science, Ministry of Defense, *Ho Chi Minh City,* 1976. Translated by Robert J. Destatte

7. The 324B Division. Published by the People's Army Publishing House (*Nha Xuat Ban Quan Doi Nhan Dan*), Hanoi, 1992. 280 pages; maps; photos.

8. Footnote: Resolution of the 18th Plenum of the Central Committee, from "The Resistance War Against the Americans to Save the Nation 1954–75: Military Events," People's Army Publishing House, Hanoi, 1980,

9. (Footnote: January 1970 Resolution of the Tri Thien Military Region Party Committee).

10. Ibid

11. "304B Division (A Chronicle) (Volume II)" Published by the People's Army Publishing House [Nha Xuat Ban Quan Doi Nhan Dan], Hanoi, 1990. 320 pages; photos; maps. Volume 2 covers the period 1954 through 1975.

12. "The 324B Division." Published by the People's Army Publishing House (Nha Xuat Ban Quan Doi Nhan Dan), Hanoi, 1992. 280 pages; maps; photos.

13. Various. This is a general reference to various101[st] Airborne Division After Action Reports, Nolan's book RIPCORD, various interviews and the author's notes.

14. "The 324B Division." Ibid

15. Various. Ibid

16. "The 324B Division." Ibid

17. Various. Ibid

18. "The 324B Division." Ibid

19. Various. Ibid

20. "The 324B Division." Ibid

21. Various. Ibid

22. "The 324B Division." Ibid

23. Various. Ibid

24. "The 324B Division." Ibid

25. Various. Ibid

26. "The 324B Division." Ibid

27. "The 324B Division." Ibid

28. Various. Ibid

29. "The 324B Division." Ibid

30. Various. Ibid

31. "The 324B Division." Ibid

32. Various. Ibid

33. "The 324B Division." Ibid

34. Various. Ibid

35. Various. Ibid

36. Lanning, Michael Lee and Dan Cragg. *Inside The VC And The NVA The Real Story of North Vietnam's Armed Forces.* New York: Ballantine/Ivy Books, 1992 P. 198

37. Lanning, Michael Lee and Dan Cragg. op. cit. P. 19.

38. op.cit. P. 21.

39. Karnow, Stanley. P. 141

40. op.cit.

41. op.cit.

42. op.cit.

43. op.cit.

44. Westmoreland, William C. *A Soldier Reports.* Garden City, New York: 1976.

45. Op.cit.

46. op.cit

47. Karnow, op.cit. P 169

48. Webb, James, "WHERE DO WE GO FROM HERE?" October 2, 2001 www.jameswebb.com

49. Adams, Sam. *War Of Numbers An Intelligence Memoir* South Royalton, VT: Steerforth Press,1994. P. 84–91

50. Adams, op.cit. P. 181–182

51. Adams, op.cit. P. 182

52. Adams, op.cit. P. 145

53. Adams, op.cit. P 141–147

54. Adams, op.cit.

55. Adams. op.cit.

56. Karnow, Ibid. P. 535

57. op.cit. P. 545

58. Ibid

59. Young, Stephen. "How North Vietnam Won the War." *Wall Street Journal* August 3, 1995

60. Langguth, A. J., *Our Vietnam*. New York: Simon and Schuster, 2000 P. 415.

61. Langguth, A. J., *Our Vietnam*. New York: Simon and Schuster, 2000 P. 415.

62. Sheehan, Neil et al. *The Pentagon Papers*. New York: Bantum Books, 1971, P. 476–477.

63. Lanning. Ibid. P. 91–94.

64. "The Southern Laos—Route 9 Counter-Offensive Campaign—1971." The Institute for Military Science, Ministry of Defense, Ho Chi Minh City, 1976. Translated by Robert J. Destatte.

65. Young. Op. cit.

66. Destatte, Robert J. Ibid. email interview

67. Dung, Van Tien General. *Our Great Spring Victory An Account of the Liberation of South Vietnam.* New York: Monthly Review Press 1977. P. ix.

68. Luong, Colonel Le Ma. Interview.

69. Ky, Brigadier General Bui Pham. Interview.

70. Ibid.

71. Lanning, Michael Lee and Dan Cragg. op. cit. P. 203.

72. Nuoi, Brigadier General Duong Ba Interview.

73. Lanning, Michael Lee and Dan Cragg. op. cit. P. 213.

74. Destatte. Ibid. email interview.

75. *Thuoc*, Major *Ho Van*. Interview.

76. Karnow. Ibid. P. 406

77. Karnow. Ibid. P. 540

78. *Thuoc*, Major *Ho Van*. Interview.

79. Adams. Ibid. P. 177

80. *Khanh*, Senior Colonel *Nguyen Quoc*. Interview.

81. *Van*, Colonel *Nguyen Ba*. Interview.

82. Narrative Message P 031916Z Sep 96 from Commander, Joint Task Force-Full Accounting to US Commander in Chief Pacific et al, Subject: Detailed Report of Investigation for Case 1648 (Search for bodies of SPC Howard and PFC Beals)

83. The author's estimate of enemy KIA during the siege at Ripcord was cal-
    culated as follows:

9 infantry battalions, each lost 150	= 1350
5 artillery battalions, each lost 100	= 500
1 sapper battalion lost 250	= 250
3 machinegun companies, each lost 50	= 150
1200 porters from 304B Division lost 150	= 150
	Total 2400

84. Lanning, Michael Lee and Dan Cragg. op. cit. P. 198–199.

85. Zagoria, Donald S. Ibid. P. 131.

86. Langguth. Ibid. P. 558–559.

87. Karnow. Ibid. P. 603

88. "The Southern Laos—Route 9 Counter-Offensive Campaign—1971."
    The Institute for Military Science, Ministry of Defense, Ho Chi Minh
    City, 1976. Translated by Robert J. Destatte.

89. op. cit.

90. Berry, Lieutenant General Sidney B. After dinner speech at the Ripcord
    Association Reunion, 24 Oct 87.

91. Langguth, A. J., *Our Vietnam*. New York. Simon and Schuster 2000. P.
    126.

92. Ibid. P. 243.

93. op.cit.

94. Young, Stephen. "How North Vietnam Won the War." *Wall Street Jour-
    nal* August 3, 1995

95. Langguth, A. J., *Our Vietnam*. New York. Simon and Schuster 2000. P. 374.

96. Sears. Ibid.

97. Gaiduk, Ilya V. *The Soviet Union And The Vietnam War*. Chicago: Ivan R. Dee, 1996 P. 65

98. Karnow. op. cit. 329.

99. Young. ibid.

100. Zagoria, Donald S. *Vietnam Triangle Moscow/ Peking/Hanoi.* New York: Pegasus, 1967 P. 78

101. Gaiduk. Ibid. P. 58

102. Sears. Ibid.

103. Sears. Ibid.

104. Sears. Ibid.

105. Gaiduk. Ibid. P. 61–62.

106. Gaiduk. Ibid. P. 72.

107. Destatte, Robert J. Ibid. email interview

108. Pike. Ibid. P. 456

109. Dung, Van Tien General. *Our Great Spring Victory An Account of the Liberation of South Vietnam.* New York: Monthly Review Press 1977. P. 232.

110. op. cit.

111. Karnow. op. cit. 328

112. Frobenius, Courtney. email interview. Courtney Frobenius was consulted by email and telephone numerous times drawing on his extensive knowledge of Vietnam, its history, people, culture and military. He served in 1969 as an infantry platoon leader and company commander in the 9th

Infantry Division and as Senior Advisor to the 43rd Vietnamese Ranger Battalion in 1970 and as a District Advisor in Phu Yen Province in 1971. Frobenius lived and studied in Vietnam 1995–1998.

113. Pribbenow, Merle L. "The Fog of War: The Vietnamese View of the Ia Drang Battle." US Army Command and General Staff College Military Review January-February 2001.

114. Karnow. Ibid. P. 254.

115. Lanning, Michael Lee and Dan Cragg. op. cit. P. 97–102.

116. Frobenius. Ibid. email interview.

117. *Ky.* Ibid.

118. Turley, G. H. Colonel, USMC *The Easter Offensive The Last American Advisors Vietnam 1927*. Navato, CA: Presidio Press,1985.

119. Andrade, Dale. Trial By Fire: *The 1927 Easter Offensive, Americas Last Vietnam Battle*. 1994.

120. Turley. Ibid. P. 309.

121. Turley. Ibid. P. 164–166

122. Turley. Ibid. P. 168–170

Bibliography

Books

Adams, Sam. *War Of Numbers An Intelligence Memoir* South Royalton, VT: Steerforth Press,1994

Andrade, Dale. *Trial By Fire: The 1972 Easter Offensive, Americas Last Vietnam Battle*. New York: Hippocrene Books, 1994

Bao Ninh. *The Sorrow Of War A Novel of North Vietnam*. New York: Riverhead Books, 1995

Del Vecchio, John M. *The 13th Valley*. New York: Bantam Books, 1982

Dung, Van Tien General. *Our Great Spring Victory An Account of the Liberation of South Vietnam*. New York: Monthly Review Press 1977

Gaiduk, Ilya V. *The Soviet Union And The Vietnam War*. Chicago: Ivan R. Dee, 1996

Giap, General Vo Nguyen. *Big Victory Great Task*. With a 17 page Introduction by David Schoenbrun. New York: Frederick A. Praeger, 1967

Karnow, Stanley. *Vietnam: A History*. New York: The Viking Press, 1983

Jones, Malcom W., Jr. *Four Condors—Four Vets On The Net*. Mac Jones, 2000

Lanning, Michael Lee and Dan Cragg. *Inside The VC And The NVA The Real Story of North Vietnam's Armed Forces*. New York: Ballantine/Ivy Books, 1992

Langguth, A. J., *Our Vietnam*. New York: Simon and Schuster, 2000

Marshall, Tom. *The Price of Exit*. New York: The Ballantine Publishing Group, 1998

McMaster, H. R. *Dereliction of Duty*. New York: HarperCollins, Publishers, Inc., 1997

Nolan, Keith. *INTO LAOS The Story of Dewey Canyon II/Lam Son 719 Vietnam 1971*. Novato, CA: Presidio Press, 1986

Nolan, Keith. *RIPCORD Screaming Eagles Under Siege, Vietnam 1970.* Navoto, CA: Presidio Press, 2000

Palmer, Dave R. *Summons of the Trumpet.* New York: Presidio Press, 1978

Pike, Douglas. *Viet Cong; The Organization and Techniques of the National Liberation Front of South Vietnam,* M.I.T. Press, Cambridge, Mass., paperback edition, March 1968, pp. 456–459.

Sheehan, Neil. *A Bright Shining Lie.* New York: Random House, 1988

Sheehan, Neil et al. *The Pentagon Papers.* New York: Bantum Books, 1971

Sorley, Lewis. *A Better War.* New York: Harcourt, 2000.

Stanton, Shelby L. *The Rise and Fall of an American Army.* Novato, CA: Presidio Press, 1985

Sun Tzu. The Art Of War. Boston: Shambala Publications, 1988.

Turley, G. H. Colonel, USMC *The Easter Offensive The Last American Advisors Vietnam 1972.* Navato, CA: Presidio Press, 1985

Vivo, Raul Valdes. *El Gran Secreto: Cubanos en El Comino Ho Chi Minh,* published by Editora Politica, La Habana, 1990; 249 pages. Robert Destatte has in his collection a Vietnamese language translation of the Cuban book. The translation is entitled *'Toi Mat: Nhung Nguoi Cuba Tren Duong Ho Chi Minh'* [Top Secret: Cubans on the Ho Chi Minh Trail]. The translation was edited by Le Tien, Pham Xuan Sinh, and Ho Quang Minh, published by Cong Ty Xuat Ban Doi Ngoai [External Relations Publishing Company], Hanoi, 1990; 174 pages, with photos.

Webb, James. *Lost Soldiers.* New York: Bantam Books, 2001

Westmoreland, William C. *A Soldier Reports.* Garden City, New York: 1976

Zagoria, Donald S. *Vietnam Triangle Moscow/Peking/Hanoi.* New York: Pegasus, 1967

Documents

'After Action Report, FS/OB Ripcord,' 101st Airborne Division (Airmobile) 1 September 1970

'Operational Report—Lessons Learned, 101st Airborne Division (Airmobile), Period Ending 31 July 1970.'

'Vietnam: Looking Back—At The Facts,' Kent G. Sears, Ph D, 1 June 2001

'Ripcord Casualty Report' Frank Marshall and Fred Spaulding, The Ripcord Association October 2000 After dinner speech by Lt Gen (Ret) Sidney

Berry, Ripcord Reunion, 24 Oct 87 Narrative Message P 031916Z Sep 96 from Commander, Joint Task Force-Full Accounting to US Commander in Chief Pacific et al, Subject: Detailed Report of Investigation for Case 1648 (Search for bodies of SPC Howard and PFC Beals)

'Vietnam: Looking Back—At The Facts' By: Kent G. Sears, PhD I June 2001 Vietnam experience dates back to 1965 and now includes nearly 19 years time 'incountry.' Currently serves as senior advisor and consultant to a variety of international business and governmental and other organizations with interests in Vietnam.

'The Southern Laos—Route 9 Counter-Offensive Campaign—1971.' The Institute for Military Science, Ministry of Defense, Ho Chi Minh City, 1976. Translated by Robert J. Destatte.

'Northern Wing Corps (Memoirs of Major General Hung Phong)'. Published by the People's Army Publishing House [Nha Xuat Ban QDNDVN], Hanoi, 1981. 140 pages. Translated by Robert J. Destatte.

'Chien Truong Tri-Thien-Hue Trong Cuoc Khang Chien Chong My Cuu Nuoc Toan Thang' [The Tri-Thien-Hue Theater during the Totally Victorious War of Resistance and National Salvation Against the Americans], a draft, published by the Thuan Hoa Publishers, Hue City, 1985; pp. 177–186. Translated by Robert J. Destatte.

'304th Division (A Chronicle) (Volume II)' Published by the People's Army Publishing House [Nha Xuat Ban Quan Doi Nhan Dan], Hanoi, 1990. 320 pages; photos; maps. Volume 2 covers the period 1954 through 1975.

The Vanguard Division (308th Division): Volume 3—a Chronicle]. Published by the People's Army Publishing House [Nha Xuat Ban Quan Doi Nhan Dan], Hanoi, 1979. 380 pages photos; no maps.

The History of the 308 Division—The Vanguard Division. Published by the People's Army Publishing House (Nha Xuat 23 Ban Quan Doi Nhan Dan), Hanoi, 1994. 328 pages; maps; photos.

The 324Bth Division. Published by the People's Army Publishing House (Nha Xuat Ban Quan Doi Nhan Dan), Hanoi, 1992. 280 pages; maps; photos.

325th Division (1954–1975), Volume 1. Published by the People's Army Publishing House [Nha Xuat Ban Quan Doi Nhan Dan], Hanoi, 1981. 280 pages; maps; photos. Covers the period from the date the division was established, 11 March 1951, through 1954.

325th Division (1954–1975), Volume 2. Published by the People's Army Publishing House [Nha Xuat Ban Quan Doi Nhan Dan], Hanoi, 1986. 335

pages; maps; photos. Covers the period from 1954, through the end of the Vietnam war. Translated by Robert J. Destatte.

Periodicals

Pribbenow, Merle L. 'The Fog of War: The Vietnamese View of the Ia Drang Battle.' US Army Command and General Staff College Military Review January-February 2001
   Guirad, Jim. 'U. S. Didn't Lose War In Vietnam.' *Dallas Morning News* April 27, 2001
   Young, Stephen. 'How North Vietnam Won the War.' *Wall Street Journal* August 3, 1995
   Webb, James, 'WHERE DO WE GO FROM HERE?' October 2, 2001 www.jameswebb.com

Interviews

Courtney Frobenius was consulted by email and telephone hundreds of times drawing on his extensive knowledge of Vietnam, its history, people, culture and military. He served in 1969 as an infantry platoon leader and company commander in the 9th Infantry Division and as Senior Advisor to the 43rd Vietnamese Ranger Battalion in 1970 and as the PSDF and RF/PF Advisor for all of Phu Yen Province in 1971. Frobenius lived and studied in Vietnam 1995–1998 and currently owns and operates Vietnam-IndoChina Tours.
   Robert J. Destatte provided an enormous amount of translations of Vietnamese books, documents and publications greatly broadening and enhancing the understanding of the North Vietnamese side of the battle for FSB Ripcord. He served nine years in Vietnam in the US Army and Defense Intelligence Agency and from 1993 until 2001 in the Defense POW & Missing Personnel Affairs Office for the Secretary of Defense.
   Ambassador Douglas B. (Pete) Peterson and the U.S. Defense Attaché, Lieutenant Colonel Frank Miller. U.S. Army, were interviewed on 5 June in the American Embassy in Hanoi.
   Colonel Pham Van Dinh was a Lieutenant Colonel in the Army of the Republic of Vietnam. He commanded the 56th Infantry Regiment and Camp Carroll in 1972 and surrendered his forces and Camp Carroll to the invading PAVN forces during the Easter Offensive of 1972. The PAVN appointed him a colonel in their army and later threw him in prison for three years. He says he is still on active duty in the PAVN. I had many discussions/interviews

with him, but have a long way to go to understand his motivations then and now.

Colonel (Ret) Nguyen Ba Van was a sergeant serving near *Khe Sanh* at the time of Ripcord, later Deputy Commander and Political Officer of the 9th Division of the People's Army of Vietnam (PAVN) and retired from the position of Political Officer of the Cu Chi District. Interviewed in Cu Chi on 4 June 2001.

Col Le Ma Luong. He had been an infantry company commander in Thua Tien Province in 1970. Col Luong is currently the Director of the Army Museum in Hanoi. Interviewed on 6 June 2001.

Mr. Nguyen The Cuong of the Foreign Press Center of the Ministry of Foreign Affairs, arranged for us to interview BG Bui Pham Ky, People's Army of Vietnam, Retired. Ky had been the Deputy Commander and Political Officer of the 324B Division in Thua Tien Province in 1970. Interviewed in Hanoi 7 June 2001.

Major (Ret) Ho Van Thuoc, who, in 1970, was the Operations Officer of the Regional forces in Quang Tri Province. Interviewed in Hue on 8 June 2001.

Brig Gen (Ret) Duong Ba Nuoi, who, in 1970 was the Deputy Commander and Political Officer Of Zone 4, which included Thua Tien, Quang Tri, Quang Binh, and Ha Tinh Provinces. Interviewed in Hue on 8 June 2001.

Senior Colonel Nguyen Quoc Khanh, who, in 1970 was the Operations Officer of the 324B Division. Interviewed in Hue on 8 Jun 2001.

Roberto Salas was and is a confidant of Fidel Castro. Salas was interviewed in Havana, Cuba 2 March 2002.

Ismail Sene served Castro in foreign intelligence for 23 years in Eastern Europe. He was interviewed in Havana, Cuba 24 Feb 2002.

Brig Gen Chu Phuong Doi, Commander of the 324B Division during the battle for Ripcord. Interviewed in Cao Bang, Vietnam 25–26 May 2004.

Index

About the Author

Benjamin L. Harrison
Major General, US Army, Ret.

Chu Phuong Doi
Maj Gen, Peoples Army of VN, Ret.

Enlisted in the Regular Army in 1946. During the Vietnam War, he served on the CINCPAC staff, commanded an aviation battalion in Vietnam for twelve months, was on McNamara's staff, was the Chief of Doctrine on the Army Staff, commanded the 3rd Brigade, 101st Airborne Division during the siege and evacuation of Firebase RIPCORD in 1970 and was the 1st ARVN Division Senior Advisor during Lam Son 719. On visits to Vietnam in 2001 and 2004, he interviewed former enemy officers including General Doi.

Enlisted in the Viet Minh in 1946. Fought under Ho Chi Minh and Vo Nguyen Giap as a Battalion Commander in 1950 in battles that forced the French to abandon the Cao Bang area. Doi was a Regimental Commander at Dien Bien Phu in 1954. In 1965, he went to the south and took command of and reorganized the 324B Division. In 1967 and 1968, he fought the US Marines at Khe Sanh. Still in command of the 324B Division in 1970, he received his first-ever division sole mission: Destroy Firebase RIPCORD.

0-595-32730-3

Made in the USA
Monee, IL
15 September 2022

14089742R00173